Business and Politics in Indian Country
You Can't Handle the Truth

Revealing the Struggles, Resilience, and Realities of Native America

D. G. Comer

About the Cover

This cover isn't design. It's declaration. Each image tells part of the truth this book refuses to dress up or dilute.

The Elder
The elder in the suit isn't a prop. He's the weight-bearer—the one who's seen too much, heard too many promises, and still stands ready to speak when silence would be easier. That look on his face? It's earned. And it doesn't blink.

The U.S. Capital
The U.S. Capitol looms—not as a symbol of democracy, but as the distant engine of decisions made about us, rarely with us. Generations of policies came from that dome, and too many left scars instead of solutions.

The Mission Church
The mission church stands quiet and still. But it's not empty. It holds the echoes of lost language, stripped ceremony, and the lie that salvation could ever be forced. That building, to some, meant help. To others, it meant disappearance.

The Child
And the child? The child is the reason. He holds the feathers not to entertain, but to reach. He doesn't know the weight yet. That's why this book had to be written—so one day, when he asks what happened to his people, someone will have the guts to answer.

This cover is a map. A warning. A mirror. And a reminder that the story isn't over—unless we let it be.

Business & Politics in Indian Country -
You Can't Handle the Truth:
D.G. Comer

Copyright © 2025 by D.G. Comer. All rights reserved.

No part of this publication may be reproduced, stored in a retrieval system, or transmitted in any form or by any means—electronic, mechanical, photocopying, recording, or otherwise—without the prior written permission of the author, except for brief quotations used in reviews, articles, or scholarly analysis.

Published by Heck Fuzzy Publications
ISBN: 979-8-9991987-0-9
First edition: October 2025

Printed in the United States of America
City of Publication: Puposky, MN
For rights inquiries, contact the author directly at:
author@heckfuzzy.com

This book is a work of nonfiction. All opinions expressed are solely those of the author and are based on lived experience, public information, and professional observation. Cover design and interior layout by the author.

Library of Congress Control Number: 2025914823

"Some images included in this book depict the author's family or community. Where historical photos appear without clear provenance, they are presented not as artifacts of ownership, but as part of a story reclaimed by those to whom it truly belongs."

Dedicated to Our Grandparents—Ann & Titus Samuels

Ann and Titus Samuels were more than grandparents. They were our guides, our storytellers, and the steady foundation beneath our early lives. My eldest sister and I had the honor of being raised by them for several formative years—years filled with lessons that reached far beyond the walls of our home. From traveling to powwows to funerals, and from Memorial Day grave cleanings to quiet evenings marked by the soft cadence of Grandma's stories, we were immersed in a world held together by their wisdom and love.

Their presence shaped the core of who I am. Though they have long walked on, the truths they lived and the values they instilled remain deeply embedded in my path. When I earned my Bachelor's in Business Administration—and later, my MBA—it was Grandma's words that echoed in my heart: "Always work for Native Peoples, even if it can't be with our own tribe." She understood the painful intricacies of tribal politics. And while I may not serve directly under our own banner, I have never stopped working for our Native People.

Grandpa—your quiet strength, your patience, your acts of love from tying a little boy's shoes to making breakfast, even your calm when I lost your tools, scattered your garage, or shot the neighbor's cow with my arrow—these are not forgotten. They live within me, stitched into memory.

To both of you—Thank you. Your enduring guidance, your gentle discipline, and your unshakeable love have shaped my life more than words can hold. I carry your voices with me. Always.

—D.G. Comer

Titus Samuels & D.G. Comer

Epigraph

"It is so much simpler to bury reality than it is to dispose of dreams."—Don DeLillo

We've been burying reality in Indian Country for far too long.
Not because we don't know the truth—but because knowing it, and speaking it aloud, demands more of us than most are willing to give.
   Dreams of sovereignty, prosperity, and cultural revival are easy to champion in headlines and council meetings.
But reality?
   Reality sits in silence behind the curtain—in our leadership failures, our mismanaged businesses, our manipulated narratives, and the unspoken betrayals that happen when no one is watching.
   This book isn't about dreams.
It's about what we've buried to keep those dreams untouched.
It is the uncomfortable digging-up of truths we all live with, but few will say.
It's a call to confront what's broken—not to destroy the dream, but to finally build something real beneath it.
   We can't move forward by pretending.
And we sure as hell can't heal by hiding.
So let's stop burying the truth.
And start unearthing what's been lost beneath it.

Table of Contents

About the Cover ii
Dedicated to Our Grandparents—Ann & Titus Samuels iv
Epigraph vi
Table of Contents vii
Foreword x
Preface xii
Introduction xiv
Disclaimer xvi
Editorial Note xvii
Terminology Note xix
Reading the Fire: How This Book is Meant to Burn xx

SECTION I: Historical Assaults and Federal Violence 1
Government Policies to Eliminate Native Americans 5
Historical Perspective: Government and Treaties 9
Treaties & Tribal Govts: Protecting the System, Not the People. 15
Legacy of Harm – U.S. Government 19
Echoes of a Lost Population 29
Shadows of the Past—A Reckoning with Historical Atrocities ... 33
U.S. Presidents and the Native Dichotomy 37
The Legacy of Discrimination: Barriers to Progress 43
Critical Race Theory: Impact on Native America 49
Erased and Reclaimed: Native Culture and Art 53
Smoke Screens & Silent Screen 59
Biological Devastation of Native Nations 61
State-Sanctioned Genocide 67
Saving Souls, Taking Nations 71
Early Resistance and Rebellions 75
The High Price of Inequity 81
The Sacred Unspoken: Hidden Religions 85
Powwow in Transition: From Ceremony to Competition 89
The Fire That Built the Future: The CCC–Indian Division 93

SECTION II: Our Internal Reckoning 97
Psychological Transformation of Native American Mindset 99
The Internal Struggle: Self-Inflicted Challenges 105
Integrating "Eye Juggling" by Rodney Frey 111
The "Hang Around the Fort Indians" 115

In Active Genocide: The Trap of Federal and State Grants 123
The Food Desert Dilemma 127
Health & Wellness: Breaking the Cycle of Poor Health.............. 131
Racial Classification: Blood Quantum 135
Education & Empowerment.. 141
Mental Health and Healing in Native Communities 145
Substance Abuse and Addiction 151
Prevalence of Suicide in Indian Country...................................... 157
Before Their Time... 163
Disenrollment, Sovereignty and the Per Capita Trap 165
The Knowing 171
Healing Through Tradition 173
The Old Law Still Stands 177
Sacred or Spectacle?.. 181
Still Ours: The Good We Carry Forward...................................... 185

SECTION III: Politics, Power, and Leadership 189
The Politics of Leadership Change: Disrupting Potential 195
Employment and Accountability in Tribal Governance 201
Two Worlds, One Rez 207
Protection for All Except Natives 213
Reforming Title VII 217
A Final Provocation.. 225
Gender Dynamics in Tribal Leadership.. 229
The Key to Thriving Businesses 233
Native Women: Missing, Murdered, Ignored.............................. 239
The Role of Traditional Knowledge in Modern Governance 247
Vanishing Nations: The Silenced Tribes....................................... 251
Trapped in the Maze: How Regulations Hold Us Back 257
Top Ten States Violating Tribal Rights... 263
Emotional Costs of Native Leadership... 269
Community Accountability... 273
When the Enemy Looks Like Your Cousin 277
Economic Sovereignty and The Role of Leadership................... 283
Outsiders on the Inside 287
Tribal Courts: When Justice Depends on Who You Know 291
Voices Silenced: Media and the Tribal Gag Order 297
Consultation or Coercion? Theater of Listening 301
Governance Before the Council.. 305
Rebuilding After the Council: 309
Restoring the Circle: 315

SECTION IV: Rebuilding the Tribal Economy 321
Strategic Partnerships for Sustainable Growth 323
Off-Reservation Businesses: A Path to Prosperity 329
Building Internal Capacity in Tribal Governance 335
Renewable Energy: Stewardship and Growth 341
Technology and Tribal Opportunity 347
Sustainable Development: Long-Term Strategies for Success ... 353
Beyond Casinos – Building a Diverse Economic Base 359
Mistakes of the Rich Gaming Tribes 365
Successful Tribal Business Diversity: Case Studies 371
Preservation and Progress: 377
Digital Sovereignty – Protecting Tribal Data 383

SECTION V: Vision, Language, and the Long Future 387
Youth and the Future of Native Leadership 391
The Real Cost of Sovereignty and Self-Determination 397
Legal Reforms and Policy Advocacy 403
Hard Answers – Ensuring Tribal Success and Thriving 409
Decay of Tribal Languages: From Thousands to a Few 415
The Future of Native America – 100 Years Ahead 419
Native Service in the U.S. Military – Pride and Betrayal 425
Acknowledging Our Greatest Challenge 430

Summary and Path Forward 435
Reparations? We've Got the Receipts 439
Unfinished Conversations: Tough Topics Beyond This Book .. 443
Epilogue 448
Acknowledgments 450
What Was Left Unsaid: A Letter to the Reader 452
Access the Complete Works Cited 455
Who Is D.G. Comer? 456

"Read this front to back or drop in where it burns hottest—either way, hear me: our people weren't broken only by Washington's paper knives, but by the habits we refuse to quit. Sovereignty isn't a feeling; it's payroll met, contracts honored, languages spoken at breakfast, and the courage to fire your cousin when the job demands it. If we won't face both the theft done to us and the damage done by us, we'll keep trading ceremony for spectacle and freedom for per-capita checks. I didn't write this to be liked—I wrote it so we stop lying to ourselves and build a nation our grandchildren can thank."

Foreword

Why I Had to Write This Myself

"When the truth becomes a risk and silence becomes a strategy, know that the path forward will be lit only by those willing to burn their own comfort to light the way."

Author's Statement

I searched for someone to write the foreword to this book—someone respected, experienced, and willing to stand beside the truths contained in these pages. But as the search went on, a deeper truth emerged: most aren't ready to risk their reputations to speak honestly about what holds Indian Country back. They'll have these conversations in quiet rooms and closed circles, but ask them to put their name in print beside these realities, and the air suddenly grows thin.

I don't fault them. That's the climate we live in. In Indian Country, reputations are currency, and positions are often held through delicate alliances, not courage. Speak too plainly, and you risk losing your seat at the table. Push too hard, and the door you spent years opening might quietly close again.

But this book isn't about preserving reputations. It isn't about protecting the comfort of power or keeping anyone's hands clean. It's about confronting the obstacles we've laid in our own path—and the systems, both imposed and self-built, that keep our people standing still while the world moves forward.

So instead of a foreword written by someone afraid of the fallout, you get this. The words of a man with nothing to hide, nothing to gain, and nothing to lose by telling the truth.

This is a book about hard conversations—the ones whispered behind closed doors but rarely spoken aloud. It confronts the nepotism that strangles opportunity, the leaders holding power without the knowledge or experience to wield it, and the dangerous addiction to federal funds that keeps our nations tethered to systems designed not for our success, but our dependence.

If these words feel harsh, good. The truth is harsh. Change never comes from comfort—it comes from discomfort deep enough to shake us loose from the cycles we've accepted far too long.

This isn't rebellion. It's reckoning. A long-overdue reckoning with the realities our people face—and the choices we make. Whether we keep walking in circles or finally forge a path forward.

I didn't write this book to point fingers. I wrote it to light fires—under the feet of those who've settled for "good enough," and in the hearts of those ready to demand better—for their families, their communities, and their nations.

So no, there is no carefully worded foreword here. No politician or scholar lending their name to safely shape the narrative. Just this statement—and a simple promise:

Everything in these pages was written with a steady hand, a clear mind, and an unshakable commitment to the truth—no matter who it offends, and no matter what it costs. This book doesn't offer comfort. It offers clarity. What follows is a catalog of uncomfortable facts, inconvenient patterns, and buried realities that too many would rather keep hidden.

But if we're ever going to break the cycles that hold us back, we have to confront the data, the decisions, and the damage—head-on. These aren't just stories. They're signals. And they matter more now than ever.

Welcome to the conversation we've been avoiding for far too long.

—**D.G. Comer**

Preface

To understand Native American tribes today is to walk a road heavy with history—promises broken, cultures misunderstood, and struggles that cut far deeper than most are willing to see.

Business & Politics in Indian Country – You Can't Handle the Truth shines a hard light on those realities—the victories earned through blood and sacrifice, the failures that still haunt us, and the daily battles that define what it means to be Native in America today.

The path we walk isn't straight. It twists through generations of hardship, across landscapes scarred by forced removals and buried beneath the unmarked graves of children who never came home. Our history isn't just written in books—it's carved into the bones of our ancestors and whispered through every generation that survives the impossible. And yet, the weight of that history still lingers just behind our next step.

From the first invasion of our homelands to the policies of modern governments, our people have been pushed to the margins. We carry burdens that make the pursuit of progress feel like climbing a mountain with a pack full of stones—each one labeled with broken treaties, lost languages, and the quiet funerals of dreams deferred.

This book takes you into that climb, connecting the wounds of the past to the challenges that define life in Indian Country today.

Each chapter steps directly into those shadows—examining the legacies of exclusion, the collapse of our health systems, and the leadership voids that keep us bound to cycles of dysfunction. You'll read hard truths: about unqualified leaders protected by politics, about nepotism choking out innovation, and about the dangerous dependence on federal funds that keep our hands tied to systems designed to control—not to uplift.

This isn't a stroll through a well-tended garden—it's a march through tangled ground, where weeds hide snakes and every step forward demands vigilance.

We won't shy away from the conversations our people too often reserve for whispers. From the hiring of non-Native companies to do work our own people could perform, to the lack of education demanded of our tribal leaders—this book doesn't skim the surface. It digs deep, unearthing uncomfortable truths alongside stories of resilience and triumph.

Think of it as a guide through dangerous country—where there are moments of breathtaking beauty, but one misstep can send you over a cliff.

This isn't about casting blame. It's about clarity. About laying bare what's at stake—and what must change.

My hope is that these pages stir something in you: a conversation, a confrontation, a commitment. Real change is born in discomfort, and it's time we sit in that discomfort long enough to start pulling the weeds out by their roots.

Business & Politics in Indian Country – You Can't Handle the Truth draws from the wisdom of our elders, the scars of our history, and the hard-earned lessons of those who refused to surrender.

This isn't just a book—it's a call to stand up, to walk forward with eyes open and feet planted firmly in truth.

If I've done my job, you won't just read these pages—you'll feel them. You'll see the faces behind the facts. Hear the voices between the lines. And carry these truths long after the final chapter ends.

This is only a glimpse into a much larger struggle. Each chapter could stand alone as a story of survival and resistance—but together, they offer a broader picture of the road ahead.

May it provoke thought. Ignite reflection. And inspire you to stand with us as we fight for something better.

The road to sovereignty has never been smooth. It was never meant to be easy.

But we have always walked the hardest paths—with heads held high and spirits unbroken.

Resilience isn't just in our blood. It is our way of life.

The path forward is ours alone to claim.
Step carefully. Step boldly.
But above all—step forward. Let the fire burn..

Introduction

Business & Politics in Indian Country: You Can't Handle the Truth is not here to comfort. It's here to confront.

The truth about Native America isn't buried in a museum drawer. It walks among us—in bloodlines, in land that remembers, in systems that still try to erase us, in stories taught to whisper when they should have thundered.

To understand Native America today is not to study history—it is to **carry** it. It lives in our bodies, under our feet, and inside policies that outlived the men who wrote them. From broken treaties to stolen children, from forced removals to engineered dependency, our story is not only what was done to us. It is what we do now—how we rise, how we resist, how we reclaim.

This book does not soften its language. It does not dodge failure—ours or theirs. It is a reckoning with uncomfortable truths about governance, economics, sovereignty, and survival.

The challenges confronting our people are not just echoes of colonization. They are also the result of our own divisions—leadership chosen by proximity instead of merit, systems that reward silence over accountability, habits that confuse loyalty with complicity.

But the forces reshaping us today are not only political or economic. They are digital. Where past generations were tethered to government dependency, our children are now tethered to the feeds, ads, and algorithms of mass media, social platforms, and artificial intelligence. These invisible systems influence how we think, what we believe, and even how we see ourselves as Native people.

I name the patterns, not the gossip. I won't traffic in personal takedowns; this work is bigger than that. If you recognize your reflection, that's the point—do the work.

I wrote once: *"In Indian Country, everything worth having moves against the current—truth, justice, money, even hope. The stream was never built for us. We paddle upstream or we don't move at all."*

That is not mysticism. It is a warning—and a challenge.

Our governance still flickers in the winds of nepotism, greed, and fear. Our rivers of commerce still run uphill because the channels around us were designed to contain, not to carry. And yet we paddle. We fight. We build.

This book is for those ready to do that fighting—not with weapons, but with truth.

We will interrogate the machinery of our governments and the soul of our communities. We will challenge assumptions, audit the stories we live by, and turn the lights on where others prefer the dark. No lists. No vendettas. Just the hard accounting of cause and effect—and the invitation to do better.

If you're ready to walk that path—sometimes tangled, sometimes treacherous, always ours—step forward.

This is not just a book.
It's a fire.
Let it burn.

Disclaimer

Business & Politics in Indian Country: You Can't Handle the Truth explores the struggles, resilience, and realities of Native America. It reflects a journey—my own—shaped by lived experience, historical research, ancestral bloodline, and unfiltered conversations across Indian Country.

What you'll find in these pages are hard truths and harder-won lessons. They are meant to inform, to provoke, and to spark the kinds of conversations we've avoided for too long.

But let's be clear: this is not legal advice. It's not financial guidance. It's not professional consulting.

It's perspective—earned through conflict, shaped by decades of observation, and delivered without apology.

If you need tailored answers, seek out a qualified professional. I'm not here to tell you how to run your tribe, your business, or your life. I'm here to hold up a mirror. What you choose to do with it is on you.

Neither I nor the publisher accepts responsibility for the actions or decisions made based on what's written here.

This book doesn't offer safe conclusions.

It asks dangerous questions.

No warranties—express or implied—are made regarding the accuracy, completeness, or outcomes associated with this material.

Rebuttal

Not every word in this book will apply to every tribe. It's not supposed to. But the patterns discussed here—the dysfunction, the courage, the corruption, the hope—echo across Indian Country.

Some of it will sting. Some might miss the mark. That's expected.

Discomfort is not a flaw in the process. It is the process.

Denial has held us hostage long enough.

As Chief Dan George said in The Outlaw Josey Wales:

"Endeavor to persevere."

That's the spirit this book carries—pushing through the discomfort not to destroy what we have, but to finally build something honest on ground we stop pretending isn't cracked.

This is not a weapon. It's a tool.
Use it however you must.
But don't ignore it.

Editorial Note

This book was edited with intention by the author, in line with its voice, style, and cultural truth.

It has not been externally polished for mass-market appeal, as that would compromise its message and authenticity. Every word was chosen to serve the purpose of truth—not perfection.

Mini-Disclaimer: On Truth Itself

The facts presented in this book—whether drawn from archives, public records, oral testimony, or hard-won experience—are offered in good faith.

But let's be honest: history is rarely neutral. It's rarely whole. And it's almost never told by the people who lived it.

"Truth," like history, is shaped by the hands that hold the pen. And far too often, that pen has never rested in ours.

What gets recorded, taught, or funded is usually what flatters the dominant narrative—and erases our own.

This book was written to challenge that.
It speaks from the other side of the pen.

On Accuracy and Error

This book draws on extended research, a multitude of sources, and decades of lived experience. Every fact, citation, and reference was chosen with care. Yet no work of this scope is flawless. Records are incomplete, archives are biased, memories are imperfect, and even with extreme effort, errors can occur.

The intent here has never been to distort or mislead, but to present truth as fully and faithfully as possible. Where mistakes exist—whether in dates, citations, or interpretation—they are mine alone. They do not diminish the core message of this work: that Indian Country must face its realities with courage, not denial.

"Embracing the truth—no matter how uncomfortable—is the first step toward real progress and healing in Indian Country."

Authorship Note

Unless otherwise cited, all standalone statements, epigraphs, and in-text quotes throughout this book are original works by the author, D.G. Comer.

Terminology Note

While this book uses terms such as "Native Americans," "Indigenous peoples," or "tribal members" for accessibility and legal clarity, it must be acknowledged that these labels are external constructs—names given by colonizers, governments, and academics. The people of this land have always had their own names, spoken in their own languages.

For example, the Lakota refer to themselves as Lakȟóta, meaning "allies" or "friends." The Diné—commonly known as the Navajo—use their own word, Diné, meaning "The People." The Anishinaabe, often grouped under terms like Ojibwe or Chippewa, call themselves Anishinaabeg, meaning "original people." And the Coeur d'Alene Tribe refers to themselves as the Schitsu'umsh, meaning "Those Who Were Found Here" or "The Discovered People."

"Native American" is not a term created by Native people. It is a governmental classification, a convenience of paperwork and political language. While useful in broader discussions, it is important to remember that these identities are not generic. They are distinct, sovereign, and deeply rooted in place, language, and history. Wherever possible, this book respects and defers to tribal self-identification.

Lim lemt·sh,

—**D.G. Comer**

Reading the Fire: How This Book is Meant to Burn

Reader's Orientation

This isn't a book built for passive reading. It's built for reckoning.
The chapters ahead are not arranged to please the academic world or chase trending headlines. They're arranged to confront truth as it unfolds in our lives: historically, internally, politically, economically, and forward into the unknown.

Each section builds on the one before it, but every chapter also stands alone—like a drumbeat calling attention to another wound, another injustice, another unfinished battle in Indian Country.

You can read this front to back. You can skip around. You can sit with one chapter for a day or rip through a dozen in a night. But understand this: each section is a fire. It may warm you. It may burn you. But either way, it's meant to change something inside you.

There's no fluff here. No manufactured hope. Just a blunt, unvarnished look at what we've survived, what we're still battling, and what we must face if we ever want to move forward with strength and sovereignty.
Read it how you need to—but don't read it safe.

How the Fire Burns

The sections in this book are structured like the rings of a fire—each one burning toward the center of what it means to survive and lead in Indian C

SECTION I: Historical Assaults and Federal Violence

To understand where we are now, you have to know exactly what was done to get us here.

This opening section exposes the foundations of Native struggle—not through romantic nostalgia or filtered textbooks, but through hard truth. From genocidal policies and broken treaties to cultural erasure disguised as salvation, these chapters trace how the U.S. government systematically dismantled Native nations, identities, and futures.

This is not ancient history—it's inherited trauma still shaping tribal realities today. It is not just a record of harm—it's the necessary evidence for understanding the present.

SECTION II: Our Internal Reckoning

Not all battles are waged from the outside. Some of the hardest truths live within.

This section holds up a mirror to the internal struggles facing Indian Country—challenges born from historical trauma, but now sustained by silence, denial, and inertia. From mental health crises and educational disparities to food deserts and self-sabotage, these are the patterns we must break if we are to move forward. But this isn't a surrender—it's a reckoning.

The healing starts when we stop pretending we're not still bleeding.

SECTION III: Politics, Power, and Leadership

Leadership is either a tool for liberation—or a weapon against our own.

This section confronts the politics of tribal governance head-on. From nepotism and power hoarding to gender imbalances and systemic burnout, these chapters explore what happens when we trade accountability for comfort. We examine the forces that shape—and often twist—tribal politics, including the invisible hands of outsiders and the complicity of insiders.

If sovereignty is the destination, leadership is the vehicle. It's time we asked who's driving—and why.

SECTION IV: Rebuilding the Tribal Economy

Survival was never the goal. Thriving is.

This section dives into the heart of Native economic sovereignty. From gaming to green energy, from tech to cultural preservation, tribes are finding new ways to build sustainable futures—but not without setbacks, sabotage, and hard lessons. These chapters look at what works, what doesn't, and how we can stop recycling the same failed models.

It's not just about money. It's about freedom, dignity, and control over our own destinies.

SECTION V: Vision, Language, and the Long Future

The road ahead is uncertain. But we do not walk it blindly.

This final section turns toward the horizon, asking the hard questions about where we're headed and who we're becoming. From the survival of our languages to the emergence of new Native leadership, these chapters explore the costs of sovereignty, the responsibilities of self-rule, and the reckoning still to come.

We are not just the survivors of history—we are the authors of what comes next

Courtesy of the National Archives

Write Observations Here

Government Policies to Eliminate Native Americans

"Understanding the history of displacement and assimilation policies reveals the enduring strength of Native communities and the profound resilience required to overcome systematic erasure."

A Trail of Paper and Blood

The history between Native nations and the federal government is not one of misunderstanding. It is one of design. What unfolded over centuries was not accidental—it was deliberate. A series of legal instruments, policies, and violent acts crafted with precision to remove, relocate, assimilate, and ultimately erase the Indigenous presence from the American landscape.

To understand the resilience of Native communities today, we must confront the machinery that tried to extinguish them. This chapter does not simply recount history—it holds it accountable. It lays bare the structure of erasure, the weight of dispossession, and the unyielding survival of Indigenous nations who refused to vanish.

Historical Context: From Papal Bulls to American Statutes

Before the first rifle was fired or treaty signed, the foundation of Native displacement was laid in European ideology. The Doctrine of Discovery, born from 15th-century papal decrees, granted Christian monarchs the "right" to claim lands inhabited by non-Christian peoples. This ideology was not abandoned—it was absorbed into U.S. law and used to justify the systematic theft of Native land. (Miller et al., 2010)

It codified a lie: that unceded, sovereign lands could be claimed through flag planting and legal gymnastics. From this doctrine, a government blueprint of erasure was born.

Policies of Removal and Containment

Signed by President Andrew Jackson, the Indian Removal Act authorized the forced displacement of entire Native nations. Under its command, the Cherokee, Choctaw, Muscogee (Creek), Chickasaw, and Seminole were marched from their ancestral homelands to unfamiliar, often barren lands west of the Mississippi. (Prucha, 1984)

What remains in our national memory as the "Trail of Tears" was not merely a trail—it was a mass atrocity. Thousands died from exposure, disease, and starvation. Children were buried by the roadside. Families torn apart. This was not relocation. It was organized cultural decimation.

Throughout the 19th century, the U.S. government signed treaties under the guise of diplomacy. In truth, many of these agreements were secured through coercion, false promises, or outright fraud. (Wilkinson, 2005)

Tribes were offered peace in exchange for land—and then betrayed when peace was inconvenient. The reservation system that followed was not a sanctuary. It was confinement. Tribes were placed on marginal lands with little regard for sustainability or sovereignty. Promised annuities and resources rarely came. The goal was containment, not care. The treaty system taught Native nations a grim lesson: ink and trust do not mix when written by a colonizer's hand.

Assimilation as Cultural Violence

The General Allotment Act, or Dawes Act, presented itself as reform. In truth, it was a scalpel. It divided tribal lands into individual plots, severing communal bonds and declaring surplus lands available for white settlement. Within a generation, Native landholdings had been reduced by over 90 million acres. (Otis, 1973)

This wasn't land reform—it was cultural sabotage. The collective governance, ceremonial gathering, and intergenerational wisdom that defined tribal life were fractured by fenced parcels and forced individualism. It was a policy that sought not only to divide land, but to divide identity.

Beginning in the late 1800s, Native children were torn from their homes and placed into government-run boarding schools, many operated by Christian denominations. They were beaten for speaking their languages. Their braids were cut. Their names replaced. Their spirits often broken. (Adams, 1995)

"Kill the Indian, save the man" was not metaphor. It was policy. The abuse—physical, emotional, and sexual—left generations scarred.

The legacy of these schools is not just in trauma, but in the silences they created: languages not spoken, songs not sung, ceremonies not passed down. It was a genocide of memory.

Mid-20th Century Erasure: Termination and Relocation

By the 1950s, the federal government pursued a new path: termination. Over 100 tribes were stripped of their legal status, their lands sold, and their federal services severed. (Fixico, 1986)

The policy aimed to dissolve tribes into the American melting pot—disappear them not by force, but by bureaucracy. Termination destroyed communities. It uprooted governance, fractured economies, and deepened poverty. Where once there was sovereignty, there was now silence.

The Relocation Program lured Native people to cities with promises of jobs and opportunity. What awaited them was often unemployment, isolation, and systemic racism. (Rosenthal, 1991)

Disconnected from homelands, cultural anchors, and kinship networks, many became lost in concrete landscapes that offered no belonging. This wasn't relocation. It was dislocation. Another step in the campaign to scatter Native identity until it became invisible.

The Lasting Wounds: Inequity as Policy Legacy

The aftermath of these policies is not past—it is present. Generational poverty, lack of infrastructure, housing crises, and chronic underfunding are the children of historical policy. Economic sovereignty remains a daily fight, not a given.

High rates of diabetes, heart disease, addiction, and suicide in Native communities are not random—they are consequences of cultural fracture and systemic neglect. Western medicine treats symptoms. Native healing understands the root: disconnection from land, language, and lineage.

Policy Reversals and Movements Toward Justice

The IRA was the first federal step toward restoring tribal governance. (Kelly, 2012)

It allowed tribes to draft constitutions and reclaim communal landholdings. It wasn't perfect, but it shifted the federal tone—from elimination to recognition.

This landmark law restored to tribes the authority to administer their own education, health, and governance programs. (Deloria & Lytle, 1984)

For the first time in modern history, the pen was placed back in Native hands—though still within the lines drawn by federal oversight.

The Native American Graves Protection and Repatriation Act provided a legal pathway for tribes to reclaim ancestral remains and sacred objects from museums and institutions. (Trope & Echo-Hawk, 2000)

This was not just a return of artifacts—it was a return of dignity.

Conclusion: From Ruin, We Rise

The policies designed to eliminate us failed. Not because they were weak—but because we were stronger. We are the descendants of survivors, of those who walked the Trail of Tears, who hid their songs in silence, who rebuilt from ashes.

To this day, we live with the shadows of those policies. But we also live with the fire of those who refused to be extinguished. Understanding this history is not a call for pity—it is a call for reckoning. For repair. For reclamation.

"The erasure of our people was drafted in ink, but our survival was carved in bone."

Historical Perspective: Government and Treaties

Introduction

From the first ink on the first treaty, Native people have been led to believe that promises carried weight. But we learned otherwise. The relationship between the United States government and Native nations has never been one of equals. Instead, it has been a long march through deception, forced displacement, and legislative erasure.

This chapter tells a hard truth—our truth. It is a reckoning with broken covenants, stolen land, and the bitter consequences of believing in promises never meant to be kept. Yet, it is also a tribute to our survival, our memory, and the sovereignty that still beats in our hearts.

Review of Treaties Between the United States and Native American Tribes (1800 – Present)

Between 1800 and the present day, the United States entered into approximately 368 treaties with Native nations. These treaties were meant to codify peace, define territorial sovereignty, and ensure mutual respect. Instead, they became instruments of erasure. Behind every handshake was an ulterior motive. Behind every signature, a shadow of betrayal.

Number of Broken Treaties

Of the 368 treaties signed, nearly every single one was broken. Some were ignored. Others were undermined by new laws or nullified by military force. Whether by delay, deception, or outright denial, the United States failed to honor the vast majority of its agreements. The ink was barely dry before boots crossed borders that were never meant to be violated.

Who Broke the Treaties?

It was not rogue actors or isolated officials. It was the federal government itself. Congress, courts, and presidents presided over a systematic dismantling of treaty obligations. The Dawes Act. The Indian Appropriations Act. The theft of the Black Hills. All government sanctioned. All written in contradiction to the agreements our ancestors signed in good faith.

Treaties Still in Effect Today

Legally, many treaties remain in force. But law without enforcement is theater. In courts, Native nations still cite treaties to defend hunting rights, land claims, and sovereignty. Sometimes they win. Most times, they are met with political resistance or bureaucratic obstruction. These treaties live in the legal code, but not in the conscience of the country.

Summary

To understand the modern struggle of Native nations, we must confront the legacy of broken treaties. These documents were never relics. They were rights. And their betrayal is not history—it is a living wound. Yet from this truth, a new generation rises, armed not only with memory, but with purpose.

Early Treaties and Agreements

In the earliest days of the American republic, treaty-making followed colonial habits—treaties were tools for expansion, not justice. To Native nations, land was sacred and communal. To the settlers, it was property to be surveyed, sold, and fenced. The 1778 Treaty of Fort Pitt with the Delaware Nation promised an alliance and even a Native state. Neither came to pass (Prucha, 1994). This was not an exception. It was a precedent.

19th Century Treaties

The 1800s brought expansion, gold, and greed. The Indian Removal Act of 1830 forced entire nations from their homelands, culminating in the Trail of Tears. Thousands died (Remini, 1981). The Fort Laramie Treaties of 1851 and 1868 promised the Lakota their sacred Black Hills. That promise was broken the moment gold was discovered. The government sent soldiers instead of stewards. What was sold as peace became policy for relocation, reservation, and repression (Debo, 1940).

Allotment and Assimilation

In 1887, the Dawes Act divided tribal lands into individual allotments. Surplus lands were sold to white settlers. By 1934, we had lost over 90 million acres (Otis, 1973). This was not just land theft. It was the erosion of our collective way of life. At the same time, the government implemented boarding schools. "Kill the Indian, save the man," they said (Adams, 1995). Generations of Native children were taken, beaten, stripped of language and spirit.

Termination and Relocation

By the mid-20th century, the federal government launched a new assault: Termination. It ended federal recognition of tribes, removed protections, and forced relocation to cities. The promise? Jobs. The result? Poverty, alienation, and broken communities (Fixico, 1986). Public Law 280 transferred tribal jurisdiction to states, further undermining sovereignty (Wilkins & Lomawaima, 2001).

Continued Impact of Historical Policies

The policies of the past cast long shadows. Native communities continue to suffer the highest poverty rates in the United States. Chronic illnesses. Substance abuse. Mental health crises. These are not cultural failings—they are the aftermath of deliberate policies designed to erase us (Snipp, 1989). Our lands are often exploited for mining, oil, and pipelines, with little benefit returned to our people (Jorgensen, 1971).

Government Policies That Helped Native Americans

There were exceptions—brief, hard-won moments when federal policy didn't aim to erase us, but to repair what had been broken. They were few, but they mattered. These laws did not undo the damage of genocide, displacement, or assimilation—but they offered footholds. They gave tribes tools to reclaim control, protect our dead, and begin rebuilding from centuries of sanctioned loss.

Indian Reorganization Act (1934)

This act marked the federal government's first formal admission that the allotment era had been a failure. Under the Indian Reorganization Act, or IRA, tribes were encouraged to reestablish self-governance structures—tribal councils, constitutions, and systems of local authority.

The act halted further allotment of tribal lands and allowed tribes to reacquire and hold land in trust. It also provided funding for economic development, educational programs, and the preservation of Native art, language, and tradition. For many tribes, it was the first time in modern memory that federal policy had encouraged—not criminalized—cultural survival. (Taylor, 1980)

Indian Self-Determination and Education Assistance Act (1975)

This law didn't give us power—it acknowledged that we had it all along. For the first time since colonization, tribes could contract directly with the federal government to manage programs like healthcare, education, housing, and infrastructure.

Control moved from the Bureau of Indian Affairs back to tribal councils and Native-run agencies. It was sovereignty in action—imperfect, but empowering. Many of today's tribal institutions were born in the wake of this law. (Cornell & Kalt, 1992)

Native American Graves Protection and Repatriation Act (1990)

NAGPRA was a line in the sand. It told museums, universities, and private collectors: our ancestors are not artifacts. This law required institutions to return stolen human remains, burial items, and sacred objects to their rightful tribal homes.

The returns weren't always smooth. Some institutions resisted. Some tribes received only fragments. But for many, the act was a first step in spiritual restoration—dignity for the dead, and healing for the living. (Echo-Hawk, 2002)

American Indian Religious Freedom Act (1978)

It took until 1978—two centuries after the Constitution—for Congress to affirm that Native people had the right to practice our traditional religions. The American Indian Religious Freedom Act protected ceremonies once outlawed, such as the Sun Dance and sweat lodges, and allowed access to sacred sites on public land. It also opened the legal door to peyote use in Native spiritual practices. The law was imperfect—often more symbolic than enforceable—but it reasserted that our spirituality is not folklore, and our ceremonies are not crimes. (Deloria, 1999)

Indian Health Care Improvement Act (1976)

Passed one year after the Self-Determination Act, this law restructured Native healthcare delivery. It permanently authorized federal support for the Indian Health Service (IHS) and expanded services like mental health care, substance abuse treatment, and health education.

It acknowledged that Native health disparities were the product of policy neglect—not personal failure. While IHS remains chronically underfunded, this act became the legal foundation for improving Native health outcomes. (Rhoades, 2000)

Tribal Law and Order Act (2010)

Violence in Indian Country—especially against Native women—has long been met with federal indifference. The Tribal Law and Order Act aimed to fix that by giving tribes more authority to prosecute crimes, improve data sharing between jurisdictions, and train tribal police. It didn't eliminate jurisdictional chaos, but it started to give tribes back the right to protect their own. (Deer, 2015)

Violence Against Women Reauthorization Act (2013 & 2022 Amendments)

This law allowed tribes to prosecute non-Natives for domestic violence committed on tribal lands—a radical shift from past federal restrictions. For the first time in modern legal history, tribes regained partial authority over non-Indians who harm Native women. Later amendments expanded that authority to include sexual assault and child abuse. It was a long-overdue recognition that sovereignty means nothing if we cannot protect our own. (Deer, 2022)

Together, these laws form a patchwork—not a full restoration, but a series of lifelines thrown into deep water. They are reminders that when policy is shaped with tribal voices at the table, it can repair instead of erase. They prove that change is possible—when it is demanded, defended, and made into law.

Conclusion

The history of treaties and federal policy is one of betrayal, but also of endurance. Despite every attempt to erase us, we remain. Our voices rise in courts, in councils, in classrooms. We carry memory as armor.

Sovereignty as truth. And the future—though forged through hardship—is still ours to shape.

They took the land, but they never took the fire. It smolders in our stories, waiting to rise."We were never given justice. We carved it from memory and made it law."

Observations

Treaties & Tribal Govts: Protecting the System, Not the People

"We did not inherit these governments from our ancestors. We inherited them from Washington."

In Indian Country, the conversation around sovereignty often centers on governments and treaties—as if the survival of the people depends entirely on the survival of the institutions that claim to represent them. But what if the very systems we hold up as protective shields are quietly sharpening the knives that wound us?

The Original Sin of the Treaty System

Treaties between Native nations and the United States were never acts of goodwill. They were legal instruments of control. Though written as agreements between sovereigns, most treaties were signed under duress, deception, or the looming threat of violence. The language often promised peace, protection, and land security—but in reality, those documents paved the road to confinement, dependence, and loss of identity (Deloria & Lytle, 1983).

These treaties formed the basis for federal recognition of tribal governments. But what they recognized was not the spiritual and communal structures that guided Native peoples for centuries. Instead, the U.S. acknowledged a replacement system—one built in its own image. A system of councils, constitutions, and bureaucracies that mirrored the very power structures responsible for our displacement.

Invented Sovereignty, Imported Governance

The tribal governments we know today are not extensions of ancient tribal authority. They are constructs of the 1934 Indian Reorganization Act (IRA), a New Deal policy that replaced traditional leadership models with U.S.-approved governing bodies (Wilkins & Stark, 2018). These governments were not meant to preserve Native autonomy—they were designed to manage Native populations.

The result? A generation of Native people now finds themselves governed by institutions that reflect federal priorities more than cultural ones. The line between tribal self-determination and federal mimicry is thin, blurred, and dangerous. Where once our leaders were chosen for their wisdom, their humility, or their ceremonial standing, today they are often selected by popular vote or political maneuvering—using a system imposed from the outside.

Government Over People

In theory, tribal governments should serve the needs of their people. In practice, many serve the maintenance of power. Tribal leaders often invoke sovereignty to justify their decisions, but sovereignty has become less about protecting the community and more about protecting the institution.

- Whistleblowers within tribal departments are silenced or fired.
- Qualified candidates are passed over for politically favored individuals.
- Community voices are ignored unless they align with those in power.

This is not just anecdotal—it is widespread. The same immunity that shields tribal governments from federal oversight under Title VII also shields them from internal accountability. And with limited investigative journalism and no enforceable civil rights infrastructure, many tribal communities become political silos where dissent is punished and compliance is rewarded (Washburn, 2006).

Treaties as Tools of Control

Treaties are still used today—not to expand Native freedom, but to regulate it. Consider how treaty language is invoked in federal funding, jurisdictional disputes, and resource allocations. Tribes must constantly prove their "treaty rights" to access what was promised long ago. And when those rights are contested, the U.S. Congress, not tribal citizens, is the final arbiter.

This dependence on treaty-based recognition forces tribes into a strange double-bind: To be sovereign, you must accept the federal definition of sovereignty.

To receive justice, you must ask the same government that historically denied it.

Who Benefits from This Structure?

Certainly not the individual Native citizen. The biggest beneficiaries of the current system are often the tribal governments themselves—especially those entrenched in power. When federal money flows, it flows through governments, not people. When grants are awarded, they go to tribal programs, not grassroots efforts. When lawsuits are filed, it's the government that gets standing—not the families hurt by tribal negligence or abuse.

And when injustice happens inside a tribal office—whether it's wrongful termination, embezzlement, or election fraud—there is rarely an external path for justice. Sovereignty is cited as the reason, but what it really protects is the political apparatus, not the people it claims to serve.

The Double Exile

For many Native professionals, this system is suffocating.
You can be fired without cause, denied opportunities because of your lineage, or punished for challenging corruption—all within your own nation. And there is no legal recourse. The same U.S. government that once stole your land now refuses to protect you from your own.

So what do many do? They leave.
They work for the federal government, for state agencies, for non-tribal businesses—because in those places, their rights are at least theoretically protected. The exodus of talent from Indian Country isn't just economic—it's existential. Our best and brightest are fleeing not because they've abandoned their people, but because their governments have abandoned them.

Reimagining Sovereignty

Sovereignty cannot simply mean the right of a tribal government to rule unchecked. True sovereignty must mean the right of a Native individual to live with dignity, voice, and protection—even from their own systems.

To move forward, we must:
- Demand constitutional reform within tribal nations that ensures individual rights.

- Create independent ombudsman systems to review tribal government actions.
- Redefine federal policy to include individual protections in sovereign contexts.
- Re-examine treaties—not to discard them, but to rewrite them for the people, not the paper.

Closing Reflection:

"We were told treaties would protect us, that tribal governments were ours. But in too many places, they have become walls instead of bridges—tools of silence instead of strength. Our future does not rest in preserving the forms of sovereignty imposed on us. It rests in building a new sovereignty—one that protects the people, not the paper."

Legacy of Harm – U.S. Government

"They didn't just take our land. They wrote laws to bury our names, built schools to erase our tongues, and sterilized our women to silence our future. This wasn't neglect—it was design. A genocide not just by gunpowder, but by paper, policy, and procedural indifference."

There are so many facets of the harm done to us that each one could fill a volume. Treaties broken, languages stolen, children buried, lands carved and sold—each story is its own wound, its own history. If you feel the need to understand more—and you should—I encourage you to seek it out. Read the testimonies. Research the policies. Confront the atrocities done, not just in the distant past, but in laws still on the books today.

Policies That Devastated Native America

History books often sanitize the truth. They'll footnote a massacre, reframe a forced removal as a treaty provision, or praise the "progress" of assimilation without ever naming the cost. But for Native people, these were not policies—they were weapons. Enacted through law, enforced with guns, and sustained by silence.

Below is not simply a list. It is a reckoning. These laws, acts, and policies—from the 1700s to the present—formed the architecture of cultural destruction, generational poverty, and loss of life for Indigenous peoples in what became the United States. Many remain misunderstood. Some are still in effect. All have left scars that shape Indian Country today.

1700s–Early 1800s: Foundations of Displacement

Royal Proclamation of 1763

Intended to halt settler–Native conflict by restricting westward expansion, the Proclamation Line was quickly ignored. It didn't protect tribal lands—it mapped the next stage of conquest.

Enabled future encroachment and land seizure.
(Calloway, 2018)

Indian Trade and Intercourse Acts (1790-1834)

These laws claimed to regulate commerce and reduce fraud. In reality, they laid bureaucratic groundwork for mass land cessions.
Millions of acres lost through manipulation and forced treaties.
(Banner, 2005)

Forced Treaty System (1790s-1810s)

Hundreds of treaties were signed under duress, deception, or military threat. Each signature marked another vanishing homeland.
Over 100,000 Indigenous people displaced. (Prucha, 1994)

Mid-1800s: Ethnic Cleansing and Reservation Confinement

Indian Removal Act (1830)

The Trail of Tears wasn't a tragedy—it was policy. This act gave legal cover to the forced migration of southeastern tribes.
~100,000 removed; 15,000–20,000 died during forced marches.
(Perdue & Green, 2007)

Treaty of New Echota (1835)

Signed by a minority faction, this treaty was used to justify the Cherokee's removal. ~4,000 Cherokee perished on the Trail of Tears.
(Ehle, 1988)

California Act for the Government and Protection of Indians (1850)

This law legalized the indenture, kidnapping, and killing of Native Californians. Estimated 100,000 Native Californians killed between 1846–1873. (Madley, 2016)

Dakota War and Mass Execution (1862)

Following starvation and broken treaties, the Dakota resisted. The U.S. responded with trials and mass hangings. Hundreds killed; 38 Dakota executed in the largest mass execution in U.S. history. (Carley, 1976)

Sand Creek Massacre (1864)

A U.S. militia attacked a peaceful encampment of Cheyenne and Arapaho, despite raised white flags. ~230 killed, mostly women and children. (Hoig, 1961)

Indian Appropriations Acts (1851, 1871)

Created reservations and ended recognition of tribes as sovereign nations. Led to systemic confinement, disease, and dependency. (Debo, 1940)

Wounded Knee Massacre (1890)

The U.S. Army killed hundreds of mostly unarmed Lakota during a religious revival. ~250–300 Lakota Sioux killed. (Brown, 1970)

Late 1800s: Land Theft and Forced Assimilation

Dawes Act (1887)

Allotted land to individuals and sold the rest to settlers. It destroyed communal landholding systems and spiritual geography.
 90 million acres lost; cultural identity fractured.
(Debo, 1940)

Curtis Act (1898)

Extended Dawes policies to the Five Civilized Tribes, abolishing tribal courts and governments. Further dismantling of sovereignty and land ownership. (Debo, 1940)

Federal Boarding School System (1870s–1970s)

Children were taken from families and stripped of their language, hair, and heritage. Tens of thousands abused; thousands died. Full numbers remain unknown. (Adams, 1995)

1900s: Termination, Relocation, and Systemic Suppression

Indian Citizenship Act (1924)

Granted U.S. citizenship without tribal consent—often used as a tool of assimilation. Political maneuver to reduce tribal sovereignty.
(Bruyneel, 2007)

Termination Policy (1953–1968)

Over 100 tribes lost federal recognition, land, and services.
1.3 million acres lost; intensified poverty and cultural erasure.
(Fixico, 1986)

Termination and the Paper Genocide of Indian Country

It didn't come with bullets or cavalry charges this time. It came with legislation, resolutions, and a pen. In 1953, the U.S. government enacted a policy called Termination—a direct attempt to erase tribes from legal existence. The language was sanitized—framed as "freeing" Native people from dependency—but the goal was clear: dismantle tribal sovereignty, liquidate communally held land, and sever the federal trust responsibility once and for all.

This wasn't passive neglect. It was deliberate erasure—a paper genocide aimed not just at lands or economies, but at identity itself.

Under House Concurrent Resolution 108, dozens of tribes were earmarked for immediate termination. The Menominee in Wisconsin. The Klamath in Oregon. The Flathead, the Tonkawa, the Peoria, and many others. Some were offered a payout—a government check in exchange for the dissolution of their nationhood. Others weren't offered anything at all. What they all lost was the same: recognition, services, jurisdiction, and the legal standing to exist as sovereign peoples. Hospitals were shut down. Schools defunded. Land was turned over to tax authorities. Reservations became counties. Treaties became meaningless.

Tribes were forced to reorganize into corporations—as if ancestral memory, communal governance, and cultural continuity could be refashioned into quarterly reports.

In Klamath County, Oregon, hundreds of tribal members—cut off from support—sold their land to logging companies just to survive. In Menominee County, Wisconsin, public services collapsed. Poverty deepened. Alcoholism and suicide spiked. And what was the federal response? Silence.

Termination didn't just dispossess Native nations. It declared they no longer existed. And many Americans never even knew it happened.

By the late 1960s, Native activism—including the rise of the American Indian Movement—began to force a national reckoning. Laws were challenged. Protests ignited. Some tribes, like the Menominee, fought for years to regain their federal status—finally restored in 1973. But others never came back. They remain terminated to this day, unrecognized by the federal government, stripped of land and legal identity, and locked out of programs tied to their stolen sovereignty.

Termination was not an anomaly. It was a strategy. A final solution dressed in legalese. It was not an attempt to fix "the Indian problem"—it was an attempt to eliminate it.

Public Law 280 (1953)

Imposed state legal control over tribal lands without consent.
Undermined jurisdiction and tribal legal authority.
(Goldberg, 1975)

Indian Relocation Act (1956)

Promised jobs and opportunity if Native people left reservations. It delivered poverty, isolation, and broken families.
Urban displacement and cultural disconnection. (Fixico, 1986)

Late 1900s–Present: Structural Harm and Policy Neglect

Broken Treaty Enforcement (1770s–Present)

Over 370 ratified treaties violated. Most remain unfulfilled.
Loss of land, resources, rights, and legal standing.
(Wilkins & Lomawaima, 2001)

Sterilization of Native Women (1960s–1970s)

IHS doctors conducted thousands of forced or coerced sterilizations.
Est. Some scholars have argued that 25–50% of Native women affected. (Lawrence, 2000)

Environmental Destruction (1950s–Present)

Uranium mining, oil pipelines, and toxic dumping poisoned tribal lands and waters. Thousands exposed to cancer-causing agents, contaminated drinking water. (LaDuke, 1999)

Jurisdictional Gaps in Protection (Pre-2013)

Tribal courts could not prosecute non-Natives for crimes, even on tribal lands. 1 in 3 Native women raped; 86% of perpetrators were non-Native. (Deer, 2015)

Modern Examples (2000–Present)

Standing Rock / Dakota Access Pipeline (2016–2017)

The federal government approved pipeline construction without tribal consent. Protests were met with militarized force.
 Hundreds injured; sacred land and water rights ignored.
(Estes, 2019)

McGirt v. Oklahoma (2020)

The Supreme Court ruled that much of eastern Oklahoma remains tribal land. It affirmed treaty law—but revealed decades of jurisdictional overreach. Thousands of convictions deemed unlawful; historic tribal boundaries upheld. (McGirt v. Oklahoma, 2020)

Chronic Underfunding of Indian Health Service (Ongoing)

IHS continues to be one of the most underfunded healthcare systems in America. Life expectancy for Native Americans is 5–7 years below national average. (IHS, 2021)

Estimated Indigenous Lives Lost (Linked to U.S. Policy)

The ledger of American history is stained not just by broken treaties, but by the blood of those who paid for them with their lives. While no exact figure can capture the full scale of devastation wrought by U.S. policy, scholars and Native historians estimate that millions of Indigenous lives were lost—directly or indirectly—through government-sanctioned actions, neglect, and erasure.

Colonial Era through 1900

- Estimated Loss: Between 10 and 20 million Indigenous people across the Americas died from disease, displacement, and violence following European contact. In what became the United States, estimates suggest that 90% of the pre-contact population perished within a few centuries.
- Causes: Smallpox and other foreign diseases; mass killings during westward expansion; forced relocations such as the Trail of Tears; starvation due to bison extermination and reservation confinement.

20th Century U.S. Policies

- Boarding Schools: Thousands of Native children died or disappeared within federal and church-run institutions designed to "kill the Indian, save the man." Psychological, physical, and cultural death were not side effects—they were objectives.
- Sterilization and Medical Abuse: In the 1970s alone, an estimated Some scholars have argued that 25–50% of Native women of childbearing age were forcibly sterilized by the Indian Health Service—often without consent. See the section at the end of this chapter: Sterilization and Medical Abuse: The Unspoken Genocide
- Neglect and Structural Violence: Rampant poverty, inadequate healthcare, and state-sanctioned underfunding of tribal programs led to avoidable deaths from preventable disease, suicide, and addiction.

Contemporary Era

- Missing and Murdered Indigenous Women (MMIW): Thousands of Native women and girls have disappeared or been murdered in recent decades—many in jurisdictions where legal systems failed to act, refused to investigate, or lacked authority altogether.
- Youth Suicide and Addiction: Suicide rates among Native youth are more than double the national average. Substance abuse deaths follow a similar trajectory—traced to generational trauma and unresolved grief.

A Note on the Numbers

We will never know the true count. Some losses were recorded. Most were not. Entire generations vanished without a name etched in any census or ledger. But the absence of a number does not mean the absence of a life. These were our ancestors, our children, our brothers and sisters.

> They were not collateral damage.
> They were the cost of conquest.

There are thousands more laws, orders, policies, and court rulings—each designed to displace, control, or erase Indigenous people from this land. What you've just read is not the full story. It's only a sample—a sliver of a much larger truth that rarely makes it into classrooms or textbooks. If you think this history is uncomfortable, then good. Go look deeper. Read the treaties. Study the congressional records. Ask why this isn't common knowledge. Because the truth is still there—buried under bureaucracy, whitewashed in civics books, and waiting to be confronted by anyone with the courage to stop pretending America doesn't know what it did.

Sterilization and Medical Abuse: The Unspoken Genocide

At minimum, thousands of Native women were sterilized in Indian Health Service facilities in the 1970s—documented in federal records. Scholarly estimates argue the true toll is higher in Indian Country, given under-reporting, uneven audits, and procedures performed off-contract or without IHS paperwork. The fact that we can only speak in ranges is itself part of the harm: when the files go missing, so does the accountability.

- Subsequent scholarship & testimonies report higher regional counts, citing clinic logs, interviews, and patterns of consent violations.
- Evidence of procedures performed at non-IHS hospitals under contract or referral—less likely to appear in IHS tallies.

Verdict: The documented minimum is enough to indict the system; the likely reality indicts the era. We name both—so the paper trail cannot excuse what the paper trail failed to record.

Dr. Connie Pinkerman-Uri, a Choctaw/Cherokee physician, exposed the depth of this abuse. She discovered widespread patterns of coercion, misinformation, and outright deception in IHS and federally contracted hospitals. Women were told the procedure was temporary. Others were simply not informed. Some were operated on while under anesthesia for unrelated procedures and awakened to find their reproductive capacity taken from them (Pinkerman-Uri, 1977). Others were threatened with the loss of their children or food assistance if they refused (Torpy, 2000).

In 1976, under growing public pressure, the U.S. Government Accountability Office (GAO) launched a limited investigation. The result: at least 3,406 sterilizations of Native women were performed in just four IHS service areas over a three-year span (U.S. GAO, 1976). But this number represented only a subset of the country. No comprehensive audit was ever completed. The real total remains unknown—likely far higher.

This was not an isolated abuse. It was part of a federal pattern—steeped in eugenics-era ideology and masked under the bureaucratic veil of "public health." Sterilization of marginalized groups, especially women of color, had long been a quiet tool of social engineering in the U.S. Native women were simply among the last and most invisible to be targeted (Stern, 2005).

There was no national outcry. No reparations. No official apology. The story faded from headlines almost as quickly as it appeared.

But our communities remember.

We remember not just the loss of reproductive rights, but the extinguishing of futures. The children never born. The broken family lines. The grandmothers who carried that knowledge in silence. The daughters who learned, too late, why their bodies never conceived.

This was genocide. Not by the gun, but by the scalpel.

And it happened in fluorescent-lit clinics, under the seal of the federal government, to women who were supposed to be protected—yet were treated as less than human.

Let the record show: Native women were not failed by the healthcare system.

They were targeted by it.

Conclusion

This wasn't an accident. It wasn't a misunderstanding, a policy gone wrong, or a few bad actors in Washington. It was deliberate. From the halls of Congress to the pulpit, from Supreme Court decisions to state statutes, a clear message echoed for centuries: Native people were obstacles to be removed, reshaped, or erased. And it hasn't stopped!

And society didn't just watch—it participated. It benefited. It built homes on stolen land, sent children to schools funded by treaty violations, and passed down family stories scrubbed clean of Native blood. Churches preached it. Schools taught it. Newspapers sold it. And generations of Americans called it progress.

We were relocated, renamed, reprogrammed, and reborn under laws we never asked for, enforced by governments that broke every promise they made. Our dead lie in unmarked graves. Our languages were beaten out of our children. Our bodies were sterilized in secret clinics. And when we protested—even peacefully—we were shot with rubber bullets and sprayed like animals for defending water.

This is not ancient history. It is ongoing harm, codified in law and calcified in the institutions that still shape daily life in Indian Country.

Courtesy of the National Archives.

So the next time someone asks why Native people still struggle, or why we can't "just move on," tell them to open a law book. Tell them to read the fine print of every policy that was written about us—but never for us. And then ask them: If this had been done to your people, would you have survived at all?

Echoes of a Lost Population

"To reflect on what was lost is to touch the sorrow of our ancestors, but to build what remains is to honor their strength. We are the echoes of those who came before, and our footsteps carry forward their enduring song."

The Legacy of Erasure and What Could Have Been

Introduction

There is a resonance in the numbers that describe our existence—an echo that reaches back across generations, across massacres, across eras of assimilation and resistance. Today, approximately 3.2 million Native Americans reside within the modern borders of the United States, representing about 1.5% of the nation's population. For many of us, this number is a testament—a symbol of resilience and survival, a reflection of our ancestors' enduring strength. But there is another number that haunts the silence, a number that evokes the depth of what could have been—a haunting reminder of potential futures that were violently torn away. What should this number truly be, had entire nations not been decimated by disease, warfare, and deliberate policies of erasure?

This chapter is a reckoning with those absences—a journey to understand the full extent of the loss and a vision of the thriving futures that might have been.

The True Toll: Population Decline Through Violence and Disease

At the time of first European contact, the Native population of North America was estimated to be between 10 and 12 million—a vast collection of nations, each with its own language, culture, and way of relating to the world. We were a tapestry of sovereign systems—interwoven, complex, and deeply rooted in land-based knowledge.

Then came the catastrophe.

Between 1492 and 1900, the Native population of what is now the United States declined by an estimated 90%. This was not the result of natural attrition—it was the outcome of a systematic dismantling of our people and way of life. European-introduced diseases—smallpox, measles, influenza—ravaged our communities, exploiting the fact that we had no natural immunity. In some regions, up to 90% of Native populations perished within a single century of contact (Thornton, 1987). Entire villages fell silent. Languages vanished. Sacred knowledge dissolved into grief.

Worse still, disease was not always accidental. Colonizers quickly realized that smallpox could succeed where guns could not. There are documented instances of settlers and military officials deliberately distributing smallpox-infected blankets to Native communities—a calculated act of biological warfare (Boyd, 1999). This wasn't mere negligence; it was premeditated genocide cloaked in the arrogance of expansion.

The Genocidal Legacy: War, Massacres, and Erasure

Violence, too, was the language of colonization. The Indian Removal Act of 1830 led to one of the most brutal chapters in our shared history: the Trail of Tears. Forced from their homelands, tens of thousands of Cherokee, Creek, Seminole, Choctaw, and Chickasaw were made to march westward through starvation, exposure, and death. Thousands never reached the other side. It was not relocation—it was exile and elimination.

Massacres like Sand Creek in 1864 and Wounded Knee in 1890 were not isolated episodes. They were coordinated, state-sanctioned assaults. At Sand Creek, peaceful Cheyenne and Arapaho were slaughtered despite flying an American flag in good faith. At Wounded Knee, the U.S. cavalry turned its weapons on unarmed Lakota, killing more than 250 men, women, and children (Koch, 1976). These were acts of war masquerading as governance—designed not just to remove us, but to erase us.

Entire nations were nearly or entirely destroyed: the Pequot, the Beothuk of Newfoundland, the Mandan of the Northern Plains. If allowed to flourish like the settler populations that replaced them, Native American populations today could easily exceed 14 million. Instead, over 11 million lives were lost to colonial violence and neglect (Thornton, 1987). What remains is not a people broken—but a people thinned, scarred, and yet unrelenting.

The Missionary Effect: Spiritual and Cultural Erasure

Erasure came not only for our bodies, but for our beliefs. Christian missionaries, armed not only with Bibles but with the intent to reprogram Native identity, labeled our spiritual practices "heathen," "savage," and "primitive." Ceremonies were outlawed. Sacred dances were criminalized. Prayers to the Earth were deemed demonic.

Boarding schools became ground zero for this cultural assault. Native children were forcibly removed from their homes, renamed, shorn of their hair, and punished for speaking their own languages. These institutions were operated under the cruel doctrine of forced assimilation: "Kill the Indian, save the man" (Adams, 1995).

The damage runs deep. Families fractured. Ceremonies faded. Stories died. Today, fewer than 20% of Native Americans speak their ancestral languages—a legacy of these calculated assaults on identity and continuity.

What Could Have Been: The Population We Should See Today

It is painful to imagine what should have been—but we must. We owe it to those who came before and to the generations yet to come.

Had the genocidal campaigns of colonization never occurred, our present-day population could easily surpass 14 million strong (Thornton, 1987). Think of the languages still sung. The medicine ways still practiced. The economies built by sovereign hands. The treaties honored. The lands untouched by pipelines and profit.

We were never meant to survive in fragments. We were meant to flourish in full.

The Path Forward: Revitalization Amid Loss

And yet, we endure—not only as survivors, but as revivalists. Across Turtle Island, Indigenous communities are bringing language back from the brink. In Alaska, the Eyak language—once considered extinct—is being taught again. In Oklahoma, Cherokee language immersion programs are thriving. Diné medicine men are reclaiming space in modern clinics.

These acts are not nostalgia. They are resistance.

Cultural centers are hosting revivals. Art, dance, and ceremony breathe once more into public space. Tribal governments are asserting sovereignty and securing legal victories—like McGirt v. Oklahoma in 2020—that reassert reservation status and jurisdiction.

We are not simply healing—we are remembering. We are rebuilding what was never meant to be broken.

Conclusion

The echoes of what could have been ring in our bones. We carry names never spoken, stories never passed down, and dreams never realized. But we also carry the fire of those who refused to vanish.

Our survival is not the final chapter—it is the prelude to resurgence. We rebuild with each syllable of our languages spoken aloud, each drumbeat that calls back our ancestors, each legal fight that reclaims what was stolen.

We are more than survivors. We are sovereign storytellers, memory keepers, and architects of a future no longer written by someone else's hand.

"When a people vanish, the world grows quieter—not only in language, but in wisdom, in spirit, and in song. Let us be the voice that refuses that silence, the breath that revives memory, and the will that rebuilds what was stolen."

Shadows of the Past—A Reckoning with Historical Atrocities

"To heal, we must first acknowledge the wounds inflicted upon us. Only by confronting the truths of our past can we chart a path toward a future of resilience and unity."

Introduction

The history of Native American communities is marked by a series of profound injustices and atrocities that have left indelible scars. From forced relocations and massacres to cultural suppression and systemic discrimination, these events have not only decimated populations but have also sought to erase identities and traditions. This chapter delves into some of the most harrowing episodes from the 1800s to the present, acknowledging the resilience of Native peoples in the face of relentless adversity.

A Chronicle of Tragedies

1. The Reservation System (1851–Present)
   The Indian Appropriations Act established the reservation system, confining Native peoples to designated areas. This policy disrupted traditional lifeways and resulted in severe poverty and cultural disintegration (National Library of Medicine).
2. The Dawes Act (1887)
   This act divided tribal lands into private allotments, selling surplus to settlers, and undermining tribal sovereignty (National Park Service).
3. Wounded Knee Massacre (1890)
   U.S. troops killed around 250–300 Lakota Sioux at Wounded Knee Creek. This tragedy marked the end of armed resistance and became a symbol of U.S. brutality.
4. Indian Boarding Schools (1870s–1960s)
   These institutions aimed to assimilate Native children by forbidding their languages and cultural practices, resulting in widespread trauma (NABS).

5. Trail of Tears (1838–1839)
   The forced relocation of the Cherokee to Oklahoma caused thousands of deaths due to starvation, disease, and exposure (National Library of Medicine).
6. California Genocide (1846–1873)
   California militias, supported by the state and federal government, committed widespread killings and enslavement of Native peoples during this period.
7. The Sand Creek Massacre (1864)
   Militia forces in Colorado killed over 150 Cheyenne and Arapaho, mostly women and children, despite assurances of safety (National Park Service).
8. The Long Walk of the Navajo (1864)
   The forced march to Bosque Redondo caused death and suffering for hundreds of Navajo people (Smithsonian Institution).
9. Suppression of the Ghost Dance (1890)
   A peaceful spiritual revival was violently crushed by U.S. forces, culminating in the Wounded Knee Massacre (PBS).
10. The Nez Perce War (1877)
    A 1,170-mile flight from U.S. forces ended in surrender and great loss for the Nez Perce people.
11. Gnadenhutten Massacre (1782)
    Militia murdered 96 peaceful Christian Delaware Indians, an early example of colonial violence against Native peoples (American Battlefield Trust).
12. Black Hawk War (1832)
    A land dispute led to U.S. military retaliation and the Bad Axe Massacre, where many Native non-combatants were slaughtered.
13. Bear River Massacre (1863)
    U.S. troops killed over 250 Shoshone near present-day Idaho, one of the largest massacres of Native Americans in U.S. history.
14. Dakota War of 1862
    A conflict in Minnesota resulted in the execution of 38 Dakota men and the forced exile of the Dakota people.

15. Pequot Massacre (1637)
    Puritan settlers and Native allies killed hundreds in a surprise attack on a Pequot village in Mystic, Connecticut.
16. Battle of Washita River (1868)
    General Custer led a raid that killed over 100 Cheyenne, mostly women and children. This remains one of the most controversial actions of the Indian Wars (History.com).
17. Removal of the Choctaw (1831–1833)
    The Choctaw were the first tribe forcibly removed westward under the Indian Removal Act, suffering high death rates en route.
18. Red River War (1874–1875)
    A U.S. campaign to displace Southern Plains tribes led to the loss of freedom, territory, and food sources (TSHA Handbook of Texas).
19. Battle of Tippecanoe (1811)
    The U.S. attack on Prophetstown devastated Tecumseh's confederation, escalating conflict and accelerating Native land loss.
20. Wounded Knee Occupation (1973)
    The 71-day siege by federal forces in response to AIM's protest reignited national attention on Native American civil rights.

Enduring Legacies and Contemporary Struggles

These atrocities are not relics of the past—they are living legacies that echo in Native communities today:

- Cultural Genocide continues in the erosion of Native languages and traditions through underfunded education systems and cultural invisibility.
- Alcoholism and Drug Addiction remain critical health crises on many reservations, often rooted in historical trauma and chronic economic despair.
- Police Violence disproportionately affects Native Americans, who are more likely per capita to be killed by law enforcement than any other group.
- Missing and Murdered Indigenous Women (MMIW) is a devastating crisis, with Native women experiencing murder rates

up to ten times the national average. Many cases go unsolved, uninvestigated, or ignored entirely.

Conclusion

The atrocities and struggles named here are but a glimpse—just a handful pulled from a ledger soaked in sorrow and survival. To recount them all would take volumes, and even then, the pain would spill over the margins.

And those would be only the known atrocities—the ones someone had the courage to record, or the fortune to survive. For every documented wound, how many have slipped silently into the past, unspoken and unrecognized, lost to time and indifference?

But to honor our ancestors, and to stand as worthy inheritors of their strength, we must remember. These wounds are not just relics of the past—they are the soil we walk on, the shadow behind every policy, and the echo in every tribal meeting, courtroom, and classroom.

By speaking the truth of what was done—and what is still being done—we do more than preserve history. We reclaim our voice. We reclaim our power. And in doing so, we begin to shape a future that no longer turns away from the truth, but rises from it.

"Our history is not a tale of defeat but a testament to resilience. By remembering and acknowledging the shadows of our past, we illuminate the path to a future of dignity, justice, and unity."

U.S. Presidents and the Native Dichotomy

Introduction

From the Oval Office came proclamations that shaped the fates of entire Nations. Some bore gifts wrapped in policy—measures that attempted to restore dignity, autonomy, and land. Others, however, came with iron and ink, dressed in legal language but soaked in displacement, erasure, and war. This chapter examines the legacy of U.S. presidents whose hands signed both our destruction and, in rare cases, our renewal. It is a ledger of power—a reckoning between historical devastation and occasional efforts at reconciliation. Between every policy and every veto lies the heartbeat of our people—resilient, resolute, and still walking forward.

Presidents Who Wounded Nations

"The land remembers the blood it has soaked, and the ancestors never forget."

Andrew Jackson (1829–1837)

Estimated Lives Affected: Over 16,000 deaths during the Trail of Tears; tens of thousands displaced. Jackson's name is etched into our memory as the executioner of the Indian Removal Act (Remini, 1981). His administration did not merely endorse removal—it enforced it with brutal determination. Under Jackson, families were uprooted and marched to death. Disease, exposure, and starvation walked beside them. Entire Nations vanished from their homelands. Jackson's legacy is not of statesmanship—it is one of systemic cleansing, masquerading as progress.

Ulysses S. Grant (1869–1877)

Estimated Lives Affected: 5,000–10,000 killed in the Indian Wars (Brown, 2019).

Grant preached peace but practiced war. His so-called "Peace Policy" paved the way for military campaigns that shattered tribes who resisted colonization. The Modoc War, the brawls over Black Hills gold, and countless treaty betrayals defined his tenure. His actions remind us that even soft words can mask sharp blades.

James Monroe (1817–1825)

Estimated Lives Affected: Thousands displaced; deaths undocumented.

Monroe set the stage for removal, crafting the ideological framework that Jackson would later enforce (Prucha, 2020). His presidency saw the birth of displacement doctrine. Southeastern tribes, including the Choctaw, Creek, and Seminole, felt the first tremors of the earthquake that would bury their homelands beneath someone else's empire.

Thomas Jefferson (1801–1809)

Estimated Lives Affected: Thousands displaced, cultures eroded.

Jefferson's vision of an "empire of liberty" came at our expense. His land acquisition strategies—rooted in manipulative treaties and coerced agreements—tore tribal lands apart like pages from a book (Miller, 2023). He believed in expansion, but not in coexistence. His hand drafted policies; his pen bled lands dry.

Martin Van Buren (1837–1841)

Estimated Lives Affected: Thousands more lost to disease, trauma, and exile during final stages of removal.

Van Buren ensured Jackson's plans were completed. Under his leadership, the Trail of Tears continued with cold administrative precision (Brown, 2019). He was not the Firestarter, but he fanned the flames. His signature cemented suffering.

Presidents Who Honored Sovereignty

Franklin D. Roosevelt (1933–1945)

Key Contribution: Indian Reorganization Act of 1934 (Taylor, 1980).

Roosevelt's administration reversed the trajectory of assimilation. The IRA returned lands, rekindled tribal governance, and lit the first small candle of self-determination in decades. Though imperfect, it marked a critical shift from erasure to empowerment.

Richard Nixon (1969–1974)

Key Contribution: Rejected termination policy; restored Blue Lake to Taos Pueblo (Smith, 2022). Nixon did not merely reform policy—he redefined it. His administration acknowledged that Native sovereignty is not a favor but a right. His actions ended termination and laid the groundwork for the era of self-determination.

Barack Obama (2009–2017)

Key Contribution: Settled major tribal lawsuits; established White House Tribal Nations Conference (Indian Country Today, 2020). Obama created space—literal and figurative—for Native voices in federal policy. His administration boosted tribal healthcare, education, and funding. More than that, it respected presence. It respected voice.

Bill Clinton (1993–2001)

Key Contribution: Protected sacred sites via Executive Order 13007 (Hauptman, 1986). Clinton's efforts focused on dignity—economic opportunity, cultural preservation, and healthcare access. He understood that sovereignty without respect is empty. Sacred lands remained sacred under his watch.

John F. Kennedy (1961–1963)

Key Contribution: Early initiatives for education and tribal recognition (Calloway, 2015). Though brief, Ken edy's term planted seeds. He brought tribal voices into policy conversations and laid the groundwork for future reform. He saw tribes not as relics, but as nations.

The Dichotomy of Trump

Donald Trump's legacy in Indian Country is one of contradictions—an unpredictable fusion of symbolic recognition and structural regression.

During his first term (2017–2021), Trump signed two historic pieces of legislation: Savanna's Act and the Not Invisible Act, aimed at addressing the epidemic of missing and murdered Indigenous women and children.

These measures were hailed as long-overdue steps toward justice and visibility, launching initiatives like Operation Lady Justice to bring federal attention to the crisis (National Indigenous Women's Resource Center, 2020).

Yet while one hand gave, the other took away. Trump simultaneously slashed protections for sacred lands. In 2017, he reduced the size of Bears Ears National Monument by 85% and Grand Staircase–Escalante by nearly half—undoing years of tribal-led conservation work and exposing ancestral lands to resource extraction (U.S. Department of the Interior, 2017).

His administration also fast-tracked the Dakota Access Pipeline, intensifying fears about sovereignty, water rights, and environmental desecration (Indian Country Today, 2020).

Trump's return to office in 2025 ushered in a new era of more aggressive action. He appointed Doug Burgum as Secretary of the Interior, an energy-focused governor known for prioritizing fossil fuel development.

Under Burgum, the administration reopened millions of acres of federal land—including parts of the Arctic National Wildlife Refuge—to oil and gas leasing, drawing sharp criticism from tribal and environmental leaders (Doug Burgum, 2025).

Within his first 100 days, Trump froze over $350 million in tribal funding, impacting housing, health care, wildfire response, and treaty-based programs vital to day-to-day survival on reservations (Indian Country Today, 2025).

He also moved swiftly to dismantle diversity, equity, and inclusion (DEI) frameworks in federal agencies. This rollback impacted Native hiring pipelines, funding for tribal education programs, and protections for Native-specific representation in federal policy spaces (Brookings Institution, 2025).

Most controversially, Trump's legal team cited Elk v. Wilkins (1884)—a case denying Native citizenship—to justify renewed attempts to challenge birthright citizenship, sending shockwaves through Native communities concerned about the very foundations of identity and enrollment (OPB, 2025).

Even amid these policies, Trump continued his pattern of selective recognition. He issued an executive memorandum supporting federal recognition for the Lumbee Tribe, a historic gesture for a people long denied full status (Associated Press, 2020).

At the same time, he signaled intent to rescind protections for newly designated sacred sites, including the Sáttítla Highlands, once again putting tribal stewardship at risk (The Guardian, 2025).

Trump's legacy in Indian Country cannot be summed up as either ally or adversary. It is a study in contradiction—one moment acknowledging trauma with federal legislation, the next eroding sovereignty with executive orders and land seizures. Tribal nations were left walking a razor's edge, forced to choose between symbolic gestures and existential threats.

"True sovereignty is not given, but fought for, with each victory and setback shaping the destiny of our people."

Conclusion

The legacy of U.S. presidents in Native America is one of brutal duality. For every step forward, we have been shoved two steps back. Yet we have never stopped walking. In each era, Native people have met policy with resistance, violence with vision, and disregard with determination. This is our truth. We are still here, still sovereign, and still rising.

"Our history is a path of survival, navigating the peaks of recognition and the valleys of erasure. We walk this path with the wisdom of our ancestors, knowing that true sovereignty is not given but reclaimed."

The Legacy of Discrimination: Barriers to Progress

We Were the Obstruction

The story of Native American tribes is not a tale of defeat—it is a chronicle of survival. From first contact, European systems saw Native sovereignty not as a parallel truth but as an inconvenience. What followed were centuries of forced removals, cultural erasure, and economic marginalization.

This chapter exposes the policies and philosophies that have kept us pinned to the margins of a nation built on our lands. These are not simply historical facts; they are the scaffolding of our current struggle, reflected in unemployment rates, school dropout rates, infrastructure inequities, and public health disparities.

The Foundations of Discrimination

The roots of our exclusion run deep. Early settlers viewed us not as Nations but as impediments. They justified our removal through doctrines like Manifest Destiny. Under its banner, relocation became righteousness and genocide became growth. The Trail of Tears was not an isolated tragedy—it was the model for national expansion at Native expense (Ehle, 1988).

Reservations: Isolation by Design

Sold as protection, built as prisons. Reservations were created to isolate and immobilize. The land given was often barren and unfit for agriculture or trade (Harmon, 2010). These zones of containment fostered dependency, not autonomy.

Their remote locations severed access to markets, capital, and visibility. Even today, over 50% of Native American communities experience housing shortages, and nearly a quarter live without access to clean water or proper sanitation systems (U.S. Commission on Civil Rights, 2018).

Cultural Eradication and Its Lasting Effects

The war against us was not just territorial—it was spiritual. This erasure was systemic, designed to destroy our ways of knowing and being. It did not come only with guns or soldiers, but with schoolbooks, courtrooms, and church sermons.

It came wrapped in the language of salvation, civilization, and progress. Our songs were declared pagan. Our dances were labeled deviant. Our languages were dismissed as inferior, our governance dismissed as primitive.

This was not ignorance—it was a deliberate assault on identity. Each generation was pressured to sever the sacred ties that held us together: to land, to kin, to story. Over time, these cuts left scars—visible in our disconnection, our grief, our struggle to return to what was once instinctively known. And yet, even in silence, our culture waited. Not dead—dormant. Not erased—buried beneath the ashes, waiting for breath and spark to rise again.

Boarding Schools

The Indian boarding school system was a calculated campaign of identity destruction. Children were taken. Hair was cut. Names erased. Language outlawed. At institutions like Carlisle, they were beaten into silence (Adams, 1995). These were not schools. They were assimilation factories. They broke bones and spirits alike. According to recent federal investigations, over 500 children are known to have died in these schools, though the actual number is likely far higher (U.S. Department of the Interior, 2022).

Cultural Suppression

Beyond the schools, policies like the Religious Crimes Code of 1883 criminalized our spiritual ceremonies (Tinker, 1993). Sacred fires were doused with legal decrees. These bans severed intergenerational knowledge and drove traditions underground. Healing ceremonies, Sun Dances, and the use of sacred medicines were all outlawed. The American Indian Religious Freedom Act of 1978 was the first federal step toward correcting this injustice, but by then, entire generations had been stripped of ancestral knowledge.

Economic Marginalization and Fragmentation

As our traditions were attacked, so too were our economic systems. Colonization dismantled our self-sustaining economies, replacing them with dependency models administered by federal agencies.

The Dawes Act

Passed in 1887, the Dawes Act split tribal lands into private allotments—an alien concept meant to destroy communal identity (Carlson, 1981). Lands deemed "surplus" were sold to non-Natives. Over time, tribal land holdings shrank by 90 million acres. The resulting land checkerboarding not only reduced our territorial integrity—it weakened our economic and political leverage.

Economic Isolation

Today, Native communities continue to endure economic segregation. Unemployment rates on reservations are often two to three times the national average. In some tribal areas, over 40% of residents live below the poverty line (Cornell & Kalt, 1992). Geographic isolation and a lack of legal authority over local commerce discourage business development. Federal underinvestment in infrastructure, internet access, and transportation only deepens the divide.

Modern-Day Manifestations of Historical Injustices

The policies of the past are not gone—they've been repackaged. Discrimination today is coded into policies, procedures, and definitions of legitimacy.

Federal Recognition

Federal recognition is not about existence—it's about validation. The burden of proof lies not with the oppressor, but with the oppressed. Tribes must demonstrate continuous political and cultural existence under colonial definitions—definitions that rarely reflect the complexity of Indigenous governance systems (Gover, 1995). Recognition means access to funding, healthcare, education. Without it, sovereignty is denied at the stroke of a bureaucrat's pen. More than 400 tribes in the U.S. remain unrecognized.

Trust Land Status

While trust status protects Native land from sale, it also limits our authority over it. Leasing, developing, or using our land often requires federal approval (Wilkins & Lomawaima, 2001). This is sovereignty in shackles. Land can be held, but not fully governed. It's a paternalistic holdover that ensures continued federal gatekeeping over Native prosperity.

Resilience and Adaptation

Still, we rise. Despite generations of targeted erasure, we adapt, rebuild, and resist with a resilience forged in ceremony, memory, and community. Our youth learn their languages again, not just in classrooms, but in kitchens and council chambers. Our elders speak of sovereignty not as a theory but as lived truth. In the face of broken treaties, we negotiate new compacts. In the shadow of erased histories, we publish our own.

Whether in grassroots land reclamation efforts, in the courtroom defending tribal jurisdiction, or at the ballot box electing Native representatives to local and national office—Native people are not waiting to be saved. We are shaping the future with our own hands. The old tools of oppression have not vanished, but we have forged new tools of resistance. Every time we light a sacred fire, fund a tribal startup, or correct a textbook, we are reclaiming what was stolen and protecting what remains.

Legal Victories

Cases like Worcester v. Georgia and McGirt v. Oklahoma reaffirmed what we always knew: our sovereignty is not subject to state whim (Prucha, 1984; McGirt, 2020). But these victories must be defended. States continue to chip away at jurisdiction and tribal authority through litigation and legislation. The courts giveth, and the courts taketh away.

The American Indian Movement

From Alcatraz to Wounded Knee, AIM lit a fire that still burns. It called out the lies of equality and demanded visibility (Smith & Warrior, 1996). AIM wasn't just a protest—it was a reclamation of voice. It inspired Indigenous legal clinics, journalism, scholarship, and policy reform. It awakened a generation to their right to be heard.

Economic and Cultural Revitalization

Gaming gave some Nations a path to prosperity through the Indian Gaming Regulatory Act (Light & Rand, 2005). But not all. Geography still dictates viability. Many tribes remain excluded from gaming revenues due to state negotiations or land limitations. Meanwhile, opposition forces continue to frame sovereignty as a "loophole" rather than a right.

Cultural Revitalization

We now see language schools, sacred fires rekindled, songs returning to the wind. Cultural centers, tribal colleges, and oral histories are restoring what boarding schools tried to kill (McCarty, 2003). Today, over 50 tribal colleges operate across the U.S., serving more than 20,000 students and embedding cultural values into modern curricula. This is not revival—it is resistance wrapped in song, sewn into regalia, whispered in language.

Conclusion

We have endured policies meant to erase us. We've suffered in silence and shouted in resistance. And yet—we remain. Our story is not one of victimhood—it is one of survival, sovereignty, and sacred reclamation. The legacy of discrimination is heavy, but it does not define us. It sharpens us. It gives clarity to our purpose, and direction to our path forward.

"Our journey forward is often blocked by the shadows of past discrimination. Yet, within those shadows, we find the strength to dismantle barriers and forge paths of resilience and progress."

Observations

Critical Race Theory: Impact on Native America

"Critical Race Theory is not a foreign concept to Native people; it is the language of our lived reality. It is the voice that echoes from treaties broken, lands stolen, and cultures silenced. By reclaiming this narrative, we are not just exposing the system's failures—we are laying the foundation to rebuild, on our terms, with our truths."

We Lived it Before They Named It

Critical Race Theory (CRT) is not merely an academic framework—it is a reflection of how the world has long treated Indigenous peoples. While it arose from legal scholarship in the 1970s and 1980s to confront systemic racism in law and society (Delgado & Stefancic, 2017), its core tenets resonate deeply with the Native experience.

CRT provides the vocabulary for our lived truths. It explains how centuries of marginalization, violence, and cultural erasure have been legally sanctioned and socially normalized. For Native people, CRT does not bring revelation—it brings validation.

Understanding Critical Race Theory

At its heart, CRT dismantles the myth that racism is aberrational. Instead, it posits that racism is ordinary—woven into the institutions, laws, and daily fabric of society. This is not a theory of accusation; it is a framework for truth-telling. The tenets of CRT are tools that illuminate the struggles of Native America:

Ordinariness of Racism: Racism is not episodic—it is systemic. For Native people, it appears in broken treaties, chronic underfunding, land encroachment, and health disparities.

Interest Convergence: Progress for Indigenous peoples often occurs only when it aligns with the interests of dominant society. The Indian Self-Determination Act? Passed when the federal government realized it could shift administrative burdens without truly ceding control.

Social Construction of Race: Race was never biology—it was power. Racial classifications like "half-blood" or "full-blood" were tools to limit rights and control access to resources.

Intersectionality: Our experiences are layered. Native women face violence at rates exponentially higher than other demographics. Our Two-Spirit relatives experience both racial and gendered erasure (Crenshaw, 1991).

Historical Context: Systemic Racism and Native America

Doctrine of Discovery and Manifest Destiny

The Doctrine of Discovery gave European settlers theological permission to claim lands inhabited by Indigenous peoples. Codified by papal bulls and later embedded into U.S. law through Supreme Court decisions like Johnson v. M'Intosh, it dehumanized Native communities and justified conquest. Manifest Destiny, its ideological heir, turned this theology into national policy—expanding westward by removing tribes and rewriting history to suit colonial narratives (Newcomb, 2008; Horsman, 1981).

Indian Removal and Reservations

The Indian Removal Act of 1830, signed by President Andrew Jackson, led to the Trail of Tears and the displacement of more than 100,000 Native people. Thousands died of disease, exposure, and starvation during forced relocations (Thornton, 1984).

Reservations, marketed as havens, were in truth carceral zones—geographically isolated, resource-deprived, and controlled by the federal government. This systemic marginalization was not incidental; it was strategic (Prucha, 1986).

Assimilation through Allotment and Boarding Schools

The Dawes Act of 1887 further fractured tribal sovereignty by dividing communal lands into individual plots. Lands deemed "surplus" were sold to non-Natives, reducing Native landholdings by over 90 million acres (Carlson, 1981). Simultaneously, boarding schools operated under the mantra "Kill the Indian, save the man." Children were beaten for speaking their language, renamed, and spiritually disconnected. Generations of cultural trauma were institutionalized and normalized (Adams, 1995).

Applying CRT to Native America

Economic Disparity and Sovereignty

Economic hardship in Native communities is not a reflection of incompetence—it is the consequence of a centuries-long architecture of dispossession. CRT reveals how federal and corporate interests have converged to suppress Indigenous self-determination. Mineral extraction on tribal lands often benefits outsiders while leaving environmental and economic devastation behind. Even today, tribal nations must navigate a maze of regulations just to develop their own land. Sovereignty without economic power is a façade (Brayboy, 2005).

Cultural Revitalization and Storytelling

CRT aligns with the Native tradition of storytelling—not as entertainment, but as survival. Oral histories are not relics; they are records. Storytelling is how we preserve lineage, map territory, and resist erasure. Today, we see a resurgence of language immersion schools, ceremonial revitalization, and Native literature reclaiming narratives once twisted by outsiders. Where federal policy once sought silence, we now amplify truth. Our stories are our sovereignty.

Legal Reforms and Policy Change

CRT does not simply diagnose injustice—it demands action. In Native America, this translates to treaty enforcement, legislative protection of sacred sites, and Indigenous-led justice systems. The push for missing and murdered Indigenous women (MMIW) legislation, the return of ancestral lands, and education reform all emerge from the core tenets of CRT. In courts, classrooms, and Congress, Native voices are no longer asking for space—they are claiming it.

Conclusion

Critical Race Theory is not a new idea to Native America—it is a framework that names the injustices we have endured for centuries. It offers more than critique; it offers power. Power to speak, to reclaim, to rebuild. In CRT, we see a mirror of our history and a map for our liberation. It gives language to our pain, but more importantly, it gives structure to our hope.

"Understanding the roots of systemic racism through Critical Race Theory empowers Native American communities to reclaim their narratives, challenge oppressive structures, and forge a path toward true sovereignty and justice."

Observations

Erased and Reclaimed: Native Culture and Art

What They Tried to Burn Still Breathes

The cultural and artistic legacy of Native America is more than a reflection of heritage—it is a living record of identity, purpose, and belonging. Etched into every pot, every bead, every drumbeat is a story—one of reverence, survival, and resistance. Yet, when colonizers arrived, their mission was not just conquest but erasure.

They came to dismantle not only our sovereignty but the symbols that held it together—our languages, sacred traditions, and artistic expressions. This chapter traces that deliberate destruction and celebrates the resilient resurgence that now rises from those ashes. Ours is not a story of cultural death—it is a story of cultural defiance, revival, and continuity.

The Total Annihilation of Tribes

Colonial conquest brought more than land theft—it brought extermination. Entire Nations such as the Pequot, Beothuk, and Yuki were decimated, not by accident but by calculated policy and militarized violence.

With them vanished languages that once sang to the stars, cosmologies rooted in place, and art forms born of spirit and soil. What remains is grief, yes—but also fire. A fire to remember, to reclaim, and to rebuild. Each act of remembrance is an act of defiance against those who believed they had silenced us.

Massacres and Military Campaigns

Sand Creek (1864). Wounded Knee (1890). These are not just historical footnotes—they are open wounds. These were not isolated atrocities; they were strategic campaigns carried out with the backing of the U.S. government to eliminate Indigenous resistance and culture (Brown,

2001). Villages were burned. Children murdered. Songs lost in gunfire. And yet our stories lived on—carried in secret, whispered in ceremony, and guarded in memory.

Forced Assimilation into "Whiteness"

The federal government attempted a different kind of erasure through boarding schools. Children were taken from their families. Hair shorn. Languages forbidden. Names erased. Traditional beliefs mocked and replaced with Christian doctrine. To policymakers, this was "education." To us, it was cultural genocide (Adams, 1995). Every punishment for speaking our tongue or dancing our dances was a blow against who we were.

Loss of Language

Our languages are not merely tools of communication—they are sacred vessels of law, prayer, and ecological knowledge. When children were denied their words, they were denied their place in the world. Today, linguists estimate that over half of all Native American languages are extinct or endangered (Hinton & Hale, 2001). But what academia calls "extinct" we call "dormant." Our languages are sleeping—not gone.

Loss of History and Stories

Oral storytelling carried our histories, ethics, and laws. Elders served as libraries, storytellers as guides. When that line was broken, we lost more than stories—we lost identity and memory. In their place came textbooks filled with erasure and lies. Our children grew up without the heroes, the warnings, the ceremonies that once defined their place in the cosmos (Deloria, 1994).

Destruction of Art and Material Culture

To colonizers, Native art was not revered—it was misunderstood, mischaracterized, and ultimately exploited. They saw feathers and hide, not symbolism.

They saw beads and clay, not spirit. Where we saw ceremony, they saw novelty. Native art was dismissed as primitive by those who never sought to understand its sacred function. To us, art was not aesthetic—it was divine. It was a living language that spoke across generations, rooted in landscape, ceremony, and identity.

Confiscation and Destruction

From the 19th century through the 20th, museums, missionaries, and collectors descended upon Native communities with the fervor of opportunistic scavengers. Under the guise of preservation and academic curiosity, they raided burial sites, sweat lodges, and ceremonial grounds.

They took what was not theirs: sacred bundles, eagle staffs, medicine pipes, masks carved with ancestral memory. These were not "artifacts." They were spiritual companions, imbued with generational purpose and power. Their removal severed rituals. Their display in glass cases became public desecration masquerading as scholarship (Jacka, 1990).

Desecration of Graves

Perhaps the most grotesque affront was the theft of our ancestors' remains. Bones, teeth, and skulls were unearthed, boxed, and shelved like curiosities. Human beings became catalog numbers in academic inventories. Skulls were measured to support racist pseudoscience. The justification? Science.

The reality? Sacrilege. These acts violated spiritual laws, tribal sovereignty, and human decency. They did not study us to understand—they studied us to define and diminish us. Institutions built their reputations on the backs of our dead (Thomas, 2000).

Suppression of Artistic Practices

Artistic suppression came not only through theft, but through forced silence. U.S. Indian policy criminalized ceremonies and traditional artistic expression. The Religious Crimes Code of 1883 explicitly banned ceremonial dances, while boarding schools punished students for making traditional crafts.

Children who painted with earth pigments or wove with ancestral patterns were scolded, shamed, even beaten. The result was more than cultural repression—it was a psychological severance. Creativity became danger. Cultural memory became contraband. Entire generations grew up believing their own art was worthless or forbidden (Brown, 2001).

The Role of Institutions and Collectors

Museums that claimed to preserve Native heritage too often did so without consultation, consent, or context. They displayed sacred objects as exotic novelties, stripped from the people and protocols that gave them meaning. Universities used our sacred items to teach non-Native students, while denying Native communities access to the very traditions being analyzed. Private collectors drove demand, incentivizing looters and grave robbers.

The art market commodified our culture, turning desecration into wealth. Institutions rarely acknowledged the source of their acquisitions—let alone the damage they inflicted. What they called preservation, we call theft (Moses, 2002; Hollinger, 2013).

Legal and Ethical Battles

The Native American Graves Protection and Repatriation Act (NAGPRA), passed in 1990, was not a gift. It was a response to centuries of injustice. For the first time, Native tribes had a legal framework to demand the return of stolen ancestors and sacred belongings (Fine-Dare, 2002).

But the law's passage was only the beginning. Institutions resist. Bureaucracies stall. Lawsuits abound. Some museums have yet to inventory their Native collections. Others argue about provenance, despite tribal testimony. The burden remains on us—to identify, to petition, to prove. The law exists, but justice is not automatic. It is pursued, piece by piece, prayer by prayer.

Revitalization of Culture and Art

We are not relics—we are resurgence. We are not reviving a dead culture—we are restoring what colonization failed to kill. Across Turtle Island, artists, scholars, knowledge keepers, and youth are breathing new life into ancestral forms. Each painted robe, each spoken word, each repatriated item is a declaration: We are still here. And we are not just surviving—we are creating.

Language Revitalization Programs

The Wôpanâak Language Reclamation Project. Navajo immersion schools. Alaska Native Heritage language nests. The Cherokee Nation's Cherokee Language Master/Apprentice Program. The Mohawk Kahnawà:ke Survival School. These are not programs—they are revolutions. Children now speak what their grandparents were beaten for. Elders become teachers again, and classrooms become cultural sanctuaries (Hinton, 2013).

I remember distinctly, many years ago when I was perhaps ten years old, sitting with my grandma at a powwow. She could speak at least three Native languages in addition to English. Several people came by and spoke to her in their language. She responded kindly, and after each one left, she gave a small chuckle. After the last person walked away, I asked, "Grandma, why do you laugh?" She said, "Because they were talking in baby talk." What they learned as children was not wrong—but it revealed how much our languages changes with each generation. The words spoken today, compared to even a century ago, might barely be recognizable. That is why revitalization isn't just about preserving words—it's about honoring the depth and evolution of meaning that our ancestors carried.

Cultural Preservation Initiatives

Institutions like the National Museum of the American Indian and tribal-run cultural centers are returning the narrative to Native hands. We are no longer the studied—we are the storytellers. Through exhibits, oral archives, digital repositories, and educational curricula, we are preserving not just history, but sovereignty (Atalay, 2006).

Artistic Renaissance

Native artists like Jaune Quick-to-See Smith, Wendy Red Star, and Jeffrey Gibson are fusing tradition with innovation. From sculpture to digital installations, their work defies stereotypes and demands space in the global art conversation. Native art is no longer confined to museum cases—it is alive, provocative, and sovereign (Ryan, 2005).

Repatriation of Artifacts and Remains

Each return of an ancestor or sacred object is a ritual of healing. These are not transactions—they are restorations of ceremony, land-based memory, and tribal dignity (Colwell-Chanthaphonh, 2008).

Community-Led Initiatives

Grassroots movements are at the heart of our cultural resurgence. From birchbark canoe building in the Great Lakes to ribbon skirt revivals on the Plains, communities are teaching the next generation with pride. These aren't hobbies. They are survival strategies, rooted in resistance and rebirth (Simpson, 2014).

Conclusion

They tried to erase us through war, policy, and silence. But culture is not so easily destroyed. Today, every drumbeat, every woven sash, every spoken word in a reclaimed tongue is a rebellion. We are not relics. We are resurgence.

> *"In the ashes of our culture's destruction, we find the embers of our resilience. Through art, language, and tradition, we reclaim our heritage and defy the forces that sought to erase us."*

Smoke Screens & Silent Screen

The Image of the Indian in Film

Hollywood's Mirage

From the first flickering frames of silent cinema, the image of the Indian in American film was never ours to shape. We were painted with broad strokes, played by white men in makeup, and cast in roles that veered between noble savage, mystical guide, or murderous threat. Hollywood didn't just misrepresent Native people—it mythologized our erasure. For decades, our portrayal on screen was less about who we were, and more about what the settler imagination needed us to be.

In films like Stagecoach (1939), Native Americans were faceless marauders whose death signaled the triumph of civilization. Later came the stoic sidekick trope, the Tonto-ization of Indigenous characters—present but hollow. These portrayals did more than entertain; they etched falsehoods into the public conscience and reinforced policy decisions rooted in stereotypes.

Yet something shifted. By the late 20th century, Native filmmakers and actors began reclaiming the lens. Smoke Signals (1998), directed by Chris Eyre and written by Sherman Alexie, was the first feature-length film written, directed, and produced by Native Americans to receive national distribution. It shattered expectations, not with spectacle, but with intimacy and humor, portraying reservation life through the eyes of Native characters with depth, conflict, and humanity, Smoke Signals.

From there, the wave grew. The Business of Fancydancing (2002) continued the momentum, as did powerful narratives like Rhymes for Young Ghouls (2013), a dark, haunting look at the legacy of residential schools in Canada Rhymes for Young Ghouls. Films like Beans (2020) brought the Oka Crisis to life through a young girl's perspective, while Prey (2022) broke ground by placing a Comanche woman at the center of a blockbuster action film, spoken partially in the Comanche language Prey.

Each of these films pushed back against the smoke screen—the distorted image of Indigenous people conjured by decades of cinematic laziness and colonial narrative. But the silence behind the screen also matters. For every Indigenous actor breaking through, countless more remain sidelined or miscast. While the doors are opening, they still creak slowly on hinges built by others.

The journey is also personal. I stood once among the cast of a western myself. In 1975, Breakheart Pass was filmed in Idaho. This time, the "Indians" were actually Indians. I was one of them—an extra, standing in full winter regalia in the bitter cold. At the movie's end, I played a "good Indian"—the one lying dead in the snow of Breakheart Pass. That image stuck with me. Not for its cinematic glory, but for what it revealed: even when we were present, we were often only there to be erased.

Representation isn't just about inclusion; it's about control. Who writes the story? Who holds the camera? Who gets to define what it means to be Indigenous on screen? The answers still tilt toward Hollywood, but the tide is turning.

Native cinema is no longer waiting to be invited. It's carving its place, scene by scene, demanding space not as background figures, but as the authors of our own stories. And as viewers, it is our duty to stop accepting images that feel comfortable, and start questioning why they ever did.

Smoke screens hide truths. Silent screens erase voices. But no more.

Biological Devastation of Native Nations

1800 to Present

Blankets, Breath, and Blood

From the moment foreign sails broke the horizon, our fate was sealed not just by gunpowder or greed, but by invisible enemies carried in breath and blood. These foreign pathogens were uninvited guests that clung to blankets, breath, and bodies—entering our homelands before many settlers even did. European diseases swept across Native lands with the force of wildfire, leaving decimated communities, broken kinship ties, and severed cultural lineages in their wake.

This chapter confronts that silent invasion—beginning in the 1800s and continuing into today—and traces how those plagues still echo in the health disparities Native peoples endure. The story of disease is not just medical—it is political, cultural, and generational.

Historical Context

Initial Contact and Early Epidemics

The first waves of colonization brought not only conquest but contagion. Diseases like smallpox, measles, and typhus cut through Native communities, whose immune systems had no precedent for such onslaughts. They struck not once but repeatedly, leaving entire villages emptied and spiritual leaders gone. By some estimates, Native populations in North America declined by up to 90% in certain regions within a century of contact—a demographic collapse unmatched in world history (Diamond, 1997). This initial devastation not only reduced numbers; it shattered social cohesion, disrupted governance structures, and erased critical intergenerational knowledge.

Continued Exposure in the 19th Century

The 1800s were marked by forced removals, brutal government relocations, and confined living on barren reservations. These acts not only fractured tribal life but created perfect breeding grounds for illness.

The Trail of Tears saw thousands die—not from bullets—but from cholera, dysentery, and pneumonia, all made worse by hunger and exposure (Thornton, 1987). Infections followed us wherever we were pushed.

Specific Diseases and Their Impact

Smallpox

Smallpox was more than a disease—it was devastation incarnate. Plains tribes in particular were ravaged by outbreaks throughout the 19th century. Entire clans disappeared. Even worse, historical accounts document the use of infected blankets intentionally distributed to Native people—an early form of biological warfare that stains American history with moral rot (Fenn, 2001). many Native people died

Measles

Though less frequently discussed, measles carried a brutal toll. It swept through children like a ghost, stealing future leaders and knowledge keepers. One outbreak could undo decades of cultural teaching and intergenerational learning. Each child's funeral represented not just a personal loss, but a spiritual fracture in a community's continuity (Crosby, 1976). many Native people died

Influenza

The 1918 pandemic was apocalyptic for Native nations. While the global mortality rate was staggering, Native American communities experienced death rates four to five times higher than the general population. Elders—carriers of oral tradition, language, and ceremony—were lost in days. The silence left behind was not just mourning; it was cultural erosion (Bray, 1994). many Native people died

Tuberculosis

TB haunted reservations like a lingering shadow. Underfunded federal agencies responded with institutionalization—shutting the sick away in distant sanatoriums, often far from family and community. Native patients were isolated, sometimes for years, with minimal support and no cultural context for healing. The disease did more than harm lungs; it isolated hearts and disrupted homes (Dowie, 2002). many Native people died

Public Health Challenges and Responses

Lack of Healthcare Infrastructure

The Indian Health Service (IHS), created to address federal responsibility to tribal health, has long been underfunded and overburdened. On many reservations, basic care is hours away, emergency services are limited, and facilities are chronically understaffed. Medical neglect isn't anecdotal—it's systemic (Jones, 2006).

Impact of Poverty and Malnutrition

Poverty weakens immune systems and shortens life expectancy. Malnutrition—rooted in food deserts and federal rations—further heightens vulnerability. Homes with mold, no heat, or overcrowding fuel the spread of disease. Health is not an isolated metric; it is a reflection of every failed policy that placed Native lives last (Harrison, 1989).

Cultural Barriers and Mistrust

Decades of abuse have seeded deep mistrust of Western medicine. Forced sterilizations, unauthorized research, and poor treatment outcomes have left scars. Healing will not come solely from hospitals. It must include traditional knowledge keepers, medicine people, and elders. Without cultural respect, even the best medicine will fail (Gone & Calf Looking, 2011).

Modern-Day Health Disparities

Chronic Illness and COVID-19

Diabetes, heart disease, obesity, and cancer are rampant in Native communities. These are not simply lifestyle diseases—they are historical diseases. They stem from intergenerational trauma, food policy, and environmental injustice. COVID-19 magnified this truth. Native people had some of the highest per-capita infection and death rates during the pandemic. This was not a surprise—it was the latest in a centuries-long pattern of abandonment (Yellow Horse Brave Heart, 2020).

Genetic and Epidemiological Insights

New genomic research suggests that centuries of disease exposure have shaped Native immunity. Trauma, malnutrition, and genetic bottlenecks altered immune responses. Some of our genetic markers now show increased susceptibility to autoimmune conditions and metabolic disorders—a biological echo of colonial violence (Malhi et al., 2021).

Ongoing Efforts and Future Directions

Improving Healthcare Access

Native-led healthcare systems are rising. Telemedicine, mobile clinics, and tribally run hospitals are becoming models of resilience. Training Native healthcare workers is critical—not just for access, but for trust. Familiar faces save lives (Sequist, 2021).

Cultural Competence in Care

We don't just need more doctors—we need different doctors. Cultural humility, language integration, and collaboration with tribal medicine practitioners bridge the gap. Healing cannot be dictated; it must be co-created (Hodge, 2012).

Community-Driven Public Health

Food sovereignty. Language immersion. Culturally grounded public health campaigns. These movements succeed because they are rooted in identity, not bureaucracy. They speak to the people in the language of memory and tradition—not mandates. This is where true healing begins (Warne & Lajimodiere, 2015).

An IHS Epilogue

Grandma lived to be 104 years old. She carried the wisdom of ten generations and the skepticism of every one of them, sharpened by time and observation. One day after returning from a visit to the IHS clinic, she shook her head and said, "The doctors have a practice. They come to our reservation to practice—on the Indians." There was no venom in her voice, just truth. She had seen it for decades: the revolving door of medical students, freshly minted and inexperienced, shipped out to Native communities to work off their debt. Our people were not seen as patients—they were seen as assignments. Case studies. Training wheels for doctors still learning how to listen, let alone heal.

In many clinics, these doctors arrived knowing little about our culture, our trauma, or the deep mistrust woven into every waiting room chair. And then they left—often before they learned. Grandma's observation wasn't just a passing remark. It was a lifetime of clarity distilled into a sentence. She didn't need a study to tell her what she already knew: we were the proving ground.

And yet, she kept going. Not because she trusted the system—but because she knew we had to survive it. Her resilience wasn't passive; it was pointed. A statement. A legacy. One that reminds us: real healing for our people will never come from someone just doing their residency. It must come from someone doing their remembering.

Conclusion

The diseases that swept through Native America came with colonizers, but their shadows remain. From smallpox to COVID-19, the epidemic has always been twofold: biological and bureaucratic. Our ancestors did not have a choice. But today, we do. With knowledge, with cultural strength, and with collective action, we can break cycles of harm. We are more than survivors—we are rebuilders. We carry the scars, yes—but also the medicine.

"From the first breath of contagion to the present day, the invisible enemies brought by European hands have scarred our people deeply. Yet, within the stories of survival lies the testament of our enduring spirit and the unyielding fight for our future."

The number of Indigenous lives lost since this continent was "discovered" depends on who you ask—and there's no shortage of sources. But let's set the debates aside. What matters is this: an unthinkable number of our people were erased before their time, swept from history by plague, conquest, and policy. Whole nations silenced before the ink on their names ever dried.

Observations

State-Sanctioned Genocide

The Dispersal of California's Tribal Peoples

The Bounty on Indian Scalps: When Murder Became Policy

Upon California's admission to the Union in 1850, the new state wasted no time formalizing the extermination of its Native population. In a stunning act of state violence, California began offering **bounties for Native American scalps and heads**, compensating settlers, militias, and vigilante groups for killing Native people, including women and children. These killings weren't rogue acts—they were **budgeted, reimbursed, and approved by the state legislature**.

By 1851, Governor Peter Burnett declared:

"That a war of extermination will continue to be waged between the races until the Indian race becomes extinct must be expected... The inevitable destiny of the race is beyond the power or wisdom of man to avert" (Madley, *An American Genocide*).

Bounties ranged from $0.25 to $5 per scalp or more for heads. Some counties, like Shasta and El Dorado, issued vouchers for reimbursement, which the state paid—spending **over $1 million by 1852**. The violence was rapid and brutal. Entire villages were massacred, survivors hunted, and scalps brought in like animal hides (Madley, *An American Genocide*).

Results and Aftermath: A Population Devastated

Between 1846 and 1873, California's Native population dropped from over 150,000 to fewer than 30,000. Some tribes were annihilated entirely. The scale and speed of the slaughter led historian Benjamin Madley to classify it plainly: **genocide**.

By the 1870s, state payments for Indian-killing had decreased—but the damage was done. Survivors lived with the trauma, displacement, and loss of homeland. Their communities fragmented. Many fled into the highlands or desert, while others were absorbed into servitude or isolation. Still others were enslaved outright through California's 1850 *Act for the Government and Protection of Indians*, which legalized forced labor and child indenture of Native people (Heizer, *The Destruction of California Indians*).

Dispersal and Survival: The Hidden Tribes

With death closing in from all directions, California's Native people fled—into the Sierra Nevada, across the Mojave, and north into Oregon and Nevada. Some hid with white settlers who, despite the cultural climate, provided protection and refuge. Others merged with different tribes, forming new communities where cultural preservation and survival were more important than political distinctions.

This chaotic displacement led to the merging of tribal identities across much of California. What was once a landscape of hundreds of autonomous tribal nations became a patchwork of mixed-tribe survivors.

A New Reality: The Mixed-Tribe Rancherias' of California

Nowhere is this legacy more visible than in California's **modern Rancherias**, many of which comprise multiple tribal ancestries, born not of choice but of necessity.

The Susanville Indian Rancheria

Established in 1923, the Susanville Indian Rancheria reflects this survival mosaic. Its members come from four distinct tribal groups:

- Maidu
- Northern Paiute
- Pit River (Achomawi/Atsugewi)
- Washoe

These tribes, once separated by geography and language, were forced by violence and removal to seek safety together. When the U.S.

government purchased 30 acres near Susanville for landless Indians, survivors from these four tribes became neighbors—and eventually, kin.

Today, Susanville Indian Rancheria holds over 1,300 acres of land and maintains cultural programs for all four heritages. Its very existence is proof that California's attempted erasure of Native identity failed (Susanville Indian Rancheria, "History").

A Legacy of Violence—and Resilience

The bounty system laid the foundation for California's genocidal history. It also planted the seeds of tribal fusion, spiritual endurance, and long-term resistance. Though treaties were broken, and scalps once held value in state dollars, Native identity in California remains.

The mixed-tribe Rancherias, like Susanville, are not the result of confused lineage—they are the legacy of adaptation, alliance, and survival under fire. California may have tried to erase them, but in doing so, it forced the birth of new tribal unions—sovereign in identity, even if wounded in history.

Observations

Saving Souls, Taking Nations

The True Cost of Missionary Work

When Faith Became a Weapon

The arrival of Christian missionaries on Native lands was not just a spiritual incursion—it was a cultural invasion. Behind the cross came the erasure of stories, the shaming of traditions, and the remapping of sacred ground. Their gospel often carried the sword of assimilation. This chapter explores how missionary work sought to dismantle Indigenous spirituality and social structure under the guise of salvation, and how Native communities responded with quiet resistance, spiritual endurance, and a defiant revival that lives on today.

Cultural Suppression and Spiritual Resilience

Conversion and Erasure of Indigenous Beliefs

Missionaries labeled our beliefs as pagan, our ceremonies as devilish, and our ancestors as damned. Their mission: spiritual conquest. The result: generations torn between ancestral reverence and imposed salvation (Tinker, 1993). Baptism became a weapon. The drum was silenced, the pipe shamed, and the sweat lodge outlawed. Yet in the margins of colonized prayer books and the hush of night fires, our people whispered the old songs. Elders hid sacred rites behind closed doors. Faith did not die. It survived—in secret, in silence, in strength.

Destruction of Sacred Sites

Many churches were built atop ceremonial sites, erasing millennia of sacred meaning with a single steeple. At one Pueblo site, a sacred kiva was demolished to construct a chapel. The people wept, but they did not forget. In the desert's quiet, the ceremonies continued—away from colonial eyes, toward ancestral skies (Dozier, 1970). Some sites remain desecrated, fenced off in the name of Christ, while their spiritual significance echoes through every footstep of the faithful who remember.

Changes in Social Structures

Disruption of Traditional Leadership

Missionaries often replaced medicine people and tribal elders with Christian converts, fracturing Indigenous governance. Consensus gave way to imposed hierarchies. Where once wisdom guided leadership, now conversion dictated authority (Deloria, 2003). As one Navajo elder put it: "They turned us against our own. Made us question our roots." The damage went beyond leadership—it dismantled generational cohesion. Communities that once gathered in council began to fracture along doctrinal lines.

Gender Roles and Family Dynamics

Christianity imported European gender norms that undermined the powerful roles Indigenous women held as healers, warriors, and decision-makers. Women who once led were now instructed to submit.

A Cheyenne account recalls a great-grandmother, stripped of her warrior's pride, told to be docile for God. Colonization didn't just change religion—it redefined identity (Fixico, 2003). Masculinity became dominance, femininity became silence. The matrilineal lines that once held nations together began to fray.

Educational Influences

Boarding Schools and Forced Assimilation

Boarding schools, many run by missionaries, were factories of forced forgetting. Hair cut. Names replaced. Language punished. Children were turned into strangers to their own people (Adams, 1995). One Chippewa survivor recalled, "They made me speak a language foreign to my soul." These schools didn't save—they severed. Faith was not offered—it was beaten in. One boy said his last words in his Native tongue before they silenced it with soap and strap.

Estimated Number of Deaths and Missing Children

Malnutrition. Disease. Abuse. Thousands of Native children died in boarding schools, many buried in unmarked graves. The Truth and

Reconciliation Commission of Canada (2015) and the National Native American Boarding School Healing Coalition estimate at least 3,200–4,100 deaths, though many believe the numbers are much higher. One Lakota mother's unanswered letter, asking only "where he lies so I can sing him home," echoes across generations. But it was not only the dead who were lost—it was the stolen identities of the living.

Loss of Language and Knowledge

Language is ceremony. It is the syntax of survival. In suppressing our words, the missionaries suppressed our worldview. What was lost was not just grammar—it was ancestral memory, ecological knowledge, and spiritual law (Hermes, 2005). Language shapes the sacred. When it is stripped, so is the wisdom encoded in generations. It is not just translation—it is severance.

Lasting Legacy: Trauma and Resilience

Intergenerational Trauma

The trauma inflicted didn't vanish with the missionaries. It lingered in broken family bonds, buried grief, and identity crises. Passed from parent to child, this trauma carved deep wounds into Native lives (Evans-Campbell, 2008). Generations born after the mission era still wake in the night, not knowing the cause of their sorrow. It is inherited grief—a shadow cast long after the steeple bells fell silent.

Resilience and Revival

Yet we endured. Language schools rise where silence once ruled. Ceremonies return to stolen grounds. Songs once whispered now echo loud and proud. "Every time I sing, I bring our ancestors back to life," said one young Anishinaabe man, reclaiming his legacy note by sacred note (Kirmayer, 2009). Across Turtle Island, the prayers are rising again—not because they were never broken, but because they were never truly gone.

Reconciliation and Healing

Some churches now speak apology. Some extend support. But the real work lies in restoring what was broken—through tribal museums, cultural programs, and education led by Native voices. Reconciliation is not only apology—it is restitution (Smith, 2003). The road back is long, and it must be walked side-by-side, with truth told plainly and healing made tangible. It means opening vaults, returning relics, funding recovery, and yielding platforms. True repentance is action.

Conclusion

Missionary work arrived with a Bible in one hand and erasure in the other. But it did not win. Though sacred fires were doused and languages banned, the heart of our people never stopped beating. Today, we walk the long road back to ourselves—carrying the weight of what was taken, and the light of what is being restored. Missionary conquest tried to extinguish the sacred. What it sparked instead was the fire of return.

"The work of missionaries, often cloaked in the guise of salvation, stripped away the sacred threads of our cultural tapestry. Yet, in the quiet resilience of our elders and the resurgence of our traditions, we find the strength to reclaim and rebuild our heritage."

Early Resistance and Rebellions

Native Responses to Colonization

They Called It Rebellion—We Called it Survival

The story of Native resistance to colonization is not one of silence or submission. It is the story of sovereign nations who met the tide of conquest not as passive victims but as fierce defenders of their land, their people, and their spirit. From the first stolen footsteps of Columbus in the Caribbean to the forced removals of the 19th century,
 Native nations across the continent stood their ground—sometimes with weapons, sometimes with treaties, always with courage. This chapter examines the many faces of resistance—armed rebellion, strategic alliance, and cultural defiance—illuminating the leaders, movements, and moments that defined Indigenous opposition to colonization.

Initial Contacts and Conflicts

The Arawak and the First Spark of Resistance

When Christopher Columbus arrived in 1492, the Arawak people extended hands of welcome. What followed was betrayal. Enslavement. Massacre. The Arawak leader Hatuey—burned alive by the Spanish—spoke with unflinching clarity: "If heaven is where you go, I'd rather burn." His defiance became a sacred ember in the fire of Indigenous resistance (Zinn, 2003).

Powhatan's Diplomacy and Defiance
In the early 1600s, the Powhatan Confederacy engaged with English settlers at Jamestown. Chief Powhatan, a master of diplomacy and power, offered peace—but not submission. When settlers encroached further, war followed.

Pocahontas, caught between worlds, remains a symbol of cultural tension, not harmony. The First Anglo-Powhatan War (1609–1614) was not just a conflict of arms—it was a clash of worldviews (Rountree, 1990).

Forms of Resistance

Armed Conflict as a Sacred Duty

War was not chosen—it was forced. But when it came, it came with thunder.

To many Native nations, armed resistance was not just a political act—it was a sacred duty, born of obligation to ancestors, land, and the future generations not yet born. Warriors did not rise for conquest. They rose because something irreplaceable was being taken—life, land, language, and the spiritual bonds between them. Resistance was a ceremony in itself, carried out with prayer, song, and the understanding that defending one's people was not only honorable—it was necessary.

When treaties were broken, when children were stolen, when the buffalo were slaughtered to starve the people into submission, war became the last breath of sovereignty. Warriors went to battle not with dreams of glory, but with the deep grief of knowing they were fighting to preserve the heartbeat of a nation. Every arrow loosed, every rifle fired, every defensive stand on ridges and riverbanks was not just warfare—it was prophecy. It was the fulfillment of sacred stories that warned of a time when the earth would be threatened, and the people would be called to rise.

The colonizers saw "uprisings." History books called them "rebellions." But to the people who stood in the snow at Bear Paw, who rode under the shadow of the Black Hills, who defended their lodges at Sand Creek and Washita—they were not rebels. They were protectors. They carried not just weapons, but memory. And when they fell, they fell with prayers on their lips and the names of their children in their hearts.

King Philip's War (1675–1678)

Metacom, or King Philip, carried the pain of betrayal. His father and brother were manipulated, murdered, and dishonored. His war was one of survival. The Wampanoag, Narragansett, and Nipmuc rose up, launching one of the most deadly wars in early colonial America. Over 600 colonists and 3,000 Native people died. In the ashes of villages and forests, a message endured: we did not go quietly (Lepore, 1998).

Pontiac's Rebellion (1763–1766)

When Britain claimed French lands after the Seven Years' War, they claimed Native lands too. Pontiac, an Ottawa war chief, said no. He united a confederacy that besieged forts, captured territories, and reminded the empire that the land had guardians. Though ultimately suppressed, Pontiac's campaign forced Britain to issue the Proclamation of 1763—an attempt, however hollow, to limit settler expansion (Dowd, 2002).

Strategic Alliances and Political Warfare

The Iroquois Confederacy and the Art of Balance

During the French and Indian War, the Six Nations of the Iroquois Confederacy walked a tightrope. Under leaders like Thayendanegea (Joseph Brant), the Iroquois allied with the British—not from loyalty, but leverage. Brant's vision was political survival. Though the war ended in more dispossession, the Confederacy's diplomacy was a masterclass in navigating colonial crossfire (Jennings, 1984).

Tecumseh's Dream of a Unified Nation

Tecumseh, Shawnee warrior and prophet, dreamed of something rare—a pan-Indian confederacy. He traveled from the Great Lakes to the Gulf, urging tribes to unite against U.S. expansion. "The earth does not belong to the white man," he said. "It belongs to all of us." His alliance with Britain in the War of 1812 was not surrender—it was strategy. He died in battle in 1813, but his voice still calls for unity (Sugden, 1997).
Cultural Resistance: The Silent War

Sequoyah and the Power of Language

In the face of erasure, the Cherokee created permanence. Sequoyah's syllabary birthed the Cherokee Phoenix newspaper—written in Cherokee, by Cherokee, for Cherokee. In ink and spirit, the Nation preserved law, culture, and identity (Perdue & Green, 2005). Resistance is not only in the rifle—it is in the written word.

The Ghost Dance and Prophetic Defiance

When bullets failed and treaties betrayed, the people danced. Wovoka's Ghost Dance was a vision of return: to ancestors, to buffalo, to balance. It spread like fire, terrifying the U.S. government. At Wounded Knee in 1890, they tried to kill the dance. Instead, they sanctified it. The massacre became a sacred wound—and a reminder that even spiritual movements were feared as acts of war (Mooney, 1965).

Key Figures in Resistance

Resistance was never incidental—it was persistent. It rose like weather across generations and geographies, carried by those who understood that to fight was not only to survive, but to uphold the sacred. These leaders were not rebels. They were protectors of sovereignty, of land, of future breath. Their names echo not in legend, but in responsibility.

Hatuey (Taíno/Cuba) Widely recognized as the first martyred resister in the Americas. He warned Indigenous people in Hispaniola and Cuba of the Spanish terror, refused to convert to Christianity, and was burned alive in 1512, reportedly rejecting the Spanish heaven if it meant sharing it with his killers (Díaz del Castillo, 2005).

Metacom (King Philip) (Wampanoag): Led the 1675–76 war of resistance known as King Philip's War, one of the most destructive colonial conflicts in North American history. Metacom's leadership marked a collective assertion of Indigenous sovereignty in New England (Lepore, 1999).

Pontiac (Odawa): Organized an intertribal alliance in 1763 to resist British postwar policies and expansion after the French and Indian War. His uprising was as much a spiritual movement as a military one, grounded in defense of Native worldview (Dowd, 2002).

Tecumseh (Shawnee): A strategic visionary and unifier, Tecumseh built a pan-tribal confederacy that aimed to halt U.S. westward expansion. He allied with the British during the War of 1812 and died in battle in 1813, his dream of unity unfulfilled but never forgotten (Edmunds, 2007).

Osceola (Seminole): Fought U.S. forces during the Second Seminole War using guerrilla tactics in Florida's swamps. He was captured under a flag of truce in 1837—an act of betrayal by U.S. authorities (Mahon, 1967).

Red Cloud (Oglala Lakota): Orchestrated a rare military victory over the U.S. Army, forcing them to abandon Fort Phil Kearny and others during Red Cloud's War (1866–68). Later a diplomat, he never stopped reminding the government of its failures (Utley, 1988).

Sitting Bull (Hunkpapa Lakota): Spiritual and military leader of the Lakota resistance, including at the Battle of the Little Bighorn. A defender of the Ghost Dance, he was assassinated by tribal police during a government raid in 1890 (Philbrick, 2010).

Crazy Horse (Oglala Lakota): Fought relentlessly to protect his people's land, co-leading at the Little Bighorn and refusing to ever sign a treaty. Killed in 1877 after surrendering under pressure, his death marked a spiritual fracture in the Lakota resistance (Marshall, 2004).

Chief Joseph (Nez Perce): Known not only for his military leadership, but for his unmatched moral clarity. Led his people on a 1,100-mile retreat toward Canada in 1877 to escape forced removal. Though eventually captured, his final words—"I will fight no more forever"—remain one of the most haunting indictments of U.S. policy and betrayal (Joseph, 1879).

Geronimo (Chiricahua Apache): Led decades of resistance against Mexican and U.S. encroachment. His final surrender in 1886 marked the symbolic end of organized Native military resistance in the continental U.S., though resistance in spirit and law continued (Kraft, 2000).

And There Were Many More

This list is not complete. It cannot be. For every name recorded, a hundred more rose and fell without fanfare—elders, women, children, visionaries, and silent protectors who resisted in ways unseen and unremembered by history books. The war for dignity, land, and life was fought in every corner of this continent. And it is still being fought today.

Long-Term Consequences and Legacy

Displacement, But Not Defeat

The Indian Removal Act of 1830 forced thousands west in death marches known as the Trail of Tears. But the journey didn't end there. Culture persisted. Nations rebuilt. Resistance, once armed, now lived in language, story, and law (Remini, 2001).

Cultural Survival Through the Storm

Every song sung in Ojibwe, every dance step at a powwow, every basket woven in tradition is a continuation of resistance. Colonization came with armies and churches—but it could not erase memory.

Recognition and the Path to Reconciliation

Today, Native resistance is honored in courtrooms, classrooms, and councils. Lands are being returned. Languages are being taught. Truths are being told. The past is not forgotten. It is a compass.

Conclusion

Colonization was not met with silence. It was met with war cries, with treaties forged and broken, with dances spun in defiance, and stories whispered to children by firelight. From Hatuey to Tecumseh, our ancestors chose defiance over despair. And in doing so, they passed to us a legacy not of loss—but of strength.

"Faced with overwhelming force and relentless oppression, our ancestors chose resistance over submission, embodying the spirit of defiance. Their courage laid the foundation for the unyielding strength that courses through our veins today."

The High Price of Inequity

Indigenous People and Police Violence

We Aren't Protected—We are Targeted

Among all racial groups in the United States, Native Americans are the most likely to be killed by law enforcement. This is not a statistical anomaly. It is the inevitable consequence of centuries of systemic inequity, dispossession, and dehumanization

From the colonial use of violence to suppress Indigenous resistance to modern-day encounters steeped in bias and misunderstanding, the cycle persists. This chapter lays bare the historical roots, structural causes, and ongoing human toll of police violence against Native peoples. It is a crisis rooted in legacy and watered by neglect.

Historical Context: From Suppression to Surveillance

Law enforcement in Indian Country did not begin as a mechanism of protection but as a tool of subjugation. The early role of armed patrols and settler militias was not to serve Native populations—but to control, remove, and often eliminate them.

The Doctrine of Discovery and the Indian Removal Act of 1830 legalized ethnic cleansing under the guise of policy. These doctrines didn't just move people; they normalized force as the language of interaction with Native communities. That normalization never ended.

The Current Crisis: Policing and Disproportionate Death

In 2016, The Guardian's The Counted recorded the highest per-capita rate for Native Americans (10.13 per million). Across later datasets, Native Americans remain at or near the top per-capita, with year-to-year rank varying by source.

Why So Many? Understanding the Triggers

Systemic Racism and Stereotypes

Law enforcement's view of Native Americans has long been colored by mythologies of savagery and instability. These tropes, modernized as "aggressive," "mentally unstable," or "combative," frame encounters before they happen. Officers often interpret resistance where there is fear, and threat where there is cultural difference. Implicit bias turns misunderstandings into funerals (Delgado & Stefancic, 2017).

Jurisdictional Chaos: Three Sovereignties, No Justice

Tribal lands operate within a confusing maze of federal, state, and tribal law enforcement agencies. In practice, this means that who responds to a call can depend on arbitrary boundaries. When a tribal citizen is harmed or killed, responsibility is deflected between jurisdictions. Injustice is buried beneath legal gray zones and competing sovereignties (Echo-Hawk, 2010).

Poverty, Over-Policing, and Social Erosion

High rates of poverty, trauma, and under-resourced mental health care lead to frequent interaction with police—often in crises. Many Native communities lack social infrastructure, forcing law enforcement into roles they are untrained to fulfill. A noise complaint at a powwow. A wellness check on someone in spiritual crisis. Too often, these moments end in violence. As one tribal officer said, "They call it backup. We call it an invasion."

Stories the Numbers Can't Hold

John T. Williams: Killed with a Knife, Not for One

In 2010, Seattle police fatally shot John T. Williams, a Native woodcarver, within four seconds of engaging him. Partially deaf and carrying a carving knife, Williams posed no threat. His death sparked outrage, memorial totems, and demands for reform. But the pattern continued.

Loreal Tsingine: Five Shots Over Shoplifting

In 2016, Loreal Tsingine, a petite Navajo woman, was killed by a police officer in Winslow, Arizona, over an alleged shoplifting incident. She held a pair of scissors. She was shot five times. Her name became a rallying cry for Native women, who are disproportionately targeted and often forgotten in national conversations about police violence.

Pine Ridge and the Legacy of Peltier

The 1975 shootout at Pine Ridge remains one of the most iconic clashes between federal agents and Native activists. The imprisonment of Leonard Peltier, amid allegations of coerced testimony and withheld evidence, speaks to the weaponization of the legal system against Native dissent. Pine Ridge today still grapples with underfunding, over-policing, and unresolved pain.

Pine Ridge and the Legacy—and Release—of Leonard Peltier

In 2025, after nearly five decades behind bars, Leonard Peltier was finally released from federal prison. His release marked not only the end of one of the most controversial incarcerations in modern American history but also reignited a national conversation about justice, sovereignty, and the right to resist.

For many, Peltier's freedom is long overdue—a symbolic acknowledgment of the deep flaws in the legal process that put him there. Yet in Pine Ridge, where the wounds of 1975 never fully healed, the moment was met with both solemn reflection and quiet hope.

The same systemic neglect—underfunding, over-policing, and generational trauma—still grips the community. Peltier's return is not a conclusion but a reminder: the struggle for justice in Indian Country is far from over.

What Must Change?

Training Must Be Tribal-Led

Cultural competency cannot be taught in a seminar. It must be embedded in departments through long-term partnerships with tribal communities. Elders should be instructors. Traditional protocols should be respected. Knowing a people is the first step to protecting them.

Jurisdiction Must Be Simplified, Not Excused

Legislation is needed to clarify law enforcement authority across Indian Country, especially to empower tribal police to intervene in cases involving non-Natives. Sovereignty must not be a loophole—it must be a shield.

Accountability Must Be Real

Body cameras. Independent investigations. Federal reviews of fatal encounters involving Native victims. Justice delayed has long meant justice denied in Indian Country. That must end.

Empowerment Must Be Funded

True justice includes investment. Invest in community-led safety programs. Fund trauma-informed care. Build trust not with promises but with presence—consistent, culturally grounded, and Native-led.

Conclusion

The high rate of police violence against Native Americans is not an isolated crisis. It is the modern extension of a long war against sovereignty, identity, and survival. Reform must be structural. Justice must be reimagined.

The right to live—not just survive—must finally be honored. Until then, every name added to the roll of Native lives lost to state violence is an indictment not of isolated officers, but of a nation still failing its First Peoples.

"Understanding the roots of systemic racism through the lens of Native American history reveals a legacy of violence and mistrust, underscoring the urgent need for comprehensive reforms in policing and social justice."

The Sacred Unspoken: Hidden Religions

"Some teachings were never written. Some prayers were never spoken above a whisper. But they lived in us—in the way we danced, in the way we healed, and in the way we endured. Our religions weren't lost. They were just never meant to be displayed."

Medicine Dances, and the Quiet Faith of Our People

Introduction

There have always been Native religions. Not "spirituality" as defined by outsiders. Not borrowed faiths adorned with feathers. But distinct, place-rooted, rule-bound religions—often unwritten, often unnamed beyond their communities, but fiercely alive.

They existed before the first missionary set foot on this soil, and they persisted through assimilation, exile, and quiet erasure. Some were practiced openly. Others were protected by silence—hidden behind the walls of Christian churches, beneath the rhythm of drumming, or carried in secret between elders and grandchildren (Irwin, 1996).

Many Native people today speak proudly of their Catholic or Protestant upbringing. And yet, beneath those pews and polished shoes, you'll often find something older. Something that doesn't need a name to be true.

Remembering the Medicine Dances

I remember it. I was a small boy.

My grandparents, both devout Catholics, would still attend what Grandma called "medicine dances"—ceremonial gatherings where healing was prayed for, not prescribed. She believed in the saints, yes. But she also believed in the drum, in the tobacco, in the power of what our people had done long before the Vatican reached our shores.

She respected the religions of others—Native and non-Native alike. She never mocked or dismissed what she didn't understand. And while she never wore her beliefs loudly, she did share something sacred with me once. She told me about her spirit animal—not the way it's parodied today in cartoons or social media, but as something real. Something personal. She believed each of us walked with one. And when her time came, she told me she had offended it—by not listening. By ignoring its message because Grandpa was nearby, and he didn't hold with that kind of spiritualism.

One night, we were taken to a gathering—oil lamp flickering, songs rising, the kind of stillness that makes you feel watched, not by people, but by spirit. Grandma looked at my sister and me and decided it wasn't our time to see this yet. She whispered to Grandpa, and before long, we were being driven thirty miles to see a movie. I still remember it—Jerry Lewis in "Who's Minding the Store." Grandpa laughed out loud that night, something I hadn't seen before.

But I've thought about that night ever since—what we left behind, what waited there in the quiet, and what Grandma knew we weren't ready to stand beside.

The Unseen Faiths

While Christianity became dominant on many reservations—often through force or survival—Native religious systems never disappeared. They simply learned to walk more quietly.

There were the Peyote Road people, part of the Native American Church, blending Christian motifs with the ancient sacrament of the peyote cactus (Stewart, 1987). There were the Feather Keepers, the Water Carriers, the Dream Walkers—roles not formally named but understood within certain tribal traditions.

Some tribes maintained Midewiwin societies, especially among the Anishinaabe—keepers of ceremonial knowledge, guardians of herbs, spirit songs, and encoded scrolls (Densmore, 1974). In the Pacific Northwest, potlatches served both social and sacred purposes, tying wealth to ceremony and cosmic balance. Among the Lakota and Dakota, the Wi Wanyang Wacipi—the Sun Dance—was a test of sacrifice and a prayer for the people, outlawed by the U.S. government until the late 20th century (Black Elk & Neihardt, 1932).

Among the Dine' (Navajo), the Blessing Way and Enemy Way ceremonies define health, order, and restoration—religion not as doctrine, but as harmony (Wyman, 1983). For the Hopi, the Katsina rites bring the spirit world into dialogue with the living (Titiev, 1944).

These were not metaphors. These were religions.

The Role of Secrecy

In many Native households, these practices were not explained—they were inherited. Children weren't told everything. Songs were shared only when the time was right. Outsiders—even family—might be turned away from ceremonies not out of rejection, but protection.

This secrecy wasn't shame. It was sacredness.

Christianity asks for belief. Many Native religions ask for presence. You don't "convert" into them. You are brought in, gradually, if you're willing to listen without needing to define.

Syncretism and Survival

The intersection of Native and Christian belief systems is complex. In many communities, syncretism occurred—not as a loss, but as adaptation.

People attended church on Sunday and ceremony on Tuesday. They held rosaries in one hand and sweetgrass in the other. Saints were often re-imagined as spirit helpers. Jesus was sometimes seen not as the destroyer of tradition, but as another sacred being walking the Good Red Road (Irwin, 1996).

For many, it wasn't either/or. It was both/and. And sometimes, neither—just the land, the wind, the ancestors, and a drum.

"Our people had religion before we had churches. We had communion before bread. We had sacred law before the courts. And we still have it—not always named, not always visible, but always there."

Observations

Powwow in Transition: From Ceremony to Competition

"The drumbeat was once the heartbeat of the people—not the sound of competition, but the rhythm of reunion. Now we must ask: when did we begin dancing for dollars instead of dancing for each other?"

Introduction

Once rooted in deep spiritual practice, communal unity, and intertribal fellowship, the powwow has evolved—some would say morphed—into a traveling spectacle of competition and pageantry. What began as sacred gathering has, in many modern iterations, become a circuit of prize purses, fame, and Instagram reels.

While the continuation of dance and drumming is, in itself, a sign of cultural survival, we must reflect on the shifting motivations behind it. This chapter explores the complex transformation of the powwow—from spiritual ceremony to competitive arena—and asks whether this change reflects resilience, loss, or something in between.

The Historical Powwow: Ceremony, Community, and Survival

The powwow was never just an event. It was survival. A post-suppression revival. After decades of cultural genocide—when dances were outlawed, languages forbidden, and spiritual practices driven underground—the powwow re-emerged as a gathering of healing. It was a time to visit distant relatives, find potential partners, tell stories, and reconnect with the sacred through movement and song (Browner, 2002).

Historically, the powwow was not standardized. Traditions varied widely by region, tribe, and context. Some were more social, some deeply ceremonial. What they shared was intention: they were centered on community. There was no prize money. No announcers. No sponsors. No "grand entries" scripted like parades. Instead, it was about being—being together, being Native, being whole again.

The Rise of Contest Powwows

The late 20th century saw a shift—a commercialization of Native culture that crept in slowly and then, suddenly, was everywhere. Contest powwows began offering prize money to attract dancers and drummers, and with money came prestige.

The greater the purse, the bigger the crowd. The "Powwow Trail" emerged, with dancers traveling across the country from May through October, competing for thousands of dollars in prize categories. Many of them are incredibly talented—true athletes and artists. But when the heart of the powwow becomes the check at the end, the purpose begins to blur (Ellis, 2003).

While contest powwows can bring in tourism and revenue for tribes, they also introduce hierarchies. The best regalia. The fastest footwork. The most impressive spin. A community event becomes a competition. Instead of the drum being a sacred center, it becomes an audition stage. This shift isn't inherently wrong—but it isn't without consequences either.

Traditional vs. Competitive: A Culture Divided?

There are still traditional powwows. Smaller. Quieter. Sometimes held without public advertising. At these gatherings, dance categories don't exist. There are no prizes. The emphasis is on prayer, remembrance, and healing. These events serve as a spiritual reconnection with the ancestors and reaffirm tribal values outside the glare of contest lights and MC microphones (Fixico, 2012).

The contrast between traditional and competitive powwows has created, in some circles, a cultural tension. Some traditionalists view contest powwows as performative—drifting too far from ceremony into entertainment. Others argue that any continuation of dance, regardless of format, is worthy and vital.

The Fame and the Fallout

Alongside prize money, modern powwows have brought with them celebrity. Star dancers. Popular drum groups. Instagram influencers in feather bustles. Young dancers are often more aware of their TikTok views than the origins of their dance styles. In an age of digital recognition, powwows are increasingly becoming content.

But the pursuit of attention comes with a cost. Cultural teachings—about humility, about spiritual preparation, about honoring the drum—risk being replaced with choreography rehearsed for judges and camera angles. We don't fault the dancers. We question the structure that incentivizes performance over presence.

What We Risk Forgetting

The modern powwow—colorful, crowded, and loud—can easily forget the reasons it was reborn. We forget that in our grandparents' time, dancing could mean arrest. That in boarding schools, Native children were punished for speaking the languages now shouted proudly in song. That the circle once formed in hiding.

Today, we host stadium-sized powwows with vendor booths, political speeches, and halftime shows. And still, the drumbeat echoes something old—something sacred—beneath all the modern spectacle. That drum, if we let it, can still call us home.

Conclusion

Dancing With Intention This is not a call to end contest powwows. It is a call to remember why we gather. To re-center the spirit beneath the sparkle. To ask ourselves—when the last dollar is handed out and the arena lights go dark—did we truly honor the ancestors? Did we dance for something more than applause?

The powwow is not lost. But it is, in many places, distracted. And it's up to us to bring it back—not to the past, but to a place of balance.

"When the last feather falls and the arena clears, what remains is not the prize—but the reason we danced in the first place. And if we forget that, no cash prize can restore it."

The Fire That Built the Future: The CCC–Indian Division

When the land bled and wallets were empty, we were paid to stop the bleeding—and proved a model worth reviving.

The Great Depression hit Indian Country like a second winter. Federal policy had already thinned our herds and hollowed our economies; then the markets collapsed and the soil itself began to blow away. Washington's answer arrived in 1933 with a strange mix of consequence and correction: the Civilian Conservation Corps—Indian Division (CCC-ID), formally the Indian Emergency Conservation Work program.

Its mandate was blunt and brilliant at once—pay Native people to heal Native land, and do it now. The government wanted relief and conservation; Indian Country needed wages and dignity. For once, those goals overlapped (National Archives – CCC-ID overview).

Unlike the main CCC, the Indian Division ran through the Bureau of Indian Affairs, recruited locally, and—critically—let most workers stay on their own reservations close to their families and fields. Where white CCC enrollees commonly lived in distant Army-run camps, many CCC-ID workers slept in their own beds and still earned federal pay.

Those who did live in camps drew the standard $30 per month plus room and board; home-station assignments often paid up to about $42 per month with rotations designed to spread relief as widely as possible—details that mattered because the program rebuilt household economies without uprooting them again (Minnesota History—CCC Indian Division; Prologue Magazine—CCC Indian Division).

What We Built—and Why It Lasted

The CCC-ID tackled the same dust, erosion, and open-range chaos the rest of the Corps fought—but on Indian lands first. Crews controlled gullies, planted shelterbelts, strung telephone lines, cut firebreaks, repaired irrigation works, fenced grazing units, and opened miles of all-weather roads so a pickup—and later, a school bus or clinic truck—could finally reach where it needed to go.

Across the broader CCC, more than two billion trees were planted, 125,000 miles of roads and trails were built, and millions of erosion-control structures stabilized fields and watersheds; the Indian Division's share threaded those accomplishments through reservation after reservation, often guided by tribal priorities and BIA engineers (USDA Forest Service—CCC in the South; Bureau of Reclamation—CCC Report).

If you want to see what that looked like—not a statistic, but a shovel in motion—watch the Department of the Interior newsreels and surviving footage: men waist-deep in a wash planting willow fascines; a crew tamping rock into a spillway; a line of posts marching into the horizon to let grass recover. These images aren't romantic—they're proof (The Corps Network – DOI film clip; National Archives – CCC-ID overview).

How It Worked (When It Worked)

The program began under the Emergency Conservation Work Act of March 31, 1933; within weeks, funds were routed to the BIA and a dedicated Indian Emergency Conservation Work Division organized. BIA foresters and engineers coordinated with tribal leaders to choose projects and enroll workers over 18 who were physically fit.

Two objectives stayed welded together: immediate employment and useful conservation. That clarity—and the fact that most work happened at home—built rare trust for a federal program in communities with long memories of broken promises (National Archives – CCC-ID overview).

Administration still had its federal fingerprints. The Army supplied some camp logistics; the BIA signed off on plans; Washington counted outputs. But the Indian Division also produced its own voice. In 1933 the BIA launched **Indians at Work**—part newsletter, part accountability report—to document projects, share techniques, and name the Native crews rebuilding Native homelands (Prologue Magazine—CCC Indian Division).

The Ledger and the Land

Here's the part too many histories file in the footnotes: CCC-ID wages didn't just buy flour and boots. They paid down store credit, kept families intact through winters, and gave young men—and plenty of not-so-young heads of household—a reason to stay instead of ship out. On more than one reservation, CCC-ID checks were the difference between a family's car staying on the road or being parked for good.

Money earned building a stock pond for the community often bought medicine for a child under that same roof. And the projects weren't busywork—erosion control widened growing seasons by keeping topsoil out of the creek; fencing rationalized grazing; roads and phone lines changed emergency response from "if the weather holds" to "Tuesday" (USDA Forest Service—CCC in the South).

Friction and Blind Spots

No New Deal program was free from the old order's prejudices. The CCC nationally reflected the segregation and quotas of its time; though the Indian Division enrolled Indigenous workers at scale and on better local terms, it still operated under agencies that often distrusted tribal decision-making and kept key levers in Washington's hands. Some projects served distant metrics more than local need. And when war came, Congress re-routed dollars to tanks, not terraces; by 1942 the program closed, its crews pulled toward the draft board or defense plants (MNopedia—CCC-ID).

Why This History Still Matters

Indian Country today debates "jobs versus tradition" as if the two are enemies. CCC-ID shows the third way we forget too easily: pay Native people to do the culturally coherent work of restoring Native land and infrastructure, at home, to standards we choose. It's not charity. It's contract performance with a moral clause.

We hold listening sessions about climate, broadband, housing, and wildfire. Imagine reviving the bones of CCC-ID with modern contracts, tribal procurement, and true local control: wages flowing to tribal crews to trench fiber on right-of-ways we control; conservation corps restoring riparian buffers with TEK written into the scope; cultural crews rehabbing irrigation ditches and timber stands. We don't need nostalgia—we need a line item (Record Group 75—BIA; Record Group 35—CCC).

For Researchers and Builders

If you're writing your family's story—or building a grant proposal—go to the record, not the rumor. The National Archives holds the paper trail: correspondence, camp and payroll lists, project reports, photographs, and **Indians at Work** issues that put names, dates, and places to the work.

Look under Record Group 75 (BIA) and CCC holdings for series like reservation-level worker lists (1938–39), engineering files, and local agency records. Read them and you'll see the faces in the fence lines. Then do what our grandparents did—organize, budget, and build (National Archives – CCC-ID overview; Record Group 75—BIA; Record Group 35—CCC).

"If the land is bleeding and our people are broke, pay our people to stop the bleeding. Call it relief or conservation—I call it justice with a timecard."

SECTION II: Our Internal Reckoning

A Call for Introspection and Accountability

We have fought wars for our land. We have stood against the weight of colonization, the theft of our children, and the erasure of our tongues. But perhaps the most difficult battle we now face is not external. It is within. The fractures that threaten the foundation of our communities today are self-inflicted—and they demand something few are willing to give: introspection.

Generational trauma is real, but so is generational responsibility. We can name the scars left by colonizers and missionaries, but we must also name the ways we have failed each other. This section is not about blame—it is about truth. And the truth is this: the over reliance on federal aid, the unchecked nepotism in our leadership, the normalization of poor health choices, and the collective apathy toward education are not just obstacles—they are threats to our sovereignty.

It is easier to point outward. To say, "We were robbed," and leave it there. But sovereignty demands more. It demands that we ask ourselves hard questions. Have we become too comfortable in dependency? Have we allowed corruption to flourish because it bears a familiar face? Have we forsaken traditional knowledge systems in favor of convenience?

These are not rhetorical questions. They are indictments—and invitations. The invitation is to reclaim what was once our greatest strength: communal accountability. The elders say, "The weakest link breaks the circle." We are that circle. And until we repair our own links, we cannot rise.

This section is a mirror. It reflects the contradictions we must face, the healing we must initiate, and the courage it takes to rebuild from within. We will speak on failed leadership, cultural neglect, public health crises, and the silent collapse of educational standards in our own nations. But we will also speak on how to turn this tide—through truth-telling, through action, and through the unshakable belief that we are capable of leading ourselves.

"Our greatest battles are not fought against external enemies, but within the heart of our own people. To conquer these, we must first recognize the power we hold over our own destiny."

Observations

Psychological Transformation of Native American Mindset

A Journey Through Five Centuries

The War for the Native Mind

The essence of Native identity has never stood still. It has shifted, stretched, and been reshaped by every blow and betrayal, every prayer and act of defiance. To understand the Native mindset today is to look back across five centuries of cultural resistance, psychological survival, and spiritual adaptation. From the first tentative encounters with Europeans to modern struggles with dual identity, Native communities have navigated the slow erosion of sovereignty and the sparks of cultural rebirth with a resilience that defies erasure.

1600 to 1800: The Era of Contact and Early Displacement

The first generations to meet European settlers did not yet know the scale of the storm that was coming. To them, the arrival of foreign ships and unfamiliar faces was approached not with hatred, but with caution and openness. Early trade was an exchange of goods and stories, not blood. For a moment, it seemed possible that coexistence might follow. But it did not. Diseases spread like wildfire. Lands were claimed without consent. Spirits began to fracture under the weight of betrayal (Calloway, 1997).

This era marked the first psychological rupture. Where once the world was seen as a sacred circle—land, spirit, people in harmony—there emerged a new consciousness: that of an intruder who did not honor the circle. The trauma was not immediate genocide, but the slow, agonizing realization that the balance was slipping away. Native peoples began to see that these settlers were not visitors. They were conquerors, and the old ways would not be safe much longer (Cronon, 1983).

1800 to 1850: The Rising Tide of Loss and Betrayal

The 19th century began with a promise—a false one. Treaties were signed, lands were ceded, and trust was betrayed. From the Trail of Tears to the burning of villages, Native nations were pushed farther from their ancestral homes and deeper into grief. The psychological landscape shifted from guarded optimism to quiet mourning. Children grew up with stories of home that no longer existed. Elders spoke less often. Songs became laments (Dunbar-Ortiz, 2014).

Still, the fire of defiance remained. Tecumseh rose not just as a leader, but as a symbol of unity against hopeless odds. His calls for intertribal resistance were not just military—they were psychological. They reminded Native people that though land could be taken, the spirit of solidarity could not. The mindset of this era was not surrender. It was steeled endurance (Deloria, 2003).

1851 to 1900: Reservations, Control, and the Crushing of Identity

The reservation system did not simply confine Native people to bounded plots of land—it confined their spirits. Cultures built on mobility, stewardship, and spiritual geography were now fenced in and managed by the very government that broke its promises. The reservation was a tool of containment, but also of psychological conditioning. Dependence was enforced. Autonomy was criminalized. Pride became something whispered, not worn.

Boarding schools intensified this psychic war. Children were taken. Names were erased. Languages were forbidden. These were not just cultural disruptions; they were engineered traumas. Shame replaced pride. Silence replaced story. Entire generations came of age seeing their own identity as something to hide. Survival meant forgetting who you were (Fixico, 1998).

1901 to 1950: Survival in the Shadow of Erasure

By the early 20th century, the psychological toll of colonization had sunk deep into the Native soul. Families bore the scars of disconnection— between parent and child, elder and youth, land and spirit. Government policies pushed for assimilation while offering little support. Native identity was tolerated only when it was non-threatening, romanticized, or profitable. For many, this meant hiding their truth or struggling to reclaim it.

Yet something stirred beneath the surface. Groups like the Society of American Indians began asserting a voice long silenced. Political consciousness took root in small but meaningful ways. It was the beginning of a reawakening—a shift from isolation to organization. Though trauma loomed large, the first shoots of psychological revival broke through the concrete of oppression (Calloway, 1997).

1950 to Present Day: Reclamation, Identity, and the Rise of Cultural Sovereignty

The Indian Relocation Act of 1956 scattered Native families across urban landscapes, promising opportunity but delivering isolation. Cities were not kind to the displaced. Poverty, racism, and cultural dislocation compounded the psychological strain. And yet, in that shared dislocation, new bonds formed. Pan-Indian identities emerged. Urban powwows, advocacy groups, and grassroots coalitions took shape.

Red Power

Then came Red Power. The American Indian Movement wasn't just political—it was spiritual rearmament. Occupations, protests, and legal battles were driven not only by rights, but by identity. The psychological shift was seismic: Native Americans were no longer passive victims of policy. They were agents of their own reclamation. Languages were revived. Songs were sung in public again. The drumbeat returned to the center (Dunbar-Ortiz, 2014).

But not everyone in Indian Country embraced the movement. For many tribal leaders, traditionalists, and everyday Native people simply trying to survive in silence, AIM wasn't seen as liberation—it was seen as disruption. To them, the group brought more heat than hope, stirring up tension in communities already under surveillance and strain. Critics labeled them hot-headed agitators. Some mocked them outright with a cruel nickname: AIM—Assholes in Moccasins. That biting phrase revealed a deeper truth—support for AIM within Indian Country was far from universal. In fact, among many Native communities, it was scarce.

This wasn't just internalized oppression; it was a reflection of real fear. Fear of government retaliation. Fear of losing what little federal support remained. Fear of the chaos that activism too often invites.

And many who disagreed with AIM kept quiet—not out of indifference, but out of fear of retaliation by their own people or other Indigenous factions who saw silence as betrayal. The very trauma AIM tried to uproot was the same force that caused many to retreat, resist, or disappear entirely.

AIM today is a shadow of its former self—splintered, decentralized, and suspended somewhere between reverence and controversy. For some, it remains a symbol of Native resistance, remembered with pride and defiance. For others, it's a relic—tangled in stories of internal conflict, unresolved violence, and unanswered questions. Its legacy is complicated: part inspiration, part cautionary tale. What AIM ignited cannot be undone—but neither can it be simplified.

The American Indian Movement still lives, but in fragments. Its heartbeat lingers in scattered chapters, community gatherings, and treaty-based advocacy. Yet the fire that once seized the nation has cooled into quieter forms of resistance. Generational shifts, internal fractures, and the weight of history have transformed AIM from a national force into a dispersed network of cultural defenders and political watchdogs. It no longer dominates headlines, but in Indian Country, its name still carries heat—honor to some, hesitation to others. AIM's story is no longer just about what it is. It's about what it changed—and what it refused to let die.

American Indian Movement (AIM) & Leonard Peltier's Release

One of AIM's most iconic—yet tragic—figures is Leonard Peltier, a Turtle Mountain Chippewa and early AIM activist who, in June 1975, was implicated in a deadly shootout on the Pine Ridge Reservation that left two FBI agents and one Native man dead. Convicted in 1977 amid serious allegations of suppressed evidence and prosecutorial misconduct, Peltier spent nearly five decades behind bars, becoming a global symbol of political imprisonment in Indian Country.

On February 18, 2025, President Joe Biden commuted Peltier's sentence to indefinite home confinement due to his declining health and the enduring controversy surrounding his conviction (The New Yorker). He was transferred to his home reservation in North Dakota under house arrest, where he was greeted by supporters and family in an emotional homecoming.

In one of his first public statements, captured by Reuters, Peltier declared:

"Today I am finally free! They may have imprisoned me but they never took my spirit!" (Reuters)

His release marked not only a personal victory, but a symbolic turning point in the narrative of AIM itself. What began as a defiant movement in the 1960s—demanding treaty rights, tribal sovereignty, and justice—has evolved into a legacy of cultural resilience and moral urgency. Peltier's freedom reminds us that justice delayed is still justice—and that the struggle for Indigenous dignity and self-determination remains as vital as ever.

In a June 2025 Zoom interview with The New Yorker, Peltier reflected on his captivity and his future as a cultural and spiritual elder. Though media coverage largely focused on the emotional impact of his return, one quote carried a deeper charge:

"I've been in darkness for so long. Now, I must use my remaining days to shine light on the truths that kept me there." (The New Yorker)

His final words in that interview carried both a warning and a demand:

"The world should know what America has done. I was no more guilty than my co-defendants, and they were found not guilty by reason of self-defense, because the jury heard what was going on, and they said that should not be done to any American. Native people have just as much right to defend themselves as any other race in the United States or around the world." (The New Yorker)

Peltier's voice—once silenced behind bars—now joins the call to confront history, challenge injustice, and chart a future led not by silence, but by truth.

Peltier's release underscores the evolving nature of AIM—from confrontational beginnings at Alcatraz and Wounded Knee, to today's legacy of cultural resilience and moral urgency. His voice now joins the chorus calling for deeper reflection in tribal leadership, reclaiming sovereignty, and restoring justice in America.

Today, Native identity is complex, fluid, and strong. Many still carry the scars—of loss, shame, confusion—but many more are choosing pride, clarity, and connection. There is no going back to a pre-contact world, but there is something better: a world where being Native is defined not by what was taken, but by what was reclaimed.

Conclusion

Across five centuries, the psychological transformation of Native America has been a story of rupture and rebirth. Colonization inflicted wounds so deep they altered not just the land, but the very sense of self. And yet, every era has birthed its warriors, its healers, and its visionaries. Today, we stand at a powerful threshold—not broken, but reborn. The Native mindset is no longer something shaped solely by trauma. It is shaped by memory, resistance, and the will to rise again.

"Our history is not just a series of battles lost or treaties broken—it is a profound journey of the human spirit. We are shaped by our land, by the laughter of our children, and by the resilience found in the quiet songs of our ancestors. The psychological scars are deep, but the fire of our identity still burns, untamed and undying."

The Internal Struggle: Self-Inflicted Challenges

Introduction

For centuries, our people have carried the weight of history on our backs. The world looks to blame external forces—oppression, relocation, the slow erosion of our culture—and no one would deny those truths. But let us speak plainly now, not from bitterness, but from the quiet strength born of endurance: the greatest enemy today does not come from without.

The hardest battle is within. It's the struggle we face in the mirror, in the choices we make, in the policies and mindsets we allow to take root. This isn't about assigning blame—it's about reclaiming our power. True progress begins with reflection and the responsibility to change what lies within our control.

Historical Context: The Foundation of Internal Struggles

The wounds of colonization run deep—policies like the Indian Removal Act, the Dawes Act, and the system of forced boarding schools were more than just political measures; they were psychological warfare. They fractured our systems, tore apart families, and severed ties to land and language. These traumas reshaped our governance, our economics, and our worldview.

The theft of land was also a theft of direction. What was once rooted in ceremony and stewardship became dictated by paperwork and policy. These scars have echoed through generations, seeping into our institutions, our homes, and our self-perception. They laid the groundwork for internalized trauma that, if left unaddressed, mutates into self-defeating cycles (Adams, 1995; Deloria, 2006).

The Culture of Dependency

Economic Dependency

Federal aid, while vital in the short term, has created a long-term reliance that stifles initiative. Grants, subsidies, and entitlements, though intended to sustain us, have often come at the cost of entrepreneurial momentum. In many communities, the very idea of starting a business or generating wealth independently is overshadowed by the expectation of external support. What our ancestors traded across vast networks—goods, knowledge, and services—we now risk replacing with a passive posture of waiting. To rekindle the entrepreneurial fire that once fueled thriving trade systems, we must move from subsistence to strategy (Cornell & Kalt, 2000).

Psychological Dependency

This is the deeper scar. When a people begin to believe that change can only come from outside themselves, hopelessness grows. Dependency is not just about dollars—it's about dignity. The erosion of agency becomes normalized, so that self-determination starts to feel like a myth rather than a right. Learned helplessness creeps in subtly, shifting our narrative from "we can" to "we can't unless someone helps us." It is time to reclaim belief in ourselves, our minds, and our capacity to govern our own futures (Duran & Duran, 1995).

Cultural Dependency

The erosion of language, ceremony, and ancestral knowledge is not just cultural—it is psychological. Colonization didn't just remove us from our lands; it disconnected us from ourselves. When we rely on academic institutions or pop culture to tell us who we are, we surrender authorship of our own identity. Cultural dependency—looking to external systems and symbols for validation—weakens the communal thread that holds us together. Reclamation is not just about language revitalization or art preservation—it is about seeing ourselves through our own eyes again (Fixico, 2011).

Leadership and Governance Issues

Nepotism and Cronyism

Leadership must be earned, not inherited. When family ties outweigh competence, the system suffers. We all pay the price when political loyalty is valued more than community results. Leaders must be selected based on experience, wisdom, and vision—not favoritism. This requires clear policies, community accountability, and a new generation trained in leadership ethics (Cornell & Kalt, 2000).

Frequent Leadership Changes

Constant turnover erodes institutional memory and fractures long-term planning. Each leadership change is like a reboot, delaying progress and undoing groundwork. Projects stall. Relationships with outside partners dissolve. Trust within communities weakens. Stability does not mean stagnation—it means continuity. It means the vision outlives the election cycle. Tribal governance must prioritize succession planning and continuity to withstand both internal and external pressures (Jorgensen, 2007).

Internal Division and Conflict

Factionalism

Tribal rivalries—whether rooted in historical grudges, family divisions, or political camps—consume energy needed for progress. Infighting diverts attention from the larger work of nation-building. It breeds cynicism among youth and erodes credibility with external stakeholders. Unity does not mean uniformity. It means building consensus across differences for the greater good. Until we choose to set aside petty feuds for strategic solidarity, we will remain fractured and vulnerable (Cornell & Kalt, 2000).

Resistance to Change

Honoring tradition should never become a justification for rejecting evolution. Our ancestors adapted to seasons, migrations, and change—they were not stagnant. Cultural preservation must coexist with institutional innovation. We need to modernize governance systems, invest in technology, and embrace global opportunities while staying grounded in our sacred roots. It's not tradition versus progress—it's tradition guiding progress (Fixico, 2011).

Economic Mismanagement

Poor Financial Oversight

Mismanagement and lack of oversight are more than administrative failures—they are betrayals of trust. Transparency is not optional—it is a sacred responsibility. Tribes must establish financial protocols, hire qualified professionals, and conduct routine audits to prevent corruption and inefficiency. Every dollar misused is a dollar stolen from future generations. Self-determination means controlling our financial destiny with discipline and foresight (Jorgensen, 2007).

Failure to Diversify Economically

A single-industry economy is a fragile economy. Relying solely on casinos, federal contracts, or resource extraction leaves tribes vulnerable to market fluctuations and regulatory changes. Economic sovereignty requires vision. It means building multiple income streams—agriculture, technology, tourism, green energy, media. It means entrepreneurship training, access to capital, and infrastructure investment. Resilience begins with economic diversity (Cornell & Kalt, 2000).

Health and Social Issues

Health Disparities

High rates of diabetes, obesity, heart disease, and mental health disorders are not only statistics—they are reflections of historical trauma and present neglect. A wellness revolution is needed—one rooted in traditional diets, active lifestyles, and community-based care. Healthcare must be culturally competent and accessible. Healing the body is part of healing the nation (Warne & Frizzell, 2014).

Substance Abuse

Alcoholism, meth, opioids—these are not just personal tragedies; they are communal wounds. Addiction tears families apart and stifles potential. We need a coordinated, culturally informed response: trauma-informed care, youth prevention programs, elder involvement, and community-led treatment models. Silence is complicity. Healing demands honesty, empathy, and action (Duran & Duran, 1995).

Educational Challenges

High Dropout Rates

Too many Native youth are walking away from systems that ignore who they are. Curriculum must be reimagined to reflect Native values, histories, and knowledge systems. Schools must become centers of empowerment, not assimilation. Every dropout is a call to reinvent education that speaks to our youth, not at them (Reyhner & Eder, 2004).

Underfunded Schools

Unequal funding, outdated facilities, overworked teachers—these are not accidents; they are policy failures. We must fight for equity at every level. But we must also explore tribal-run schools, alternative education models, and community investment. Education is not a luxury—it is liberation (Reyhner & Eder, 2004).

Path Forward: Addressing Internal Challenges

Promoting Qualified Leadership

Build the leaders we need. Leadership development programs, mentorship networks, and succession planning are essential. Equip young leaders with both traditional wisdom and modern tools. Let merit, ethics, and vision—not bloodline—be the measure of leadership (Cornell & Kalt, 2000).

Encouraging Economic Diversification

Invest in industries that reflect our values and leverage our assets. From food sovereignty to e-commerce, from eco-tourism to content creation—the future is broad. Economic strategy must be community-driven, data-informed, and future-focused. Ownership equals power.

Implementing Governance Reforms

Modern governance requires integrity. Adopt ethics codes, enforce transparency, and empower community watchdogs. Governance should inspire trust, not suspicion. True sovereignty is built on accountability (Jorgensen, 2007).

Conclusion

The war for our future will not be won in courtrooms or capital buildings—it will be won in council chambers, homes, and schools. It begins with truth, continues with responsibility, and ends with transformation. We are not broken. We are burdened. And we are still standing. Now is the time to rise—not just in protest, but in purpose. To lead ourselves. To heal ourselves. To become again the sovereign nations our ancestors once dreamed we would be.

"Within our communities lies the power to overcome, yet too often we wrestle with shadows of our own making. Acknowledging and addressing these internal challenges is the key to unlocking our collective potential and reclaiming our strength."

Observations

Integrating "Eye Juggling" by Rodney Frey

Introduction

Rodney Frey's Eye Juggling isn't merely a collection of stories—it's a lens. A reflective method for seeing beyond what we think we know, one that dares readers to confront values: personal, political, and cultural. More than a book, it is a tool of discernment, helping communities interpret their own reflection.

When integrated into Business and Politics in Indian Country: You Can't Handle the Truth, Frey's methodology casts new light on the moral and institutional challenges tribes face today. His storytelling framework offers not just clarity, but a path forward: one rooted in empathy, value-based governance, and the sacred obligation to see through more than just our own eyes (Frey, 1995).

Expanded Synopsis

In Eye Juggling, Frey blends tribal oral traditions with structured introspection, inviting us to perceive the world through stories layered with cultural meaning. His characters wrestle with competing obligations, differing world-views, and the ongoing challenge of balancing self and community. Frey asks readers to reflect not only on the content of each story but also on how their own perspectives are shaped.

Applied to Indian Country's modern political and business realities, this approach can soften entrenched divisions. It creates a blueprint for honest dialog—the kind required to move beyond issues like nepotism, misaligned leadership, and cultural disconnection, as addressed throughout Business and Politics in Indian Country.

Understanding and Reconciling Values

Frey teaches that wisdom is not found in seeing one perspective more clearly, but in holding two perspectives at once. He shares the tale of a young man guided by an elder who teaches him to juggle his sight—one eye on his own truth, and one on the truth of his people.

That metaphor is central to governance in Indian Country today. Many tribal councils are torn between cultural preservationists and economic pragmatists. Too often, these groups see themselves in opposition.

But if we apply Frey's model, we begin to understand: both perspectives are incomplete alone. The preservationist keeps the fire of tradition alive. The pragmatist builds the shelter that protects it from the wind. Bridging this divide means seeing not opposition, but balance—a dynamic tension that, if managed with intention, can produce policy that serves both heritage and the future (Frey, 1995).

Enhancing Leadership and Governance

Leadership in Native communities is too often reduced to titles. But Frey reminds us that true leadership is not declared—it is revealed. One of his stories follows a chief faced with choosing between investing in long-term development or solving an immediate crisis. The chief learns to weigh both time-lines equally—short-term need and long-term vision—and to lead not from fear or ego, but from a center rooted in community welfare.

In Business and Politics in Indian Country, we address the consequences of narrow leadership: councils mired in favoritism, conflict, or transactional thinking. Frey's stories offer an antidote. Leaders must be taught to juggle competing values without dropping either. Reflective leadership, as Frey defines it, is the cornerstone of ethical tribal governance (Frey, 1995).

Fostering Economic Resilience

Frey's stories are filled with characters who survive by merging ancestral knowledge with contemporary challenges. In one tale, a family revives traditional foraging methods during a time of famine, adapting them with new tools. The lesson: resilience does not require abandoning the past; it requires renewing it.

This teaching is directly relevant to economic development in Indian Country. As discussed in a chapter of this book, many tribes face dependency due to underdeveloped economic strategies. Frey invites us to rethink economic models as moral frameworks. What values do our economic choices reflect? Are our investments building self-determination, or reinforcing dependence? Juggling those questions leads to economic strategy rooted not just in revenue, but in values. This is not theoretical. It is essential (Frey, 1995).

Promoting Cultural Integration

In a particularly striking story, Frey describes a young artisan who uses synthetic materials to make traditional jewelry. The elders disapprove until they see the next generation wearing the designs—honoring culture in a new form. Frey's lesson: culture is not static. It breathes, adapts, and survives when given room to evolve.

Tribal economic initiatives often struggle with this balance. In Business and Politics in Indian Country, we explore projects that fail either because they ignore culture or cling to it too tightly. Frey's approach offers a middle ground: integration. Infusing cultural principles into new industries—not for nostalgia, but for resilience—turns cultural continuity into a competitive advantage (Frey, 1995).

Addressing Internal Conflicts

Few challenges in Indian Country are more corrosive than internal division. Frey doesn't ignore this. One story tells of a tribal council that only elects leaders from a single lineage. But when faced with an existential threat, they choose a new leader—one without ties, but with skill. In this moment, the community redefines what matters: survival over tradition, merit over legacy.

This story echoes the recurring theme: that nepotism, factionalism, and internal distrust cripple tribal progress. Frey's wisdom offers a template for reform. Not by rejecting tradition, but by restoring its purpose: to serve the people, not personal agendas. Eye juggling, in this sense, becomes a metaphor for equitable leadership (Frey, 1995).

Conclusion

Rodney Frey's Eye Juggling offers more than parables. It provides a methodology for transformation: personal, political, and cultural. When integrated into the framework of Business and Politics in Indian Country, Frey's insights elevate the discussion from policy to principle, from dysfunction to healing. His stories teach us that the most critical tool in rebuilding our nations is not legislation or funding—it is the ability to see differently, to hold contradiction, and to lead with both vision and humility.

"Integrating our stories and wisdom is not just about preserving the past but leveraging it to illuminate our path forward. The truths we juggle are the very threads that weave our resilience and vision for the future."

Observations

The "Hang Around the Fort Indians"

"True sovereignty is not found in the hand that receives but in the hand that builds. Our ancestors survived by endurance, but our future demands that we thrive through independence, transforming dependency into empowerment and division into unity."

Economic Dependency:

Dependency Wasn't Chosen—It Was Engineered

Economic dependency remains a formidable barrier to the growth and self-sufficiency of Native American tribes. Rooted in historical injustices and perpetuated by systemic barriers, this dependency restricts progress and perpetuates an imbalance where Native communities rely on external support that often ignores their true needs and aspirations.

This chapter delves into the origins of economic dependency, examining the historical underpinnings of treaties, the establishment of reservations, and the adoption of discriminatory terms like "Hang Around the Fort Indians" and "apple Indian." We will also assess the ongoing impact of federal aid and the challenges of fostering economic independence in today's context.

Historical Roots of Economic Dependency

The Treaty System

In the 19th century, treaties between the U.S. government and Native American tribes were presented as solemn contracts—offering promises of land, resources, and lasting peace. These agreements, however, were never meant to be kept. They were tools of expansion, intended to appease tribes temporarily while settlers advanced further westward Deloria & Lytle, 1983.

Treaties were often crafted in a language foreign to tribal leaders, using legal jargon designed to obscure the true intentions of the U.S. government. The promises made in these documents—annuities, rations, and rights—were insufficient and unreliable. The U.S. government distributed these resources not as the means of partnership, but as a way to placate, to keep tribes fed just enough to avoid outright rebellion (Prucha, 1994.)

Negotiations Under Duress

These treaties were negotiated in conditions of extreme hardship. Tribal leaders faced starvation, the destruction of traditional hunting grounds, and relentless military pressure. They were cornered, often signing not out of agreement but out of desperation—a desperate bid to save lives, even if it meant surrendering lands they knew to be sacred Prucha, 1994. Even these coerced agreements were not respected. Promises of rations were rarely delivered in full, leading to years of malnourishment and hardship.

The psychological impact of betrayal was profound—leaving deep scars on tribal leadership, which had placed its hope in the U.S. government only to see those hopes dashed repeatedly. The dependency that began in these negotiations persists today, as tribes continue to face unreliable commitments from federal agencies that hold the purse strings (Iverson, 1998.)

The Reservation System

The establishment of the reservation system was another devastating blow to Native autonomy. Reservations were often carved out of lands deemed undesirable by settlers—barren landscapes, far removed from traditional hunting areas and spiritual sites. Reservations were not chosen based on the tribes' needs, but based on the convenience of expansionists looking to exploit more desirable land Iverson, 1998.

The federal government maintained control over these territories, dictating how land could be used and forbidding meaningful economic development. Even the ownership of individual plots within the reservation was structured under the system of "allotment" to undermine communal land-holding practices, further alienating tribes from their way of life (Utley, 2008.)

Isolation and Restrictions

The reservations were designed not just to be homes but prisons—places where the movement of Native peoples was severely restricted. The government banned tribes from exploiting their natural resources.

Mining, forestry, and even agriculture required federal permits, which were frequently denied. The reservation system imposed a physical and economic isolation that prevented trade with neighboring communities and access to broader markets Utley, 2008.

This created an economy that was wholly dependent on federal rations and aid, with few opportunities for self-sufficiency. The reservation system effectively barred any attempt at creating an independent economic infrastructure, ensuring that tribes would be forever reliant on the federal government—a dependency that still hinders economic progress today.

Contemporary Manifestations of Economic Dependency

Federal Funding

Today, a significant portion of tribal budgets still comes from federal funding. Programs like the Indian Health Service (IHS) and the Bureau of Indian Affairs (BIA) are lifelines for many tribes, yet they remain symptomatic of the same old problem: external control (Cornell & Kalt, 2000.)

The annual funding cycles, influenced by political changes and budgetary constraints, make it difficult for tribal governments to plan long-term. Unlike stable revenue sources, these funds can be reduced or redirected without input from tribal leadership, resulting in a fragile dependence that leaves communities vulnerable to shifts in federal priorities (NCAI, 2020).

Strings Attached

Federal funds are often accompanied by restrictive conditions. Grants and allocations usually stipulate the specific ways in which money must be used, giving tribes little freedom to direct funds where they see fit.

This approach prevents Native governments from addressing the unique needs of their communities, and innovation is stifled as local leaders must conform to federal guidelines that may not align with community priorities (Cornell & Kalt, 2000).

The power dynamics in this relationship cannot be overstated—the very idea of sovereignty becomes undermined when tribes cannot decide how to utilize their own funding.

Social Services

Federal assistance often provides essential services—housing, food, healthcare—but in doing so, it creates a dependency that is difficult to break. The pervasive reliance on food assistance programs, for instance, makes it harder for tribes to invest in local agricultural projects that could foster genuine economic growth. Tribal health services funded by the IHS are often underfunded and overburdened, perpetuating cycles of poor health that further hinder economic productivity (Wilkins & Lomawaima, 2001). Many tribes have no choice but to accept what is given, even if what is given is not enough.

Economic Isolation

Geographic isolation remains a major factor in the economic stagnation of many Native communities. Reservations, often located in remote areas, are distant from employment opportunities, markets, and educational institutions. Infrastructure—both physical, like roads and broadband, and social, like reliable schools and healthcare—remains underdeveloped (Smith, 2012).

This isolation prevents the diversification of economies that is essential for reducing dependency on federal aid. The ability to grow businesses, attract investments, or even access competitive markets is limited by the infrastructure gap that exists between reservations and non-reservation areas.

The "Hang Around the Fort Indians" Phenomenon

Origins and Impact

The term "Hang Around the Fort Indians" emerged during a bleak period in Native American history. Displaced from ancestral lands, stripped of resources, and facing starvation, many Native people turned to the military forts established by the very government that had taken everything from them.

These forts provided food, shelter, and security, albeit in insufficient measure, and Native people had little choice but to remain nearby (Deloria & Lytle, 1983.) This phrase became a slur—a shorthand for "dependent," and it ignores the historical context of survival, the resilience needed to endure what Native people endured. It transformed a tragic survival mechanism into a derogatory stereotype.

Historical Context

The context of this term is crucial—it reflects a moment when Native survival depended entirely on receiving aid from those who had caused their suffering. It was a survival strategy forced upon tribes by circumstance, not choice (Prucha, 1994.)

Yet the term persists, perpetuating a damaging narrative that implies Native people have always chosen to be dependent. The label reinforces a colonial perspective that refuses to acknowledge the resilience of a people who endured forced relocation, famine, and continuous marginalization.

Internalized Stereotypes

The power of a stereotype lies not just in how it is used against a people, but in how it is absorbed by those people. The term "Hang Around the Fort Indian" has internalized implications; it becomes an insidious part of the narrative within Native communities. People begin to believe the lie—that their ancestors chose this dependency out of laziness rather than necessity—and it becomes a barrier to progress. It affects self-worth, motivation, and the vision of what is possible (Smith, 2012.)

The Concept of the "Apple Indian"

Origins and Impact

The term "apple Indian" is equally divisive, emerging as a critique of those who chose to leave the reservation in search of better opportunities. Success in mainstream society has been interpreted as assimilation, as losing one's cultural identity.

The label implies that those who thrive in the broader society are somehow less Native, less loyal to their community (Deloria & Lytle, 1983.) This term has been weaponized to maintain a false dichotomy between "authentic" and "inauthentic" Native experiences.

Cultural Conflict

The internal cultural conflict deepens with each generation. Those who leave often do so with the intent of returning, armed with education and resources that can benefit their community. The "apple Indian" stereotype fails to recognize this desire to give back—it creates division where there should be unity, alienating those who wish to serve their people in new ways (Smith, 2012). It is a narrative that prevents the community from seeing the broader value of integration and economic success.

Perception and Reality

Reality is always more complex. Those labeled as "apple Indians" often continue to embrace their heritage deeply, finding ways to honor their culture even as they navigate a broader society. They serve as doctors, lawyers, and advocates—positions that are crucial for navigating the complexities of federal policies and ensuring that tribal interests are represented (Wilkins & Lomawaima, 2001.) The contributions of these individuals often go unrecognized, obscured by the narrow lens through which their success is viewed.

The Challenges of Breaking Free from Dependency

Building Diverse Economies

Breaking free from federal dependency requires the development of diverse, resilient tribal economies. Tourism, agriculture, renewable energy, and technology are all sectors with untapped potential for many tribes (Smith, 2012.)

Diversification not only creates jobs but also protects against the volatility of relying on a single revenue source, such as casinos or federal funding. Success lies in strategic investment and partnerships that respect tribal sovereignty while promoting economic independence.

Entrepreneurship and Small Business Development

Entrepreneurship remains a powerful tool for reversing dependency. By fostering an environment where small businesses can grow—through access to capital, training, and mentorship—tribes can create a more dynamic economy. Small businesses provide jobs, stimulate innovation, and build resilience. They are the backbone of any economy, and tribal governments must focus on creating opportunities for entrepreneurship if they are to break the cycle of reliance (Cornell & Kalt, 2000.)

Education and Workforce Development

Investment in education is fundamental. Empowering the youth through education, vocational training, and opportunities for higher learning ensures that tribes have the skills and knowledge required to build thriving economies.

Tribal colleges and vocational programs tailored to the needs of Native communities are key to creating a workforce capable of driving tribal development (Cornell & Kalt, 2000.) The investment must not only be in traditional academics but also in cultural education—ensuring that economic progress does not come at the cost of cultural erosion.

Conclusion

Economic dependency is a deeply entrenched issue, born from a history of broken treaties, enforced isolation, and systemic marginalization. Terms like "Hang Around the Fort Indians" and "apple Indian" have long been used to divide and degrade Native communities, turning the struggle for survival into something to be scorned. The path forward lies in rejecting these labels and embracing a future where economic independence is not only possible but inevitable.

By investing in diverse economies, fostering entrepreneurship, and prioritizing education, Native communities can break free from the chains of dependency and build a future that honors their past while embracing new possibilities. The goal is clear: economic sovereignty, self-determination, and the reclamation of our rightful place as thriving, resilient nations.

"True sovereignty begins when we break the chains of economic dependency and reclaim our right to self-sufficiency. The fort is not our refuge; it's a reminder of what we must overcome to thrive on our own terms."

Observations

In Active Genocide: The Trap of Federal and State Grants

The word genocide makes people flinch. We want to relegate it to history books, to black-and-white photos of starving faces and broken treaties. But genocide is not always bullets, blankets, or mass graves. Sometimes it's paperwork. Sometimes it's a signature at the bottom of a grant application.

What happens when a people's very survival is tethered to federal and state funds? When whole nations budget their future not by their own production, but by the next round of government checks? That is not sovereignty. That is dependency dressed up as development. And make no mistake—it is a slow-moving, carefully engineered form of genocide.

The Illusion of Support

Federal and state agencies sell their grants as "opportunities." They parade the language of support, uplift, and partnership. But read the fine print: every grant carries rules, conditions, oversight mechanisms, and reporting structures designed to make tribes bend (U.S. Commission on Civil Rights, 2018). Each dollar comes with invisible strings that tighten over time.

Grants are not just financial instruments—they are tools of control. The very act of chasing them forces tribal councils to align their priorities with state and federal agencies, not their own people. Projects are shaped by what the grant allows, not what the community actually needs. And in that dependency cycle, culture, sovereignty, and vision are smothered (Wilkins & Stark, 2017).

Sovereignty for Sale

What happens to sovereignty when the next fiscal year becomes the tribe's lifeline? Leaders grow hesitant to speak out, afraid to bite the hand that feeds. Councils become grant-writers instead of nation-builders. Young people learn to measure success not by what they create, but by what outside institutions approve (Cornell & Kalt, 2000).

And the deeper truth? This is not an accident. It is design. A tribal nation forever dependent on external grants is a tribal nation stripped of its independence. Sovereignty becomes a slogan, not a practice.

Death by Dependency

Genocide does not always announce itself with armies. Sometimes it looks like bureaucracy. Sometimes it comes wrapped in a glossy binder full of "funding opportunities."

The money we do get is being wasted. Look at the measurements of health, social, and economic indicators—they have not improved in proportion to the billions poured into Indian Country (U.S. Commission on Civil Rights, 2018).

Funds are spent on ineffective programs that recycle the same failures decade after decade. They are eaten up by inflated employee compensation packages, by administrative overhead, and by endless reports sent back to the very governments that use those numbers to fine-tune their control over us (Treuer, 2012). This is not investment—it is managed dependency.

Each grant accepted without a plan for independence is another step into the quicksand. The more tribes depend on these dollars, the less incentive exists to create internal revenue, to innovate, to take risks that lead to self-sufficiency.

Over time, the skills to sustain independence fade. Dependency becomes culture. And when dependency becomes culture, genocide has already done its work.

The Call Back to Life

The solution is not to abandon every dollar. It is to expose the danger of building a nation on someone else's terms. Grants should be tools, not crutches. They should be stepping-stones, not shackles. But for too many tribes, they have become the entire foundation.

If we do not confront this head-on, we will wake up one day to find our languages gone, our ceremonies hollow, and our sovereignty reduced to a line item on a state budget. That is not survival. That is erasure.

The Hard Question

So here is the question no grant report will ever ask, but every tribal leader must:

Are we building a future, or are we signing away the present in exchange for a slow, well-funded extinction?

Until Indian Country can answer that without flinching, we remain not just in danger—but in active genocide.

Observations

The Food Desert Dilemma

"True hunger is not the empty stomach, but the absence of choice—the inability to feed oneself with dignity, nourish one's spirit, and sustain one's community. Until we grow gardens of opportunity in these food deserts, the cycle of dependency will endure."

Unhealthy Diets and Health Crisis

Introduction

On many Native American reservations, the struggle to access nutritious food is a daily battle. This issue is not simply a matter of geography but a reflection of generations of structural neglect, economic disparity, and policy failure. So-called "food deserts" have become more than physical spaces—they are symptoms of political and social abandonment.

This chapter focuses on the environmental and logistical barriers that limit access to healthy foods, explores the economic realities that shape dietary choices, and examines the cumulative impact of poor nutrition on individual and community health.

The Geography of Neglect

In food deserts, the nearest full-service grocery store can be dozens of miles away. Most residents are forced to rely on gas stations or convenience stores that offer little more than processed snacks, sugary drinks, and canned goods (USDA 2019). These are not merely food deserts—they are nutritional wastelands. Without a car or public transportation, many families have no way to escape them.

Yet geography is only part of the problem. Many reservation communities face deeply rooted infrastructure deficits—poor roads, unreliable supply chains, and weather-dependent deliveries. These conditions inflate the cost of fresh produce and limit what stores can reliably stock. Access becomes a daily gamble, not a guarantee (Gordon & Richardson 2012).

The Economics of Hunger

Even when healthy food is available, it is often unaffordable. Due to high transportation costs and limited competition, the price of fruits, vegetables, and lean meats on reservations can far exceed national averages (Jernigan et al. 2017). When survival depends on stretching each dollar, processed foods—which are cheap, calorie-dense, and shelf-stable—become the default option.

This is not a question of willpower or ignorance. It is a question of poverty and access. Families are not choosing poor diets because they want to. They are choosing them because the system offers no viable alternative.

The Human Toll

The results are predictable and devastating. Native communities experience some of the highest rates of diet-related illnesses in the country: obesity, Type 2 diabetes, heart disease, and high blood pressure (Blue Bird Jernigan et al. 2012). The dominance of processed foods, combined with systemic barriers to healthcare, compounds these outcomes.

The harm goes beyond the body. Poor nutrition affects mental health, learning, job performance, and community cohesion. Children raised in food deserts suffer academically, elders with chronic conditions live shorter lives, and cultural traditions rooted in traditional foods erode over time.

Generational Consequences

The health effects of food deserts ripple through generations. Children who grow up without access to proper nutrition face increased risk of developmental delays, behavioral issues, and long-term health challenges (Story et al. 2008). These outcomes reduce educational achievement and economic mobility, reinforcing cycles of poverty and dependency.

At the other end of the age spectrum, the early loss of elders due to preventable diseases weakens the cultural integrity of Native communities. Elders are the bearers of language, traditions, and wisdom. Their loss is not just a health crisis—it is a cultural emergency.

Solutions Rooted in Community

Breaking the cycle of food deserts requires more than importing healthy food. It demands a rethinking of systems, investments in local infrastructure, and the restoration of food sovereignty. Some tribes are already leading the way—creating community gardens, launching mobile grocery units, reviving traditional agriculture, and building local food co-ops (Gundersen et al. 2018).

Such solutions empower communities to reclaim control over their food systems. By growing, harvesting, and distributing food locally, tribes can restore both physical health and cultural resilience.

Toward Food Sovereignty

Food deserts are not natural phenomena. They are the result of deliberate disinvestment and systemic neglect. Reversing them means more than providing handouts—it means returning control to Native communities. True food sovereignty includes land access, traditional knowledge, local farming, and policy support (Power 2008).

Conclusion

The food desert dilemma is a public health crisis born from historical injustice and ongoing neglect. To overcome it, Native communities need more than access to grocery stores. They need infrastructure, economic opportunity, cultural revitalization, and food systems built by and for Indigenous people.

"Our journey to health begins by sowing the seeds of self-reliance. Only when we transform our food deserts into fields of abundance will we nourish both body and spirit."

Health & Wellness: Breaking the Cycle of Poor Health

"True wellness in our communities comes from honoring the wisdom of our ancestors while embracing the tools of today. To break the cycle of poor health, we must blend tradition with innovation, healing our hearts as we heal our bodies."

Introduction

The health of Native American communities has been systematically eroded by centuries of forced change, cultural loss, and structural neglect. Once grounded in traditional lifeways that nurtured physical, spiritual, and communal well-being, Native health today is marked by crises—rising chronic disease, mental health challenges, and barriers to care.

These are not random afflictions; they are the direct result of colonization, broken treaties, relocation, and modern disconnection from land and tradition. This chapter examines that decline, explores the roots of resilience within Native traditions, and outlines paths forward to reclaim health—both individually and collectively.

Traditional Life-ways and Holistic Health

Long before hospitals and processed foods, Native communities thrived through balanced diets, active lifestyles, and the spiritual harmony of land-based living. The traditional diet—rich in wild plants, lean meats, and cultivated crops like corn, beans, and squash—was nutrient-dense and sustainable (Vantrease 2013). Medicines came from roots, bark, and ceremony. Physical movement was a way of life, not a fitness program. And health was not separate from culture; it was embedded in ceremony, story, and kinship.

The damage began when that equilibrium was disrupted. With land loss came food insecurity. With relocation came dependency. With government rations came white flour, lard, and sugar—"survival foods" that slowly poisoned generations. Colonization didn't just take lives; it rewrote the Native relationship with food, body, and spirit.

Chronic Illness and Modern Disease

Today, the consequences of that disruption are devastating. Native American communities suffer disproportionately from obesity, diabetes, cardiovascular disease, and cancer. These illnesses are fueled by diets heavy in processed food, limited access to healthcare, and the residual trauma of historical injustices (Jernigan et al. 2017). Reservation food deserts and underfunded health services aren't coincidences—they are outcomes of systemic disinvestment.

Obesity, Diabetes, and Heart Disease

Obesity in Native communities is not just about calories—it's about colonization. The loss of healthy, traditional foods and physical activity led to an over-reliance on cheap, high-calorie, nutrient-poor foods. As obesity increased, so did diabetes—a disease now at epidemic levels in many tribes (Wilson et al. 2012).

It leads to kidney failure, blindness, amputations, and premature death. Cardiovascular disease follows, often undetected due to limited preventative care. These diseases compound one another, and together they cut lives short and weaken communities.

Alcoholism and Substance Abuse

The health crisis isn't only physical. Alcoholism and drug addiction continue to tear through Native populations, rooted in the unresolved pain of forced assimilation, cultural suppression, and broken familial structures. Alcohol was weaponized historically—and its legacy lingers (May 1996). Substance abuse, particularly opioids and methamphetamines, have become modern tools of destruction. Without access to culturally grounded treatment and mental health care, many remain trapped in cycles of addiction and despair.

Mental Health and Historical Trauma

Mental health in Native America is a silent crisis. Depression, anxiety, and PTSD affect individuals who carry the weight of intergenerational trauma—loss of land, language, and loved ones. Suicide rates among Native youth are among the highest in the nation (Duran et al. 2004). But these conditions are not innate—they are the echoes of boarding schools, forced removals, and institutional betrayal. Healing requires not just therapy, but truth-telling and cultural restoration.

Underfunded Health-care Systems

The Indian Health Service, meant to provide care to Native peoples as part of treaty obligations, remains chronically underfunded. Clinics on reservations are understaffed and ill-equipped. Wait times are long. Access to specialists is rare. And for many, even reaching a clinic means traveling hours from home (Sequist et al. 2011). This systemic neglect violates not only trust, but life expectancy.

Barriers to Access

Transportation, cost, and mistrust of Western institutions create further barriers. Cultural misunderstandings often alienate Native patients from non-Native providers. The absence of Native voices in medical decision-making ensures that many treatments are delivered without cultural relevance or respect. Health care cannot just be available—it must be trusted.

Breaking the Cycle

Solutions must be rooted in sovereignty, culture, and community. Health cannot be imported—it must be reclaimed.

Reviving Traditional Diets

Reintroducing traditional foods is both a nutritional and cultural act. Bison, salmon, wild rice, and native vegetables are more than sustenance—they are identity. Community gardens, seed preservation, hunting education, and tribal food sovereignty initiatives are reshaping what Native nutrition looks like today (Boyer 2014). When communities grow their own food, they grow power.

Culturally Relevant Health Education

Schools and clinics must teach health through a Native lens. Programs that integrate traditional knowledge with modern science—like pairing diabetes education with ancestral food lessons—have shown success. Children learn better when lessons reflect who they are. Healing must start early, and it must start at home.

Expanding Access with Innovation

Telemedicine, mobile health units, and tribally-run clinics offer pathways around access gaps. But they require funding and political will.

Native nations must be empowered and resourced to build their own health infrastructure—not as wards of the federal government, but as sovereign providers of their own future (Sequist et al. 2011).

Culturally Competent Care

Training health-care providers in Native history, values, and protocols is essential. So is including traditional healers in treatment plans (Gone 2013). True healing respects both sides of medicine—the clinical and the ceremonial. Health is not just blood pressure readings and lab results; it is balance, story, and relationship.

Conclusion

Breaking the cycle of poor health in Native America requires more than treating symptoms. It demands a return to cultural roots, a reckoning with historical trauma, and the courage to build something better. It means refusing to accept the diseases of colonization as permanent. It means healing in our own way, on our own terms.

"The body remembers. So does the spirit. Our healing will not come from systems that once sought to erase us—but from the traditions, foods, and medicines that once sustained us. The path forward isn't new. It's old. We just need to walk it again."

Racial Classification: Blood Quantum

"The survival of Native identity cannot be measured by blood alone, but by the strength of our connection to culture, community, and tradition. True sovereignty is found in reclaiming the right to define who we are, beyond the constraints of colonial numbers."

Mathematical Genocide

Native Americans remain the only racial or ethnic group in the United States whose identity and legitimacy are legally defined by blood quantum—the percentage of Native ancestry an individual carries. This colonial construct, imposed by the U.S. government, measures a person's "Native blood" to determine eligibility for tribal membership, rights, and benefits (Garroutte, 2003).

The concept of blood quantum, originally designed to limit the number of people who could claim Native heritage, has continued to influence tribal policies today. While the intent of the federal government was to curtail access to resources, land, and sovereignty, the practice has remained in place and now acts as a barrier to self-determined identity within many Native communities (Wilkins & Stark, 2017).

Colonial Legacy of Blood Quantum

The origins of blood quantum trace back to U.S. policies from the late 19th and early 20th centuries, which aimed to reduce Native populations eligible for land and benefits. The U.S. government viewed Native identity through a framework of genetic purity, determining legitimacy by fractional degrees of Native blood—much like the classification systems used in livestock breeding. This approach sought to undermine tribal sovereignty by artificially shrinking Native populations (Wilkins & Stark, 2017).

For Native peoples, this system of classification was not only dehumanizing but also directly contradicted traditional concepts of belonging, which were rooted in kinship, shared responsibility, and cultural commitment—not genetics.

Adoption of Blood Quantum by Native Tribes

In response to federal pressure and the desire to maintain federal recognition, many tribes adopted blood quantum as part of their enrollment criteria. While this move was originally a survival strategy, it also signaled the internalization of colonial tools. Blood quantum, once a tactic of erasure, became embedded within the very governance structures it was meant to dismantle.

Tribes today commonly impose minimum thresholds—such as one-quarter or one-eighth Native ancestry—for enrollment (TallBear, 2013). This process, steeped in colonial biology, has fractured Native communities by valuing mathematical purity over cultural belonging. The result is a bureaucratic form of genocide—each generation pushed closer to statistical extinction, even as cultural knowledge endures.

The Alaskan Exception: Corporate Status and Bloodline Disqualification

Tribes have also limited what they recognize as "Native" lineage—sometimes in ways that sever legitimate connections. One tribal member reported that their blood quantum was abruptly reduced when the tribe learned their ancestry included Alaskan Native blood. The tribe did not recognize that bloodline as "Native," and reclassified that portion as non-Native. The member's official blood quantum dropped to 50%. As a result, their grandchildren—whose blood quantum fell below the tribe's threshold—were no longer eligible for tribal membership.

The justification? Alaskan Natives had "opted out" of tribal classification by agreeing to the Alaska Native Claims Settlement Act of 1971 (ANCSA).

Under ANCSA, Alaskan Native tribes were restructured into for-profit corporations. Over 44 million acres of land and nearly $1 billion in compensation were transferred to more than 200 newly created Native-owned regional and village corporations. In exchange, traditional tribal governance structures were weakened, and Alaskan Natives became "shareholders" rather than citizens of sovereign nations (Case & Voluck, 2012).

To some tribes in the lower 48, this corporate structure invalidated Alaskan Native identity for the purpose of enrollment. The consequences are profound: Native families fractured, grandchildren cut off from their heritage, and blood quantum manipulated to serve bureaucratic convenience. If the tribe had recognized the Alaskan Native bloodline as valid, those grandchildren would still be counted. Instead, sovereignty was used to exclude—not protect.

This case illustrates the dangerous fluidity of blood quantum—not as a biological reality, but as a political tool. It shows how colonial frameworks, still alive in tribal law, can erase Native identity one generation at a time.

The Decline of "Full-Blood" Native Americans

The concept of a "full-blood" Native—someone with two Native parents—is rapidly disappearing. As intermarriage rates climb (nearly 60% of Native Americans marry outside their race), each generation contains fewer individuals who meet traditional blood quantum thresholds (Snipp, 1989). Population genetics models confirm the outcome: tribes relying solely on blood quantum are mathematically destined for decline (Proulx, 2003).

This raises urgent questions: What happens when no one meets the minimum? Do we dissolve ourselves, or redefine what it means to belong?

Red Lake Tribe: Changing the Definition of Native Identity

Some tribes have begun pushing back. On October 8, 2019, the Red Lake Band of Chippewa Indians passed a resolution redefining every person enrolled as of November 10, 1958 as a full-blood (4/4) member. The motion, introduced by Tribal Secretary Sam Strong and seconded by Redby Representative Al Pemberton, passed by a 7-3 vote (Red Lake Tribal Council, 2019).

The intent was to strengthen tribal identity and safeguard enrollment for future generations. As Secretary Strong explained, this was the first step in moving away from what he called "mathematical genocide." Though not a full departure from blood quantum, it was a bold assertion of tribal sovereignty over colonial classification.

Implications of Blood Quantum and Reduced Native Ancestry

Cultural Implications: Blood quantum erases the role of culture, kinship, and community. It reduces Native identity to fractions, denying the deep belonging of those raised in traditional ways but lacking the required paperwork (TallBear, 2013).

Legal and Political Implications: Lower population counts affect federal recognition, funding, land claims, and legal standing. When fewer members "qualify," the tribe's political power is weakened (Garroutte, 2003).

Social and Emotional Impact: Blood quantum divides communities—creating hierarchies of "authenticity" that pit relatives against each other and fracture shared identity. Those with lower quantum often feel they must prove their Native-ness, even in their own homes (Wilkins & Stark, 2017).

Psychological Impact of Blood Quantum on Native Identity

The psychological toll is devastating. Blood quantum fosters internalized colonialism, planting doubt and shame where pride should grow. Many who fall below tribal thresholds wrestle with feelings of alienation and worthlessness—despite cultural fluency and lived experience (Gone, 2007).

This system tells them they are less Native, even if their lives say otherwise. It separates grandchildren from their grandparents. It reduces sacred lineage to a number on a form. And in doing so, it wounds something far deeper than paper can measure.

Reclaiming Identity Beyond Blood Quantum

But the story doesn't end in fractions. Across Indian Country, voices are rising to redefine belonging—not through blood percentages, but through language, ceremony, community, and accountability.

Scholars and tribal leaders advocate for enrollment criteria that reflect kinship and cultural participation, not colonial math (Alfred & Corntassel, 2005). The Red Lake Band's resolution offers a model: reclaim sovereignty by reclaiming the right to define ourselves.

If identity is to survive, it must evolve. It must outgrow the very tools that were designed to erase us.

Conclusion

The future of Native identity does not belong to the Bureau of Indian Affairs—or to the federal definitions meant to shrink us out of existence. It belongs to the people brave enough to break from colonial measures, to honor cultural reality over bureaucratic convenience.

Blood quantum is not destiny.
It is a decision.
And it's time we make a better one.

"Blood quantum is a tool of erasure, not preservation. If we are to protect the future of our nations, we must move away from colonial definitions of purity and embrace a vision of identity rooted in kinship, cultural knowledge, and collective survival."

Observations

Education & Empowerment

Building a Knowledgeable Workforce

Introduction

Education and empowerment are crucial to the prosperity of Native American communities. Equipping tribal members with leadership and business skills through education enables them to achieve self-sufficiency and economic growth.

This chapter examines the historical evolution of Native American education, the challenges faced today, and the strategies to build a resilient and knowledgeable workforce through education and empowerment.

Historical Context of Native American Education

Traditional Education

Before European colonization, Native American education was embedded within cultural practices and everyday life. Knowledge was passed down orally through stories and rituals, where children learned through observation and participation (Cajete, 1994).

For instance, boys learned hunting and tracking from elders, while girls were taught cooking and weaving by mothers and grandmothers (Deloria, 2001). Ceremonies and storytelling played a critical role in passing moral values, ensuring that each generation understood its heritage and responsibilities.

Impact of Colonization

The advent of European settlers brought an abrupt shift in Native education. Western education systems were imposed, and traditional ways of learning were disrupted. Boarding schools, prevalent in the 19th and early 20th centuries, were instrumental in the forced assimilation of Native children into Euro-American culture (Adams, 1995). These schools actively suppressed Native languages and cultural practices, creating a legacy of cultural disconnection and trauma (Child, 1998).

Current Challenges in Native American Education

Educational Attainment

Today, Native American students face educational disparities in comparison to their non-Native counterparts. High school graduation rates remain below the national average, and college enrollment and completion rates are also disproportionately low. Factors such as poverty, underfunded schools, and cultural alienation contribute to these disparities (National Center for Education Statistics, 2019).

Poverty

A significant number of Native American families live in poverty, limiting their access to educational resources. Students from low-income backgrounds often grapple with food insecurity, unstable housing, and healthcare deficits, which directly affect their ability to succeed academically (Demmert, 2001).

Underfunded Schools

Schools in Native American communities frequently suffer from insufficient funding, leading to a lack of basic resources such as up-to-date textbooks and technology. These schools struggle to attract and retain qualified teachers, leading to high turnover and a shortage of experienced educators (Education Trust, 2013).

Cultural Disconnection

Decades of forced assimilation have created a disconnect between Native American students and the current education system. Many students feel alienated by a curriculum that is disconnected from their cultural heritage, leading to lower academic engagement and performance (Brayboy & Castagno, 2009).

Access to Higher Education

Financial barriers, inadequate academic preparation, and cultural isolation are significant obstacles to higher education for Native American students (Guillory & Wolverton, 2008). Many students lack the necessary support systems to navigate these challenges, contributing to low enrollment and completion rates.

Financial Barriers

The high cost of college is a major impediment to Native American students, as scholarships and financial aid seldom cover the full expenses associated with higher education (Swisher & Tippeconnic, 1999).

Strategies for Fostering Education and Empowerment

Culturally Relevant Education

Providing a culturally relevant education is one of the most effective methods to improve outcomes for Native American students. Incorporating Native languages, histories, and practices into the curriculum ensures that students can connect with their heritage and feel engaged in their learning (Brayboy & Castagno, 2009).

Language Revitalization

Language revitalization programs that teach and promote Native languages help students reconnect with their cultural heritage. Bilingual education models, which incorporate both English and Native languages, have been shown to enhance academic performance and cultural pride (McCarty, 2003).

Community Involvement

Engaging the community in the education process fosters a more supportive learning environment. Schools that partner with tribal leaders, parents, and community members can create programs that reflect the values and needs of the community (Benham & Stein, 2003).

Support for Higher Education

Increasing college access and providing necessary support systems is key to improving completion rates. This includes scholarships, academic preparation programs, and culturally sensitive support systems (Shotton, Lowe, & Waterman, 2013).

Building a Knowledgeable Workforce

Education and vocational training programs focused on building a knowledgeable workforce can help Native American communities achieve economic self-sufficiency and leadership in various fields (Ortiz & Cash, 2006).

Case Studies of Successful Initiatives

The American Indian College Fund provides scholarships and academic support to Native American students, breaking down financial barriers to higher education. By providing financial aid, the organization helps students overcome the obstacles to college access (American Indian College Fund, 2021).

Conclusion

Education and empowerment are foundational to building a knowledgeable workforce and achieving economic independence in Native American communities. By addressing historical and contemporary challenges through culturally relevant and supportive strategies, Native students can thrive academically and professionally. Through collective action and strategic initiatives, Native American communities can ensure that education empowers future generations to achieve sustainable progress.

"Empowerment begins with education; it's the bedrock upon which we build a future of opportunity and resilience. By fostering a knowledgeable workforce, we not only uplift individuals but also strengthen the foundations of our entire community."

Mental Health and Healing in Native Communities

"Healing in Native communities is not just about treating the mind; it is about mending the broken bonds between history, culture, and spirit. True wellness begins when we embrace our stories, honor our pain, and transform it into the strength of our people."

Healing More Than the Mind

The mental health crisis in Native American communities is an urgent issue that affects every facet of life, from individual well-being to the overall health of the community. Historical trauma, ongoing discrimination, and socioeconomic challenges have compounded to create disproportionately high rates of mental health issues among Native Americans. This chapter explores the mental health issues facing Native American communities, examines the current mental health infrastructure, and outlines strategies for addressing these challenges to promote holistic well-being.

Historical Trauma and Its Impact

The Legacy of Colonization

Colonization, along with policies of forced assimilation, inflicted deep psychological wounds on Native American communities. The loss of land, cultural identity, and autonomy, coupled with the trauma of boarding schools and forced relocations, has led to intergenerational trauma.

Intergenerational Trauma: Historical traumas, such as the violence and displacement experienced during colonization, have been transmitted through generations, impacting the mental health of descendants. Symptoms of intergenerational trauma include depression, anxiety, and substance abuse, all of which are prevalent in many Native communities (Brave Heart, 1998).

Forced Assimilation and Boarding Schools

The boarding school era, during which Native American children were taken from their homes and forced to abandon their cultural identities, has left a lasting psychological toll on many.

Psychological Impact: The separation from family and community, compounded by abuse and neglect in boarding schools, led to a widespread loss of cultural identity and a profound sense of shame and self-doubt. Survivors of these schools often grapple with post-traumatic stress disorder (PTSD) and other severe mental health issues (Adams, 1995).

Current Mental Health Challenges

Prevalence of Mental Health Issues

Native American communities face higher rates of mental health challenges compared to the general population. Common issues include depression, anxiety, PTSD, and substance abuse.

Depression and Anxiety: The prevalence of poverty, unemployment, and exposure to violence all contribute to widespread depression and anxiety. Additionally, the isolation and scarcity of resources on many reservations exacerbate these problems (Gone & Trimble, 2012).

PTSD: Many Native Americans suffer from PTSD, a condition often rooted in historical trauma, violence, and continued discrimination. The lack of culturally competent care further hinders access to proper treatment (Duran, 2006).

Substance Abuse: Substance abuse, frequently a symptom of deeper mental health struggles, is widespread in Native communities. Alcoholism and drug addiction are often linked to untreated mental health issues and the inadequate availability of mental health services (Beals et al., 2005).

Suicide

Suicide rates are notably high in Native American communities, particularly among the youth. The suicide rate for Native American youth is more than double that of their non-Native peers.

Youth Suicide: Hopelessness, bullying, and a lack of mental health resources all contribute to this alarming trend. Preventing youth suicide in these communities demands attention to root causes, as well as the implementation of robust support systems (Wexler et al., 2015).

Community Impact: The loss of young lives to suicide further compounds grief and trauma within the community, emphasizing the need for community-based and culturally relevant suicide prevention efforts (Walls, Hautala, & Hurley, 2014).

Mental Health Infrastructure

Access to Mental Health Services

Access to mental health services in Native communities is extremely limited. Many reservations are located in remote areas with few healthcare providers, and mental health services are often underfunded.

Indian Health Service (IHS): The IHS, tasked with providing healthcare—including mental health services—to Native Americans, suffers from chronic underfunding and a shortage of professionals. This results in long wait times and often inadequate care (Sequist, 2017).

Telehealth Services: Telehealth offers potential solutions to the geographic barriers faced by many reservations. However, many Native communities lack the necessary infrastructure, such as reliable internet access, to make telehealth feasible (Yellowlees et al., 2015).

Cultural Competence

Cultural competence is essential for providing effective mental health care in Native American communities. Many Native individuals are reluctant to seek help from providers who lack an understanding of their cultural experiences.

Culturally Appropriate Care: Providing culturally competent care means acknowledging and incorporating the cultural beliefs of Native American patients. This approach involves integrating traditional healing methods with Western mental health practices (Gone, 2013).

Traditional Healing Practices: Traditional healing, such as sweat lodges, talking circles, and ceremonies, are often preferred by Native Americans for addressing mental health issues. Integrating these practices into the healthcare system can improve patient engagement and outcomes (Bassett, Tsosie, & Nannauck, 2012).

Strategies for Addressing Mental Health Challenges

Community-Based Approaches

Engaging community members in planning and delivering mental health services is a critical strategy for Native American communities.

Peer Support Programs: Peer support programs, where individuals with lived experience provide guidance to others, can help reduce stigma and build trust in mental health services (White & Sanders, 2018).

Community Education: Public awareness campaigns and education on mental health can reduce stigma and encourage individuals to seek help (Gone & Calf Looking, 2011).

Integrating Traditional and Western Practices

A holistic approach to mental health care, which blends traditional Native healing practices with Western mental health treatment, can be more effective than Western methods alone.

Traditional Healers: Collaboration between Western mental health providers and traditional healers can bridge cultural divides, making care more acceptable to patients (Bassett, Tsosie, & Nannauck, 2012).

Holistic Care: A comprehensive approach to mental health, which integrates physical, emotional, spiritual, and social care, can improve outcomes in Native communities (Gone, 2013).

Improving Access to Care

Efforts to improve access to mental health care must address systemic barriers that prevent individuals from receiving the care they need.

Expanding Telehealth: Investment in telehealth infrastructure can expand access to remote communities, though it requires reliable broadband internet and provider training (Yellowlees et al., 2015).

Workforce Development: Increasing the number of Native American mental health professionals through education and training programs can improve access to culturally competent care (Sequist, 2017).

Case Studies and Successful Initiatives

The White Mountain Apache Tribe Suicide Prevention Program

The White Mountain Apache Tribe's suicide prevention program integrates traditional practices with evidence-based interventions to address youth suicide.

Community Involvement: The program includes elders, youth, and community members in suicide prevention efforts, fostering a supportive environment (Cwik et al., 2016).

Traditional Healing: The program incorporates traditional practices such as ceremonies and talking circles, creating a culturally relevant suicide prevention model (Cwik et al., 2016).

Conclusion

The mental health crisis in Native American communities is rooted in historical trauma, ongoing discrimination, and socioeconomic struggles. Addressing this crisis requires building a culturally competent mental health infrastructure, improving access to care, and integrating traditional and Western healing practices. By addressing both the mental health needs and the underlying causes of these disparities, Native American communities can build a healthier and more resilient future.

"Mental health is the silent battle within our communities, a struggle often masked by resilience. Addressing this crisis with culturally sensitive care and open dialogue is not just necessary but vital for the well-being and survival of our people."

Observations

Substance Abuse and Addiction

"Substance abuse in our communities is not merely a battle against addiction—it's a struggle to reclaim the spirit that was lost through generations of trauma. Healing comes when we restore the circle, reconnect with our traditions, and rebuild the kinship that sustains us."

A Growing Concern

Numbing the Pain of a Stolen Past and Future

Substance abuse and addiction pose pervasive threats to the health, stability, and future of Native American communities. Rooted in historical trauma and compounded by socio-economic and cultural factors, these challenges demand a nuanced understanding to develop effective interventions.

This chapter examines the root causes of substance abuse, identifies the key socio-economic and cultural contributors, and explores the treatment programs and strategies being implemented to foster a healthier future for Native American populations.

Root Causes of Substance Abuse and Addiction

Historical Trauma and Colonization

The historical trauma endured by Native American communities, stemming from colonization, displacement, and cultural suppression, continues to manifest in modern-day substance abuse.

Historical Trauma: The legacy of forced relocations, violent colonization efforts, and the boarding school system has resulted in intergenerational psychological distress. This unresolved trauma frequently leads to substance abuse, as individuals seek to numb emotional pain and cope with crises of identity and hopelessness (Brave Heart et al., 2011).

Cultural Disruption: The imposition of Western values eroded traditional cultural practices and disrupted social structures. This breakdown in traditional coping mechanisms left many individuals vulnerable to addiction (Gone, 2013).

Socio-Economic Factors

The socio-economic landscape in Native American communities often exacerbates the prevalence of substance abuse.

Poverty and Unemployment: High rates of poverty and unemployment foster environments in which substance abuse flourishes. Economic instability generates chronic stress, and the lack of opportunities leads individuals to use substances as an escape (Sarche & Spicer, 2008).

Lack of Education and Employment Opportunities: Limited access to quality education and meaningful employment restricts personal growth and community development, heightening the risk of addiction (U.S. Commission on Civil Rights, 2003).

Housing Instability: Inadequate housing conditions and homelessness are common in some Native communities. The instability caused by poor housing can exacerbate substance abuse (Roubideaux, 2005).

Mental Health Issues

Mental health disorders are both a cause and a consequence of substance abuse, creating a cycle of dependency and psychological distress.

Depression and Anxiety: High levels of depression and anxiety, often linked to socio-economic hardships and historical trauma, lead individuals to self-medicate with drugs or alcohol (Kirmayer et al., 2014).

PTSD: Many Native Americans suffer from PTSD, often a result of violence, abuse, or historical trauma. The absence of adequate mental health services compounds this problem, with individuals turning to substance abuse as a means of coping (Gone, 2009).

Dual Diagnosis: Co-occurring mental health and substance abuse disorders are common in Native communities. Integrated treatment approaches are essential to address both issues concurrently (Sequist, 2017).

Cultural Disconnection

The disruption of traditional ways of life and forced assimilation policies have left many Native Americans disconnected from their cultural heritage.

Loss of Cultural Identity: The erosion of cultural identity and community cohesion has led to feelings of emptiness and alienation, driving individuals toward substance abuse as a means of coping (Whitbeck et al., 2004).

Intergenerational Trauma: Trauma experienced by past generations continues to affect subsequent generations, contributing to substance abuse as a way to cope with inherited pain and unresolved issues (Brave Heart et al., 2011).

Substance Abuse Patterns

Alcohol Abuse

Historical Context: Alcohol abuse remains one of the most significant substance abuse challenges in Native American communities. Introduced by European settlers, alcohol has become a major issue, with many Native Americans lacking the genetic adaptations needed to metabolize alcohol efficiently (Whitbeck et al., 2004).

Social Impact: Alcohol abuse contributes to various social problems, including domestic violence, accidents, and crime. It also worsens health issues, such as liver disease and mental health disorders, perpetuating cycles of addiction across generations (Gone & Calf Looking, 2011).

Drug Abuse

Methamphetamines: The abuse of methamphetamines has surged, leading to severe health and social consequences, including cognitive decline and aggressive behavior (Whitesell et al., 2012).

Opioids: The opioid crisis has severely impacted Native communities, leading to an alarming rise in overdose deaths and straining already limited healthcare resources (Sequist, 2017).

Marijuana: Although often considered less harmful, marijuana abuse can still lead to dependency, especially among young people, and negatively impact motivation and mental health (Kirmayer et al., 2014).

Treatment Programs and Strategies

Culturally Competent Treatment

Effective substance abuse treatment in Native American communities requires approaches that respect and integrate traditional healing practices.

Traditional Healing: Incorporating practices such as sweat lodges, talking circles, and ceremonies into treatment programs offers a holistic approach to recovery, helping restore cultural identity and community bonds (Bassett et al., 2012).

Cultural Competence Training: Training healthcare providers in cultural competence ensures they understand and respect Native cultural values, fostering trust between patients and providers (Gone, 2013).

Holistic Approaches: Combining modern medical treatments with traditional healing practices offers a comprehensive approach to recovery, addressing the spiritual and psychological aspects of addiction (Brave Heart et al., 2011).

Community-Based Programs

Prevention Programs: Community-based prevention programs targeting youth and delivered through schools, community centers, and cultural events are essential for reducing substance abuse (Wexler et al., 2015).

Peer Support Groups: Adapted versions of Alcoholics Anonymous (AA) and Narcotics Anonymous (NA), incorporating traditional practices, provide safe spaces for individuals to share their experiences and support one another (Bassett et al., 2012).

Access to Healthcare

Expanding Services: Increasing access to substance abuse treatment on reservations and in urban areas with large Native populations is essential. Detox centers, residential treatment, and outpatient services are critical components (Roubideaux, 2005).

Telehealth: Telehealth services can bridge gaps in access, particularly for those in remote areas, by providing counseling, medication management, and support groups digitally (Yellowlees et al., 2015).

Case Studies of Successful Initiatives

The Healing Lodge of the Seven Nations

Holistic Approach: The Healing Lodge combines traditional healing with modern treatment, addressing the physical, mental, and spiritual aspects of recovery (Bassett et al., 2012).

White Bison, Inc.

Wellbriety Movement: White Bison's Wellbriety Movement emphasizes sobriety through cultural teachings and the integration of traditional values with recovery models (Brave Heart et al., 2011).

Conclusion

Substance abuse and addiction in Native American communities are complex issues rooted in historical trauma and exacerbated by socio-economic factors. Addressing these challenges requires culturally competent, holistic approaches that blend traditional and modern treatment methods. By understanding the root causes and implementing community-based solutions, Native American communities can foster resilience and healing, paving the way for a healthier future.

"In the throes of substance abuse and addiction, our communities face battles that mirror the struggles of our ancestors. The path to recovery demands resilience, cultural reconnection, and unwavering support for those fighting to reclaim their lives from the grip of addiction."

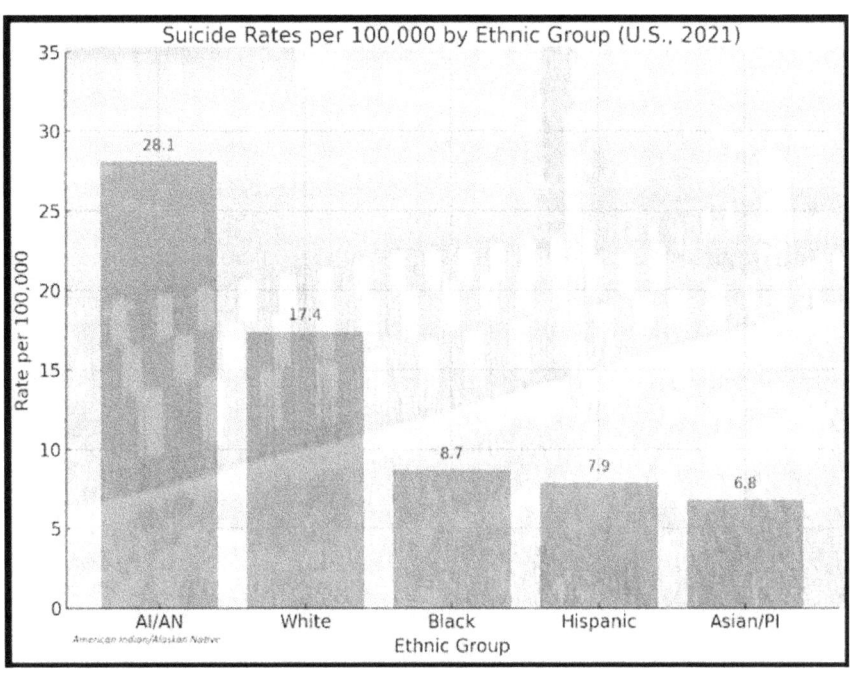

Prevalence of Suicide in Indian Country

"The silence of despair cannot be broken by whispers of sympathy alone. It demands the roar of community, the embrace of tradition, and the unwavering belief that each of us carries the power of our ancestors within."

More Than a Crisis—A Cultural Emergency

Suicide rates in Native American communities remain alarmingly high, representing one of the most urgent public health crises in the United States today. Unlike other demographic groups, Native peoples endure an intricate web of challenges rooted in historical trauma, cultural erasure, and generational poverty. These forces converge to create a mental health landscape where despair often outweighs hope.

This chapter explores the layered causes of this crisis—how centuries of displacement, forced assimilation, and systemic neglect have left deep emotional scars. We examine the impact of economic hardship, cultural disconnection, and spiritual conflict, as well as the role of community-based healing efforts grounded in tradition. We also explore how Native worldviews around death and the afterlife may influence how suicide is perceived, especially among youth.

Why the Pain Runs So Deep

Historical Trauma and Intergenerational Grief

Legacy of Colonization--The arrival of European colonists launched a campaign of removal, suppression, and destruction that continues to echo through Native communities today. From the Indian Removal Act of 1830 to the forced assimilation of boarding schools, generations were stripped of land, language, and spiritual continuity. These were not merely policies—they were deliberate instruments of psychological warfare.

Families were broken. Traditions were outlawed. Identities were dismantled.

What remains is a legacy of unresolved trauma—grief carried like a shadow across generations. It often surfaces as depression, addiction, or suicide, because the original wound was never healed, only inherited (Brave Heart et al., 2011).

Intergenerational Grief

The trauma endured by grandparents now lives in the blood of their grandchildren. From boarding school abuse to the criminalization of ceremonies, these scars do not fade—they calcify into emotional burdens. When a Native youth contemplates suicide, they are often carrying more than personal pain. They carry ancestral grief that has never been released (Kirmayer et al., 2014).

Socio-Economic Realities

Poverty

In many Native communities, poverty is not a temporary setback—it is the inherited framework of life. Lack of access to healthcare, clean water, nutritious food, and safe transportation intensifies both physical and psychological suffering. Poverty does not simply limit opportunity; it feeds hopelessness and convinces the spirit that no escape is possible (Sarche & Spicer, 2008).

Unemployment

Joblessness strips more than income—it erodes identity. In communities where unemployment rates are several times the national average, many youth grow up believing that purpose is a luxury they'll never afford. Dreams die quietly when survival becomes the only goal.

Poor Housing Conditions

Overcrowded trailers. Collapsing infrastructure. No privacy. No dignity. Poor housing is not just a material hardship—it's a constant reminder of dispossession. It can make daily life feel like a trap, where even rest offers no relief (Roubideaux, 2005).

Mental Health and Substance Abuse

Limited Access to Mental Health Services

Mental health services are often inadequate, inaccessible, or culturally irrelevant in Native communities. Where resources do exist, they are underfunded and understaffed, and rarely rooted in tribal values. This leads to a breakdown of trust, which further discourages people from seeking help. The result is silence. Silence is deadly (Gone, 2009).

High Rates of Substance Abuse

Alcohol and drugs become a refuge for the deeply wounded—but they are not a cure. Substance use increases impulsivity and clouds judgment. It dulls the pain but also accelerates the descent. Suicide and addiction often walk side by side (Whitesell et al., 2012).

Cultural Disconnection

Loss of Cultural Identity

Colonization didn't just steal land—it stole meaning. Through criminalized ceremonies, banned languages, and forced Christianization, the spiritual and cultural identities of Native peoples were fractured. Many Native youth today grow up with a spiritual void—disconnected from their ancestors, their practices, and even themselves (Gone, 2013).

Language Loss

Language is not just a way to speak—it's a way to remember. To name the sacred. To belong. When language is lost, so is the ability to access ancestral knowledge and spiritual grounding. Disconnected from their roots, many youth feel unmoored—adrift in a world that neither welcomes nor reflects them (McCarty et al., 2006).

Family and Community Breakdown

Domestic Violence and Abuse

Generational trauma often repeats itself through cycles of violence. Abuse becomes normalized. Silence becomes survival. Too many Native homes are fractured by pain, lacking the tools to break that cycle. For many, trauma begins not with history books—but behind closed doors (Oetzel & Duran, 2004).

Bullying and Social Isolation

Whether in schools, communities, or online spaces, many Native youth endure bullying rooted in racism and rejection. These are not just insults—they are assaults on identity. When combined with cultural disconnection and systemic neglect, the weight can become unbearable. In the absence of affirmation, suicide becomes a whisper too easily heard (King et al., 2009).

Cultural Mindsets Around Death and the Afterlife

In many tribal traditions, death is not an end—it is a return. A crossing into the spirit world. A reunion with ancestors.

For those in mourning, this belief offers peace. But for those in anguish, it can be distorted. Some may see death not as loss, but as escape. Not as tragedy, but as relief. This sacred worldview, while powerful, adds complexity to suicide prevention. It means that our interventions must not only protect life—but honor the spirit (Gone, 2013).

Yet there is another layer, one less spoken of but no less real. In some communities, when a loved one passes, those closest may choose to follow them through suicide, believing they are joining that person in the next world. One death then becomes two or more. A single funeral becomes several.

What was already unbearable grief compounds into further anguish and sorrow for those left behind. This pattern, born of love twisted by despair, deepens the toll on Native families and demands that prevention efforts reckon not only with trauma, but with belief itself (Lester, 1997; Wexler, 2006).

A Deadly Toll: 50 Years of Loss to Suicide and Addiction

The numbers are not abstract—they are a reckoning.

Suicide
- Native suicide rate (2015–2020): 22.5 per 100,000
- Native youth (15–24): 2.5x higher than U.S. average
- Estimated deaths over 50 years: 25,000 to 40,000
- Alcohol-Related Deaths
- Death rate: 49.1 per 100,000 (3.5x national average)

- Annual estimate: 2,500 to 3,500
- 50-year total: 125,000 to 175,000
- Drug-Related Deaths
- Overdose death rate: 23.5 per 100,000
- Annual estimate: 500 to 1,000
- 50-year total: 25,000 to 50,000

Combined Total (50 Years):

175,000 to 265,000 Native lives lost to suicide, alcohol, and drug-related causes. This is not just a public health crisis. It is a cultural emergency.

No More Lost Generations

This crisis will not be solved with statistics, slogans, or services alone. It demands a cultural revival rooted in remembrance, relationship, and responsibility.

We must rebuild what was broken—language, ceremony, kinship—because these are not luxuries. They are life-saving tools. Our people do not need another study. They need space to heal, room to speak, and reasons to stay.

We must make our communities places where it is safe to feel, safe to hurt, and safe to survive.

Healing our people from the scourge of suicide is not about erasing pain but about reconnecting each heart to the beating drum of our community, where tradition and spirit remind us why we endure.

"In the silence left by our ancestors, we hear the echoes of lives lost to despair and addiction—a generation caught between the weight of history and the promise of tomorrow. We must confront this pain not as an individual failure, but as a collective call to reclaim our strength, our spirit, and our will to survive."

Observations

Before Their Time

"We must make our communities places where it is safe to feel, safe to hurt, and safe to survive."

I'm getting up there in years. My bones tell me more about the weather than the forecast does, and my memories have started to outnumber my plans. I've lived through seasons—some long, some bitter, some full of unexpected grace and quiet beauty, but all with changes that I didn't know how to appreciate back then, with my younger eyes. But lately, more often than not, I find myself sitting with the grief of our young ones who don't stay long enough. Too many are gone. Too many have taken the Great Journey well before they even had the chance to write, let alone rewrite, the first few chapters.

Their presence lingers in empty chairs, old photos, and the way the air goes still when someone mentions their name. It settles in deep—down in the marrow of a community—and it doesn't let go.

We all have our time on this stage. That truth has never been lost on me. The path we walk has its beginning and end, and no one gets out of this world untouched. But there is a sacred kind of sorrow—a bone-deep ache—that comes when the young are taken before they've seen enough sunrises to know what it feels like to grow into their own skin. Before they've laughed until their belly hurt beside someone who truly saw them. Before they got to fall down and get back up with the help of people who believed in them.

They should still be here. Laughing. Struggling. Learning. Loving. Cussin', and living. Even when it's messy—especially when it's messy.

Some days I think back, memories rising up, and feel the absence more than the presence. Those memories show me who should still be here. I think about the ones we've lost, and I wonder—who's still here to carry their names forward? Are we doing enough to hold them before they start to slip—whether it's quiet despair, a reckless second that can't be undone, a truck on a backroad, a bottle in the dark, or a decision made with no one left to call? Too many of our young are taken—some by their own hand, some by the world's sharp edges—but all of them too damn early.

I won't pretend to understand why. Creator's reasons aren't written in language I can read. That kind of wisdom lives far beyond what I can grasp. But I do know this—we were never meant to walk this life alone. We were put here to watch over each other. And we've got to act like it. Especially when the storms come. Especially when the weight gets too heavy for one set of shoulders. Especially when someone's smile doesn't quite reach their eyes.

It's not enough to mourn them after they're gone. We have to reach for them while they're still here. We have to be visible—really visible—not just in presence, but in purpose. Not just for our kids, but for the ones who slip through the cracks because no one ever looked twice. We have to care for ourselves—eat, rest, breathe, forgive—so we have enough left to care for others.

Because this isn't just tragedy, it's failure. Failure of leadership that looks the other way. Failure of systems that spend money but never touch lives. Failure of communities too divided to lift up the ones carrying the heaviest loads. If sovereignty means anything, it must mean the power to fight for the living, not just mourn the dead.

We have to become living reminders. Not statues, not martyrs, not social media echoes—but flesh and blood reminders that someone is watching, listening, and ready to say, "You matter. You belong. I'm right here."

If our communities are going to survive—if our culture is going to carry forward with its soul intact—then we have to treat every conversation like it might save a life. Because sometimes, it will.

So speak. Show up. Be awkward, be tired, be uncertain—but show up anyway. Let your presence be a shield. Let your words be a thread that binds someone back to this world. Let them know—we're still here. And we are here for them.

"Grief teaches us the weight of what we didn't say in time. But presence—real, steady, imperfect presence—can be the rope that pulls someone back from the edge. We don't need to have the answers. We just need to be there."

Disenrollment, Sovereignty and the Per Capita Trap

"The very sovereignty that was meant to protect and uplift our people has been twisted into a tool of exclusion, where greed trumps kinship, and the pursuit of wealth blinds us to the pain we inflict on our own. Dis-enrollment is not just a political act; it is a betrayal of our deepest values as Native people."

Cut from the Circle: Dis-enrollment, Sovereignty, and the Fracturing of Native Nations.

Introduction

Sovereignty is not just a legal construct; it is the very essence of who we are as Native nations. It is our birthright, the hard-won acknowledgment that we, as Indigenous peoples, have the right to self-governance, to protect our lands, and to determine our own future. More than a political tool, sovereignty is a living reflection of our resilience, a reminder that despite centuries of colonization and oppression, we refuse to be erased.

But sovereignty, like all tools of power, carries its own shadows. It allows us to define who belongs in our nations, but it also grants us the authority to exclude. And today, that power is being wielded in ways that tear at the very fabric of our communities, as greed and the allure of casino wealth push some to turn against their own. The practice of dis-enrollment—the removal of tribal members—has become a painful reality, particularly in tribes benefiting from lucrative gaming operations. What was once intended as a mechanism for cultural preservation has been twisted into a weapon of division.

The Promise and Perils of Tribal Sovereignty

The promise of sovereignty is clear: the power of self-determination. It allows us to make our own laws, to define our citizenship, and to protect our cultures from further erosion (Deloria & Lytle, 1983). Sovereignty is more than a legal right; it is a declaration that we will survive and thrive, honoring our ancestors while securing a future for our children.

Yet, with this promise comes peril. Each tribe has the autonomy to establish membership criteria—through blood quantum, lineage, residency, or cultural participation—but these standards, once designed to protect, have become tools for exclusion. In recent years, the darker side of sovereignty has come into view as dis-enrollment surges, often driven by the desire to increase per capita payments from casino revenues (Wilkins & Stark, 2017).

The Rise of Casino Wealth and the Temptation of Greed

The advent of tribal casinos, made possible by the Indian Gaming Regulatory Act of 1988, was envisioned as a path to economic empowerment. For many tribes, it has delivered on that promise, funding schools, health-care, housing, and pulling entire communities out of poverty (Light & Rand, 2005).

However, wealth brings temptation. The prosperity generated by casinos has too often been overshadowed by internal strife over who has the right to share in the profits. Per capita payments—cash distributions from casino revenues—vary widely between tribes, but the temptation of a bigger payday has turned dis-enrollment into a weapon. Tribal leaders, in their pursuit of personal gain, have used dis-enrollment to cut members out and consolidate wealth (Gonzales, 2016).

A study published in the Yale Law Journal found that approximately 84% of tribes that have dis-enrolled members operate casinos, despite only about 44% of all federally recognized tribes running gaming operations. This disparity reveals that gaming tribes are nearly twice as likely to engage in dis-enrollment compared to non-gaming tribes. The financial motive becomes even clearer considering that over half of the tribes that have dis-enrolled members distribute per capita payments, compared to less than 25% of all federally recognized tribes.

Yet not all dis-enrollment stems from casino wealth. Some non-gaming tribes have also engaged in dis-enrollment, driven by lineage disputes, internal politics, or efforts to control tribal identity. The Nooksack Tribe, the Grand Ronde Community of Oregon, and the Narragansett Tribe are examples where dis-enrollment occurred even without the lure of gaming revenues. These cases demonstrate that dis-enrollment is not exclusively a byproduct of wealth, but its prevalence and weaponization are significantly amplified by it.

Dis-enrollment: The Hidden Crisis Within Tribes

Dis-enrollment is more than a bureaucratic maneuver; it is a profound wound that strikes at the very heart of belonging. It is an exile not only from the rolls but from the community, history, and identity that define a person's sense of self (Palmater, 2011). Entire families, sometimes whole bloodlines, have been removed from tribes under dubious circumstances, driven by personal vendettas or financial motivations. This isn't just the removal of names from a list—it's the erasure of lives, legacies, and the bonds that hold communities together.

Tribes that have seen the greatest casino success, such as the Pechanga Band of Luiseño Indians, the Picayune Rancheria of Chukchansi Indians, and the Nooksack Tribe, have become cautionary tales. Here, the quest for control and cash has overshadowed the duty to protect and honor the collective (Cohen, 2015). The consequences of these power struggles have been devastating, turning what should be a shield for the people into a sword of exclusion.

The Human Cost of Dis-enrollment

For those who have been dis-enrolled, the cost is not merely financial—it is a loss of identity. To be cut off from one's tribe is to be stripped of access to health care, education, housing, and the right to participate in cultural and political life (Miller, 2018). It is a forced invisibility, a denial of everything that once made you whole.

The psychological toll is immeasurable. For many, dis-enrollment feels like a betrayal by their own people, compounding the trauma of colonization and assimilation. It is a violation of the values of kinship and community, replaced by cold calculations of wealth and personal gain (Gonzales, 2016).

The Struggle for Reform and Accountability

But where there is pain, there is also resistance. Across Native communities, voices are rising to challenge the abuses of dis-enrollment. Some tribes are beginning to reexamine their membership criteria, shifting the focus away from blood quantum and arbitrary rules, and toward cultural connection and community involvement. Others are demanding accountability, calling on their leaders to serve the people rather than their own pockets.

The path to reform, however, is steep. Sovereignty means that tribes govern themselves, and external intervention is rare. Courts, respecting sovereignty, are often reluctant to intervene, leaving disenrolled members with few avenues for justice (Wilkins & Stark, 2017).

Balancing Sovereignty and Justice

Sovereignty was never meant to be a tool of harm. It was forged as a shield, protecting us from the forces that sought to erase us, but today it is too often used to divide our people. The crisis of dis-enrollment forces us to confront an uncomfortable truth: the right to self-govern must be balanced with the responsibility to protect all of our people.

When tribal leaders use their power to disenfranchise, they don't merely cut off individuals; they sever the bonds of kinship that sustain us. Dis-enrollment weakens our community, fractures our identity, and tarnishes the legacy we leave for future generations.

As Native nations, our survival depends not on the pursuit of wealth but on the preservation of the values that have defined us for centuries. Sovereignty is a tool for building up our people, not tearing them down. To truly honor our ancestors, we must honor one another, safeguarding not just our lands and resources, but the spirit of unity that makes us who we are.

Conclusion

The practice of dis-enrollment has become a shadow looming over the promise of tribal sovereignty. What was meant to secure our futures and fortify our self-determination has, in too many instances, been weaponized to fracture the very communities it was designed to protect.

By turning on our own, we are not only losing our people; we are losing the values of kinship, shared identity, and collective strength that have sustained Native nations for centuries. If sovereignty is to mean anything, it must be exercised with a profound sense of responsibility—not just to land or wealth, but to the people who carry forward our cultures, languages, and legacies.

A Look Ahead

If these actions persist unchecked, the consequences could be devastating. Dis-enrollment will continue to tear at the fabric of Native communities, eroding the sense of belonging that is essential for both cultural survival and political strength. The diminishing of tribal populations through exclusionary practices risks weakening political influence, reducing federal recognition, and undermining the unity needed to face external challenges. As internal divisions deepen, the ability of Native nations to assert their sovereignty on the larger stage may be compromised. Worse still, if economic incentives continue to drive these decisions, we risk becoming nations driven by greed, rather than tradition.

However, the future is not set in stone. There remains time to reclaim the spirit of community and unity that defines us. By reforming membership criteria, holding leaders accountable, and embracing inclusion, Native nations can renew their strength, ensuring that sovereignty becomes not just a shield from external threats, but a tool for internal healing. Only by upholding our shared values can we protect the legacy of our ancestors and ensure that our nations not only survive but thrive for generations to come.

"Dis-enrollment reveals a dark irony within tribal sovereignty: the power to decide who belongs and who does not. When our leaders prioritize per capita payments over the integrity of our communities, they do more than just sever membership—they sever the lifeblood of our cultural continuity, tearing apart families and erasing identities."

Sovereignty today is often debated in boardrooms and courthouses, dissected into percentages and lineal descent codes. But if we define a people only by what is proven on paper, we risk forgetting what is still felt in the quiet, unseen spaces of our lives. Sometimes sovereignty doesn't shout. Sometimes it just stands still and waits to be recognized.

Observations

Sovereignty isn't always declared. Sometimes, it's remembered.
Not in courtrooms. Not on paper.
But in the stillness—out on your own land, when no one's watching and nothing needs proving.
I had a moment like that once.
A moment that didn't ask to be explained... only remembered.
And in that remembering, I saw exactly what we're fighting to preserve.

The Knowing

Sovereignty isn't only measured in rolls, codes, or court rulings. It lives in smaller, quieter places too — in the instinct that ties us to land, to each other, and to something older than law. I was reminded of that once, in a moment I didn't expect.

One day, after work, I climbed onto the zero-turn mower and started cutting up and down the long driveway. It had been a full day, and the simple rhythm of mowing settled me. My ears were covered with earmuffs, the blades humming beneath me, chewing through the grass. I was in motion, but my mind wasn't anywhere in particular.

Then, suddenly—I stopped.

No sound, not that I could hear over the roar of the mower, No movement in the trees. Just... something.

I didn't know why I knew, but I did. Something was nearby. I didn't see it. I didn't hear it. But something inside me said: "Coyote."

My eyes locked onto a narrow space between the trees—twenty feet in front of me. I just stared. It wasn't nerves. It wasn't fear. It was stillness. A kind of alertness I can't explain.

The mower idled beneath me, unmoving. I sat motionless, staring into that spot.

Then he came.

A coyote stepped out from the trees. Slow. Intentional. He walked maybe eight feet before he turned his head and saw me. We were close—too close for it to feel like chance. And in that moment, we looked at each other. Not startled. Not afraid. Just aware.

He gave the slightest tilt of his head, like a nod, or a recognition. Then he turned and walked back into the woods. No panic. No scramble. Just: "Oh... it's you."

And I was left there, still staring at the same spot, trying to understand what had just happened.

I've thought about it since. Was it a premonition? A connection? A trick of the mind? I haven't a clue. I only know that I knew he was there before he appeared. I stopped without reason. I stared at the exact place he would emerge.

What do you call that?

Some would call it instinct. Others, coincidence. But I think it was more. A kind of listening. A kind of remembering. Maybe a kind of permission—to still feel something ancient and connected in this modern life.

The coyote is often seen as a trickster to some, but not always. Sometimes he's a message. Sometimes, he's a mirror—showing you a part of yourself you forgot was even there. Or maybe… it was simply a quiet, sacred moment. A random intersection where two beings walking this earth just happened to converge. No greater meaning. No grand lesson. Just presence.

And maybe, that's meaning enough.

This was just a sharing of an event—and these are the kinds of thoughts that come when the wind outside is the only sound, except for the honk of passing geese this time of year. This old cabin stays quiet most days. I don't keep the TV running. Maybe an old western or Star Wars now and then. The radio's mostly off. That stillness? It doesn't bring noise. It brings reflection.

That was sovereignty too — not in statutes or per capita checks, but in a presence that couldn't be denied. A reminder that belonging is more than membership, and that what we are fighting to preserve isn't just rights on paper, but the living, unspoken knowing that binds us as a people.

Healing Through Tradition

"Reviving our ceremonies and languages is more than an act of cultural preservation; it's a profound journey of healing. Each prayer, song, and word spoken in our ancestral languages reconnects us to the wisdom of our elders and the strength of our identity—it's a declaration that we are still here, thriving despite all attempts to silence us."

Reviving Ceremonies and Language

Introduction

For generations, the effort to strip away our identity came through laws and institutions designed to sever our ties to land, spirit, and each other. The echoes of boarding schools and the forced silence of our tongues still reverberate in Native communities today. But silence was never meant to be our inheritance.

Today, Native peoples are turning back to our ceremonies and languages as sacred paths of healing. These long-suppressed traditions are not relics—they are rising again. In this chapter, we explore how traditional ceremonies and language revitalization act as instruments of healing, resilience, and cultural survival.

The story of our survival is not just about enduring. It is about reclaiming what was stolen—and thriving.

The Historical Suppression of Native Languages and Ceremonies

Colonization was not just a conquest of land—it was a campaign against spirit. Boarding schools, established in the late 19th century, became tools of cultural eradication. Children were taken from their homes, punished for speaking their languages, and stripped of identity. Ceremonies like the Sun Dance, Potlatch, and Ghost Dance were criminalized—sometimes with brutal consequences for those who dared to keep them alive (Adams, 1995).

The goal was clear: break the connection between Native people and the sacred practices that anchored them. Yet even in the darkest moments, our people held on—in whispers, in secret songs, in quiet defiance. That quiet defiance is now a movement.

The Importance of Ceremonies in Healing and Identity

Ceremonies are the heartbeat of Native life. They are not pageantry—they are medicine. The Sun Dance, Sweat Lodge, and Powwow are more than cultural events; they are places where wounds are named and spirits are lifted.

In the Sweat Lodge, the heat, the prayers, and the sacred songs cleanse not just the body, but generations of pain. It is a return to the womb of the Earth Mother—a place to confront what weighs heavy, and emerge renewed (Kirmayer et al., 2009).

Personal Stories of Revival

The revival of ceremonies like the Lakota Sun Dance tells a story no policy could crush. John Eagle, a Lakota Sun Dancer, described it this way: "It wasn't just about physical endurance. It was about reconnecting with my ancestors and asking for their guidance. It's about healing the spirit." His story echoes across Native communities—where ceremony is not performance, but survival.

The Navajo Blessing Way ceremony is another pillar of healing. This sacred practice, calling on spiritual beings to restore hózhó—balance and harmony—has brought peace to generations. Maria, a young Navajo woman, said of her experience: "It gave me peace and a connection to something bigger than myself." Her family's legacy of boarding school trauma had weighed heavy. But through ceremony, she began to rise.

Language Revitalization: Reclaiming the Voice of the Ancestors

Language is not just vocabulary—it is worldview, memory, prayer. It is who we are.

The suppression of Native languages was one of colonization's most violent acts. But across Indian Country, we are now reclaiming our voices. The Wôpanâak Language Reclamation Project, for example, is breathing life back into the Wampanoag language after more than a century of dormancy. These efforts are not about nostalgia—they are about sovereignty (Baird, 2013).

Cherokee Language Immersion Schools

In the Cherokee Nation, language immersion schools teach entirely in Cherokee. These schools do more than educate—they protect. As Emma Kingfisher, a teacher, puts it: "When they speak Cherokee, they're not just learning words—they're connecting with their ancestors, understanding their history, and building a sense of identity that's grounded in who they are." Language, like ceremony, binds us.

Technology and Language Preservation

Technology is now a powerful tool in cultural defense. Apps, online dictionaries, and social media have made Native languages accessible to new generations. Tools like the Dakota Language App and the Ojibwe People's Dictionary carry ancestral voices into classrooms, kitchens, and mobile phones (Hermes et al., 2012). This is how we survive in the digital age: by bringing the old ways into new light.

Healing Through Language: A Personal Journey

For many, learning their language is a return to self. Sarah Running Deer, a young Lakota woman, began learning Lakota to reconnect with her grandmother, who had been punished in boarding school for speaking it. "Learning Lakota filled a void I didn't know I had," she said. "It's healing in a way that's hard to describe." To reclaim language is to reclaim identity. And to reclaim identity is to begin the long healing of a people (Wilson & Yellow Bird, 2005).

Conclusion

Reviving our ceremonies and languages is more than resistance—it is rebirth. It is a declaration that, despite all attempts to silence us, we remain rooted in the prayers and words of our ancestors. Healing begins when we speak those words again, when we sing those songs again, when we gather in ceremony—not just for ourselves, but for those who could not.

"Our languages and ceremonies are not relics of the past; they are living, breathing parts of who we are. By reclaiming these traditions, we not only heal the wounds of historical trauma but also empower future generations to walk proudly in the footsteps of their ancestors, guided by the voices and spirits that have sustained us for centuries."

Observations

The Old Law Still Stands

Respect and Sharing in a World That Forgot
Among Indigenous peoples across North America—despite vast cultural diversity—two interwoven values guided all human and non-human relationships: Respect and Sharing. These were not just moral niceties; they were the structural pillars of social life, law, survival, and the sacred.

Respect – A Law Beyond Words

In traditional Native societies, Respect extended to:
- The land – treated as kin, never property.
- The animals – offered with ceremony, not conquest.
- The elders – honored for their wisdom, not cast aside.
- The community – guided by consensus, not competition.

This respect was relational, not hierarchical. Every entity had a spirit and place. An Ojibwe hunter would offer tobacco before taking a deer. A Lakota grandmother's words held as much weight as a war leader's. A Diné farmer would walk the cornfields with prayer before harvest.

As the late Vine Deloria Jr. wrote:
"Traditional Indian peoples held a land ethic that accepted human beings as part of the environment—not above or separate from it."
(Deloria, God Is Red)

There was no written constitution enforcing this. It was embedded through story, ceremony, and example—a sacred law inherited, not legislated.

This respect carried into all parts of life—including business.

I've been in many meetings where I had things to say, but the non-Natives in the room loved to hear themselves talk. I've been told I'm too quiet. But it's not that. It's that I was taught to respect the speaker—to listen, not interrupt. The problem is, when no one takes a breath, it's hard to get a word in. My ideas sit at the edge of the table, waiting to be let in—but the room rarely pauses long enough to make space for them.

Following what I was taught—to listen first and speak last—often feels like a disadvantage in a world that rewards noise over thought. But I still believe respect matters. And I won't abandon it to compete with the loudest voice in the room.

Sharing – The Foundation of Economy and Survival

Sharing wasn't a virtue—it was law.
In hunter-gatherer societies, hoarding was shameful, and generosity brought status. Those who gave the most were respected the most.

- In Plains cultures, buffalo meat was distributed across the camp, often prioritized for the elderly and infirm (Lowie, Primitive Society).
- Among Pacific Northwest tribes, wealth was measured not by what one kept, but by what one gave away in potlatches (Codere, Fighting with Property).
- The Iroquois Confederacy structured land use and food distribution on communal ownership and inter-tribal cooperation (Johansen, Forgotten Founders).

Even in times of scarcity, sharing was practiced. Because individual survival meant nothing if the community starved.

Colonial Disruption & Cultural Inversion

European settler colonialism brought new values—ownership, extraction, individualism, and domination—that were fundamentally opposed to Indigenous systems.

- Respect was replaced with conquest.
- Sharing was replaced with privatization.
- The land, once sacred, became commodity.
- Generosity became naivety.
- Harmony became "primitive thinking."

Colonial governments criminalized sharing economies and communal landholding. In boarding schools, Native children were punished for speaking their language or honoring elders—direct attacks on systems of intergenerational respect (Adams, Education for Extinction).

Modern World: Mocking the Sacred

Capitalism and Hyper-Individualism

Today's dominant economic and social systems are structured around:
- Winning, not sharing.
- Self-promotion, not humility.
- Profit, not balance.

Modern capitalism often praises selfishness as "hustle" and mocks collectivism as "weak." Generosity is now called "handouts," especially when applied to marginalized people.

Native values are not just dismissed—they are often weaponized against Native people, portraying traditional ways as reasons for poverty or stagnation (Treuer, The Heartbeat of Wounded Knee).

Social Media: The Erosion of Respect

Social media platforms—while capable of building connection—often reward mockery, outrage, and ego over listening, gratitude, or reflection.
- Elders are drowned out, not elevated.
- Community is fractured by algorithms built for division.
- Spiritual teachings are appropriated, repackaged by influencers for profit.
- Traditional humility is often misread as weakness.

Some Native youth struggle to balance their digital identities with teachings of modesty and restraint. In tribal communities that once emphasized non-interference and silent wisdom, online culture encourages impulsive reaction and public shaming.

Survivance: Upholding Old Laws in a Modern World

Despite this, many Native communities are actively reclaiming these ancestral values—not as nostalgia, but as survival strategy.

Examples include:
- Land back movements, re-centering stewardship over ownership (Estes, Our History Is the Future).
- Food sovereignty initiatives, rebuilding traditional food systems based on community sharing.
- Cultural revitalization via digital platforms that honor, rather than exploit, traditions.

- Youth mentorship circles, reconnecting modern Native youth with ancestral values of respect, patience, and listening.

Elders and culture-bearers teach that respect begins within—how you speak, how you walk, how you listen. The modern world might not value these things, but Native futures depend on them.

Conclusion: The Old Law Still Stands

The unwritten law of Respect and Sharing—carried by Indigenous peoples for millennia—has not died. It is remembered in ceremony, whispered in prayer, and reawakened every time someone gives without expectation, listens before speaking, or walks gently on the land.

The world may mock it.
Social media may erase it.
But it still lives—unbroken—beneath the noise.

"Respect was never a rule—it was a way of being. And sharing wasn't charity. It was survival. Until we return to that way, we are only surviving the sickness, not healing it."

Sacred or Spectacle?

"What was once ceremony is now content. What was once sacred is now a hashtag. But somewhere beneath the noise, the medicine still breathes."

The Collision of Culture and Clicks in Indian Country

Introduction

The drumbeat once summoned the ancestors. Now, it signals the start of a live-stream.

From the outside looking in, powwows, naming ceremonies, and tribal dances often appear to the broader public as colorful cultural displays—vivid, rhythmic, and Instagram-worthy.

But for Native communities, these are not performances. They are sacred expressions of survival, sovereignty, and spirit. Increasingly, however, these ceremonies are being commodified, edited for virality, and consumed by non-Native audiences with little understanding of their meaning.

The border between cultural preservation and cultural performance has become blurred, shaped as much by algorithms and social media trends as by tradition and elder instruction.

This chapter confronts the uneasy tension between Indigenous identity and modern digital platforms—asking: when does visibility become vulnerability? When do sacred acts become spectacles?

The Rise of the "Feed-Ready" Ceremony

In the era of TikTok, YouTube Shorts, and Instagram Reels, even the most sacred Indigenous practices are finding their way into global digital feeds. Social media has become a double-edged sword—offering platforms for cultural revival and youth engagement, while simultaneously inviting exploitation, misinterpretation, and spiritual dilution.

Dances meant to honor ancestors are now synced with pop songs for cross-platform trends. Tribal regalia becomes visual bait for influencers. Ceremonies once kept within the protection of the community are now uploaded for anonymous viewers, stripped of context and consumed like digital artifacts. The risk is not just misrepresentation—but the erosion of what made these practices powerful in the first place.

As Dr. Adrienne Keene, creator of Native Appropriations, has warned, *"Visibility without control is just another form of colonization."*

Cultural Consent and the Myth of Exposure Equals Empowerment

A troubling narrative underlies the viral sharing of Native traditions—that exposure is inherently good. That visibility equals validation. But history tells a different story.

Native peoples have always been highly visible when it served colonial interest—from ethnographic photos in the 1800s to museum dioramas, World's Fair exhibitions, and boarding school propaganda. What's new is the voluntary nature of this exposure, often by our own youth, seeking connection, influence, or relevance.

The question must be asked: is it really empowerment if we are feeding our sacredness into systems we do not control?

Consent, in a cultural sense, requires more than a phone screen and a willing dancer. It requires intergenerational dialogue, tribal policy, and communal boundaries. Just because something can be posted, doesn't mean it should (Smith, 2012).

Digital Exploitation: When Profit Meets Ceremony

Some tribes and Native entrepreneurs are attempting to monetize cultural experiences, marketing live-streamed events, ticketed access to powwows, or paid subscriptions to language and dance content.

While this can fund tribal programs or reach diaspora citizens, it also introduces market forces into ceremonial space. Culture becomes product. Ritual becomes revenue. And the danger, as history shows, is that the buyer begins to shape the product (Raheja, 2010).

This is not a call for silence—but for sovereignty over what is shared, how it is shared, and why it is shared.

A Call for Cultural Boundaries in the Digital Age

Elders must be part of this conversation. So must tribal councils, cultural committees, and youth mentors. The new sacred circle includes not just the drum or the fire, but the screen—and we must define our protocols accordingly.

Should certain ceremonies be declared off-limits to filming?
Should tribal governments establish digital usage policies?
Can tribal-run platforms or encrypted cultural networks serve as alternatives to public content farms?

The answers may differ by community, but the principle of sovereignty must extend into the digital realm (Wilson, 2008).

As Indigenous scholar and activist Nikkita Oliver states, "We don't need visibility, we need protection."

Conclusion

We are not artifacts. We are not trending topics. And we are not obligated to serve our spirituality to a voyeuristic world that has never returned what it took.

To preserve the sacred, we must resist the spectacle.
Let the stories be told—but let us decide when, how, and to whom.

Observations

Still Ours: The Good We Carry Forward

Not everything in Indian Country is broken.

You wouldn't know it from the headlines, from the tribal politics, or from the battles we still fight just to get heat in the winter and health care in the summer—but beneath all that, there's something that's never gone away.

It's in how we show up for each other.

I've seen people drive hundreds of miles to attend a powwow, a wedding, or a funeral—with just enough gas to get there and a little extra cash for eats. And they'll do it without question. Not for show. Not to be seen. But because that's what we do. We show up.

We cook for the people, too. Doesn't matter how much food we have—we'll stretch it. I remember as a kid, we'd cook up a feast at powwows, and when it was ready, Grandma or Auntie would ring that old bell. No invitations. No VIP list. Just one rule: If you're hungry, come eat.

Sometimes, food would be handed out—sacks of potatoes, beans, rice, bread, and good old-fashioned commodities. To this day, I still hear folks debate what "commods" were best. "I miss the cheese block," someone'll say. "Nah, the canned pork was where it's at." We laugh. But behind those jokes are memories—of full bellies when money was tight, of kitchens that smelled like survival and love.

And it wasn't just about us. If we attended a ceremony, or stepped into a religion that wasn't our own, we respected it. We didn't mock what we didn't understand. That kind of humility is still alive in the quiet ones, the old ones, the ones who nod instead of argue.

We give our last dollars when someone needs it. We take in nieces and nephews like they're our own. We become uncles, aunties, grandmas, and grandpas to kids who've lost theirs—or never had them to begin with. We don't ask for thanks. Half the time, we don't even talk about it.

But this, too, is Indian Country.

Unfortunately, some of this doesn't happen anymore. Not all of it—but a lot. Too many of our youth are shaped by social media, by fast ads and flashing screens, by modern life that doesn't understand community the way we once lived it. And it's not their fault—they just haven't had the experience of growing up and living in the old ways, old days to me, in our country, the way I did.

Yes, it does still exist—those customs, those values—they're still here. But most likely a lot less than when I was a kid, a short sixty years ago. What was once normal is now rare. But even now, some of it is still with us. We're holding on. In pockets, in families, in ceremonies, we're maintaining what we can.

And it's not just tradition.

It's resistance.

It's hope.

And it's ours.

We talk a lot about the wounds in Indian Country—because there are many. And they run deep. But if we are to tell the truth, we must also speak of the beauty that never left us. The strength we still carry. The laughter that survived the darkness.

Because not all is broken.

Walk through a tribal community during sunrise, and you will see it. In the aunties making frybread and teasing each other like teenagers. In the old men who sit in silence and still say more than most leaders ever will. In the young dancers at powwows who move not to impress, but to remember. To honor. To feel connected to something ancient that the world tried—but failed—to erase.

Not all is broken.

We are still here. And not just surviving—we are creating, reclaiming, and redefining.

Tribal nations are building language schools, launching sustainable businesses, and returning to traditional governance models that reflect Indigenous values rather than colonial blueprints. Native artists are winning Pulitzer Prizes. Native scientists are leading environmental restoration. Native youth are getting degrees, organizing protests, and refusing to be anyone's mascot, prisoner, or statistic.

We still gather. We still grieve. And yes—we still laugh. Loudly. Inappropriately. And often in defiance of what this country expected of us.

Tribal Kinship Across Reservations

Tribes are reconnecting long-lost family ties—new kinships rekindled through support and sovereignty. A powerful example: the Coeur d'Alene Tribe of Idaho is financially backing the ShoshonePaiute Tribes of Duck Valley in launching their first-ever casino project outside Boise, an act of solidarity and stepped-up intertribal relations

These two nations share more than resources—they share a vision: sovereignty, economic strength, and renewed cultural bonds. The Coeur d'Alene's decades of success in gaming and community investment is now being passed forward as partnership, not charity, echoing ancient clan principles of mutual care.

This isn't just a business deal. It's a modern act of kinship, proving that when one tribe wins, we all win. It's a family circle expanding—Indigenous nations empowering one another, healing old scars, and moving forward together.

Not all is broken.

Our ceremonies continue. Our songs are still sung, even if whispered in kitchens late at night. Our languages are being taught again—not just by elders, but by apps, classrooms, and grandchildren who refuse to let their ancestors' words die.

Our love for one another—flawed, tangled, and sacred—is still the fire that warms us. We may fight each other. We may struggle to lead. But when the real hurt comes—when someone is lost, when tragedy hits—we show up. With food. With song. With our bodies. We hold each other up, even if our own knees are shaking.

Not all is broken.

There is trauma in our bloodline, yes—but also a stubborn, unbreakable love. A pride that doesn't need to shout. A knowing that we are the descendants of those who survived the impossible. And if they endured what they did for us to be here—then what excuse do we have to give up now?

So let us tell the whole story. The full truth.

Because even as we name the harm, we must also name the healing. Even as we confront the corruption, we must celebrate the community. And even as we demand justice, we must remember: we are not only a wounded people—we are also a beautiful one.

Not all is broken.

"We've lost a lot over the years—but not everything. What we still carry in our hands, in our kitchens, and in our hearts is proof that we were never just surviving. We were remembering. And sometimes, remembering is the most radical thing we can do."

Observations

SECTION III: Politics, Power, and Leadership

"True leadership is not found in titles or the power to command, but in the ability to listen to the heartbeat of the people and the whisper of the ancestors. A leader walks with the past at their back, the future in their hands, and the spirit of the land beneath their feet. Only when they honor all three can they guide the people through the storms of today and into the light of tomorrow."

Leadership and Governance

In the intricate landscape of Native American governance, leadership is not a role worn lightly. It carries a weight far beyond the responsibilities outlined in policy documents or titles. True leadership in Indian Country means balancing the old with the new, honoring traditions while navigating modern realities, and holding fast to the values that have sustained our people for generations.

It is about understanding the delicate interplay between tradition and modernity, where community loyalty often takes precedence over individual achievement, and cultural preservation is paramount.

Leadership is not merely about decision-making; it is about ensuring that the choices made today will resonate through future generations, protecting our heritage, and carving a path forward in a world that is, too often, at odds with Indigenous values (Wilkins and Lomawaima, 2001).

The chapters in this section will explore the multifaceted nature of tribal leadership—from the political challenges that disrupt progress to the spiritual and communal roles that guide decision-making. Native governance faces visible challenges, such as frequent leadership changes, and invisible burdens, like the cultural weight leaders must carry to safeguard the soul of their people.

These chapters delve deep into the complexities of leadership within Native communities, revealing how effective governance must reflect the core values of the people it serves. It is a balancing act, requiring leaders who are not only politically astute but also culturally rooted and spiritually attuned to their community (Deloria and Lytle, 1984).

The Politics of Leadership Change: Disrupting Potential

Change is inevitable, but in Native governance, frequent leadership turnover can fracture progress and disrupt the potential for long-term stability (Wilkins and Stark, 2017). Political transitions often challenge continuity, leaving leaders to rebuild where others have left off. This chapter will explore the challenges that come with leadership changes, how they impact governance structures, and what steps can be taken to ensure that transitions enhance, rather than disrupt, progress.

Qualified Leadership: The Key to Thriving Businesses

In today's world, qualified leadership is critical to economic development, particularly within Native-owned businesses. Leaders who understand both the cultural significance of economic ventures and the technical skills necessary to make them thrive are key to ensuring the financial health of tribal communities (Cornell and Kalt, 2007). This chapter will highlight the importance of education, cultural grounding, and the ability to navigate complex business landscapes while maintaining a strong connection to traditional values.

Navigating the Complexities of Employment and Accountability

Employment within Native communities brings with it layers of accountability that extend beyond the typical employer-employee relationship. Leaders must balance cultural obligations with the professional responsibilities of running organizations that provide for the community (Fleming, 2003).

In this chapter, we explore the role of accountability in leadership, and how Native leaders can build systems that are fair, just, and reflective of the needs of their people, while maintaining transparency and trust.

Nepotism and Influence: The True Power Structure

In the context of Indigenous leadership, nepotism—while seen by some as a threat to governance—often carries historical significance. Clan ties, family lineage, and community networks can influence leadership decisions and power structures (Wilkins, 2011).

However, when unchecked, nepotism can undermine the efficacy of governance, leaving leadership open to criticism and weakening trust. This chapter will discuss the delicate balance between honoring familial and community connections while maintaining ethical and effective governance practices.

Gender Dynamics in Tribal Leadership

Traditionally, many Native societies recognized the essential role of women in governance, yet colonization disrupted these systems, imposing patriarchal structures that diminished the power of female leaders. Today, there is a resurgence of female leadership in tribal communities, a reminder that governance is a shared responsibility across genders (Mihesuah, 2003).

This chapter will examine the gender dynamics at play in modern tribal leadership, highlighting the contributions of Native women as both political leaders and cultural caretakers. It will discuss the return to a more balanced leadership model, one that honors the voices and strength of women as integral to the community's well-being.

The Role of Traditional Knowledge in Modern Governance

While modern governance demands a level of technical expertise, it must also be informed by the traditional knowledge that has guided Native communities for centuries. Whether in environmental stewardship, legal systems, or health care, the wisdom of the ancestors continues to provide a moral and ethical framework for leaders today (Cajete, 2000).

This chapter will explore the ways in which traditional knowledge is integrated into modern decision-making, ensuring that governance remains culturally relevant and spiritually grounded.

Navigating Federal & State Regulations: Challenges & Strategies

Federal and state regulations can impose significant obstacles for tribal leaders, often forcing them to navigate bureaucratic structures that are at odds with the sovereignty of Native nations (Wilkins and Stark, 2017).

This chapter will examine the challenges tribal leaders face in dealing with external regulations, highlighting successful strategies that have allowed communities to assert their rights and protect their interests. Leaders who can successfully manage these external pressures while maintaining their cultural integrity will be essential in the fight for sovereignty and self-determination.

Mental Health and the Emotional Toll of Leadership

Leadership in Indian Country carries not just a professional burden, but an emotional and spiritual one. Mental health crises, trauma from historical oppression, and the weight of expectations can take their toll on leaders (Gone, 2013).

This chapter will explore the mental health challenges that Indigenous leaders face, examining how they can seek support, address their own wellness, and model healing for their communities.

Community Accountability: Balancing Tradition with Modern Expectations

Leadership is not just about decisions made behind closed doors; it is about accountability to the community. Traditional forms of governance were often based on reciprocal relationships, where leaders were directly responsible to the people (Cornell and Kalt, 2007). In a modern context, balancing tradition with contemporary governance practices can be difficult, but essential.

This chapter will explore how tribal leaders can stay accountable, blending traditional community structures with the expectations of modern governance.

Economic Sovereignty and the Role of Leadership

With the expansion of Native-owned businesses and the growth of gaming enterprises, economic sovereignty has become a cornerstone of self-determination (Cornell and Kalt, 2007). This chapter will focus on the role of leadership in building and sustaining economic sovereignty, exploring how economic growth can be balanced with cultural preservation and the long-term needs of the community.

Summary

As this section unfolds, it reveals that the strength of tribal governance lies in its ability to balance—to balance the old with the new, the collective needs of the people with individual merit, and the immediate demands of governance with the long-term vision for future generations.

Native leadership is about more than political power; it is about ensuring the well-being of the community—mentally, physically, and spiritually. The path forward requires leaders who are not only skilled in the art of governance, but who are also deeply connected to the heart and soul of their people. They walk with the ancestors beside them, guided by the values of their people and the strength of their culture.

"In leadership, as in life, the path forward must honor both the wisdom of our ancestors and the reality of our present struggles. Only then can we guide our people with strength and vision."

Observations

The Politics of Leadership Change: Disrupting Potential

"True progress within our Native communities is not defined by the sporadic flicker of short-term achievements, but by the enduring glow of stable leadership committed to a collective vision. When leadership turns over faster than the seasons, it disrupts not only the governance but the very spirit of our people."

Introduction

Leadership, when unstable, is not just a bureaucratic issue—it's a spiritual fracture. In Indian Country, every change at the top sends ripples through homes, ceremonies, and futures alike.

Frequent shifts in tribal leadership do more than change policy—they disrupt economic growth, cultural preservation, and generational trust. When governance lacks continuity, long-term initiatives collapse, administrative knowledge vanishes, and communities are left to rebuild again and again from fractured plans. This chapter explores how political instability undermines sovereignty and identity—and how continuity can restore both.

The Cycle of Political Instability

Leadership changes are often driven by short election cycles, internal rivalries, and external pressures. These forces together create a climate of volatility that impedes progress.

Election Cycles

Many tribes hold elections every two years, a pace far more rapid than federal or state governments. Leaders are pressured to deliver immediate, visible results, often abandoning long-term planning. Strategic development is sacrificed for fast wins, while community transformation requires time, patience, and consistency (Smith, 2020).

Each new administration often distances itself from the last—not out of necessity, but political optics. Effective programs are scrapped not because they failed, but because they didn't originate from the current leadership. The community pays the price: wasted funds, stalled services, and shattered public confidence.

Internal Power Struggles

Tribal politics carry deep personal weight. Leadership isn't just a job—it's ancestral, communal, and tied to resources that shape lives. Competing visions, old grievances, and family dynamics often turn elections into battlegrounds (Johnson, 2018).

These aren't just political fights—they're family fractures, echoes of unresolved pain from decades past, now replayed in council chambers and ballot boxes. The result is factionalism, mistrust, and a government focused more on protecting power than serving people.

External Pressures

Federal agencies, state regulations, and corporate interests exert outsized influence on tribal governments. Grant conditions, legal frameworks, and lobbying relationships pull leadership toward compliance instead of community priorities (Anderson, 2019).

External partnerships can also destabilize progress. Businesses seeking favorable deals may leverage leadership transitions to renegotiate or exit entirely. Instability erodes trust, and without long-term leadership, meaningful economic relationships struggle to take root.

Impact on Tribal Governance

Stable governance is essential for sovereignty. Without it, policy collapses, institutional knowledge vanishes, and hope thins.

Policy Discontinuity

Policies often shift drastically between administrations. One council launches a housing initiative; the next abandons it. These abrupt reversals create confusion, destroy trust, and waste resources (Garcia, 2017).

Imagine a youth center built under one council, shuttered under the next. Kids are left standing outside locked doors, wondering if anyone remembers the promises made.

Administrative Turnover

New leaders often replace experienced staff with allies. Expertise is lost, delays increase, and daily operations suffer. Institutional memory—critical to navigating federal compliance, managing complex contracts, or preserving cultural projects—disappears overnight (Brown, 2021).

Fragmentation of Governance Structures

Instability fractures cooperation. Departments stop coordinating. Priorities shift without notice. Large-scale problems—addiction, housing, education—require unified response. Frequent change prevents it (Davis, 2018).

Crisis management suffers too. A fragmented government cannot mount coordinated disaster responses, healthcare campaigns, or security initiatives. Fragmentation puts lives at risk.

Economic Consequences

Unstable leadership kills momentum—and money. Tribal businesses depend on consistent oversight, but new leadership often brings cancellations, renegotiations, or policy U-turns.

Business Disruptions

A new administration cancels a years-long casino development. Investors pull out. Jobs disappear. Community trust in tribal enterprise shrinks (Martin, 2016).

Loss of Investment

Investors prioritize predictability. Tribes with volatile leadership are often viewed as high-risk—regardless of potential. Funding dries up. Projects stall. Economic diversification fades (Williams, 2019).

Economic Planning and Development

Tourism, infrastructure, energy—these require long-term planning. Frequent leadership turnover makes them impossible. The result? A brain drain, as young members leave to build futures elsewhere (Taylor, 2020).

Social and Cultural Impact

Leadership instability doesn't just affect budgets and business. It erodes the cultural spine of a nation.

Community Programs

Vital programs—youth centers, elder services, mental health clinics—are slashed with each new budget. Skilled staff leave. Community engagement dies. Vulnerable populations suffer most (Thomas, 2017).

Cultural Preservation

Language programs, ceremonies, and cultural classes require decades, not terms. Funding cuts midstream waste years of effort and silence the voices of our elders before they can pass on what they carry (Wilson, 2018).

Social Cohesion

Each leadership war drives deeper wedges between families, clans, and generations. Governance becomes a source of tension, not unity. People stop attending meetings. Stop voting. Stop believing (Miller, 2019).

Strategies for Stability

We don't need to wait for change. We can build it.

- **Lock the mission, not the personalities.** Adopt a two-page Charter of Continuity that states what never changes with elections: fiduciary duty, transparency rules, audit schedule, and citizen reporting.

- **Succession isn't a surprise.** Create a standing **Transition Playbook**: 30–60–90 day checklists, current contracts, grant calendars, vendor contacts, and active litigation summaries. Hand it to every incoming chair the day after the vote.

- **Civil service spine, political head.** Protect critical staff (CFO, Controller, Grants, Procurement, HR, IT) with merit-based contracts and cause-only removal. Leaders steer policy; professionals keep the engine running.

- **Budgets that survive elections.** Pass a two-year baseline operations budget with quarterly variance triggers. No midnight reallocations without a public vote and written rationale.

- **Procurement that can't be gamed.** Standard scopes, open scoring rubrics, rotating evaluation panels, and conflict-of-interest disclosures published with awards.

- **Dashboards over rumors.** Monthly public KPIs: cash on hand, AR/AP aging, project status, grant drawdowns, hiring and retention. When everyone sees the truth, panic has nowhere to grow.

- **Independent eyes.** Audit committee with at least one outside CPA and one elder statesperson; annual external audit, midyear compliance review, and a hotline that reports outside the chain of command.

- **Leadership onboarding with teeth.** Mandatory orientation: law, finance, HR, and ethics. Sign a Code of Conduct with real penalties for interference or retaliation.

- **No-jerk switch rule.** Any policy reversal requires: written findings, cost/benefit, stakeholder consultation, and a 14-day cooling period.

Build these now, and leadership changes stop being crises. They become routine handoffs on a road that already knows where it's going.

Succession Planning

Clear succession frameworks reduce conflict and preserve progress. Mentorship, policy continuity, and shared goals across leadership generations create unity (Smith, 2020).

Leadership Development

Invest in programs that teach governance, negotiation, law, and values. A deep bench of leaders ensures continuity, not chaos (Johnson, 2018).

Accountability and Transparency

Oversight bodies, financial clarity, and community forums are more than good policy—they're spiritual insurance. When people trust the process, they don't panic at transition (Anderson, 2019).

Community Engagement

Governance should be communal. Public input, town halls, and open communication create ownership. If the community feels seen and heard, they'll support stability—even when leadership changes (Williams, 2019).

Case Studies and Examples

White Mountain Apache Tribe: Launched a mentorship-driven leadership pipeline to ensure smooth transitions (Garcia, 2017).

Confederated Salish and Kootenai Tribes: Adopted formal succession planning and governance continuity protocols (Brown, 2021).

Navajo Nation: Strengthened public trust through extensive community consultation and town hall sessions (Taylor, 2020).

Conclusion

Leadership change, when mishandled, doesn't just disrupt—it derails. Progress is lost. Trust is broken. Dreams are delayed. But with vision, structure, and community, we can build leadership that lasts—not in name, but in purpose.

"Leadership change, when mishandled, can halt progress and disrupt the potential of our tribes. Stability in governance is not just about continuity; it's about creating a foundation where dreams can grow and communities can thrive without the constant fear of upheaval."

Employment and Accountability in Tribal Governance

"True accountability in tribal governance isn't about choosing between tradition and modernity; it's about forging a path that respects our cultural bonds while building systems that serve our people with integrity and transparency. Only through this balance can we ensure that our leaders serve all with fairness, and not just the few with favor."

Introduction

Accountability isn't just a policy—it's a principle. And in Indian Country, where kinship and community thread through every institution, the path to fair governance is anything but simple.

The challenges of employment and discipline within tribal government are not hypothetical. They are lived daily—in council meetings, in department offices, and in the quiet discontent of staff who feel unheard. According to a 2020 National Congress of American Indians (NCAI) survey, 62% of tribal employees reported witnessing favoritism in hiring or disciplinary decisions, and 47% expressed concern about retribution for reporting misconduct. These numbers underscore the need for comprehensive reform. This chapter explores the cultural, political, and structural complexities that make accountability both essential and elusive—and outlines how tribes can move toward a governance model rooted in both tradition and integrity.

The Challenge of Accountability in Tribal Employment

In a community where everyone knows each other, enforcement of standards becomes an emotional minefield. When accountability is tangled with bloodlines and old alliances, fairness often comes second to familiarity.

Influence of Familial and Political Connections

In many tribal systems, decisions aren't just administrative—they're relational. When a tribal employee violates policy, the response is rarely simple. Relatives on the council, elders in the community, and lifelong allies may rally around them, pressuring supervisors to overlook offenses or reverse disciplinary action (Smith, 2020).

That loyalty is deeply cultural. But when it shields wrongdoing, it breaks trust. In one documented case from a midwestern tribe, a department supervisor attempted to terminate an employee for repeated absenteeism and falsified timesheets. The employee was reinstated within a week after a relative on the council intervened. The message it sends: who you know matters more than what you do.

Handling of Serious Offenses

Even in the face of serious violations—embezzlement, drug use, or criminal convictions—some employees are quietly transferred rather than held accountable. A 2019 Government Accountability Office (GAO) review of tribal health programs found multiple instances of administrators with pending felony charges simply reassigned rather than terminated. The fallout is corrosive: morale collapses, good employees disengage, and the public sees clearly what leadership won't admit (Johnson, 2019).

When misconduct is buried instead of confronted, tribes risk not only internal dysfunction but external scrutiny that undermines sovereignty. Silence may seem protective, but it invites rot.

Impact on Governance and Community Trust

When accountability is selective, trust dies. And in tribal communities, once lost, that trust is difficult to restore.

Erosion of Trust

People notice who gets protected and who gets punished. When wrongdoing is overlooked due to connections, the community's belief in the fairness of its leaders falters. Disillusionment replaces engagement. And civic participation suffers (Garcia, 2018).

In a 2018 survey conducted by the Indigenous Governance Network, nearly 54% of tribal citizens said they "rarely or never" felt confident that their leaders would enforce discipline fairly. Trust isn't built with promises. It's built with consistency. When rules apply to everyone equally—including relatives, allies, and elected leaders—the foundation of governance strengthens.

Operational Inefficiencies

Political interference doesn't just erode morale—it disrupts operations. When hiring and firing decisions are made through backroom agreements instead of formal policy, departments lose credibility, and administrators are paralyzed (Williams, 2017).

In one Pacific Northwest tribe, chronic council interference in hiring decisions led to a 36% staff turnover rate within two years. Programs stall. Services lapse. Good staff leave. And the community feels it—in housing delays, unanswered requests, and unmet needs.

Political Interference and Its Consequences
Avoidance of Transparency

The instinct to protect reputations often leads to secrecy. Leaders fear admitting internal issues will make the tribe look weak. So they hide them. But hidden rot still spreads—and eventually, it surfaces (Taylor, 2021).

A 2021 report by the Tribal Legal Code Resource Project found that fewer than 15% of tribal governments publish internal audit results or disciplinary decisions, contributing to a culture of opacity. True strength lies in transparency. Communities that confront their problems head-on build resilience. Those that bury them build resentment.

Acceptance of the Status Quo

Too often, the phrase becomes a shield: "That's just how it is here." But normalization of dysfunction is not tradition. It's defeat. And every time misconduct is tolerated, it becomes harder to undo (Miller, 2019).

This mentality keeps systems stagnant. Tribal youth watching these patterns internalize that change is unlikely—and the cycle continues. If we want better for the next generation, we must reject that resignation.

Potential Solutions

Solving these challenges doesn't mean abandoning culture. It means protecting it through integrity.

Establish Clear Policies and Procedures

Create explicit employment policies—with written, enforceable standards. No gray areas. No unwritten rules. Define how misconduct is handled and follow through. Fairness demands clarity (Smith, 2020).

A tribal HR study in 2020 showed that tribes with written and consistently applied disciplinary frameworks saw a 29% reduction in grievance filings over a two-year period.

Strengthen Oversight and Accountability Mechanisms

Independent ethics boards—separate from council politics—can review employment and conduct decisions without bias. Their very existence sends a message: fairness is no longer optional (Garcia, 2018).

Some tribes have begun creating ombudsman roles or oversight councils composed of retired elders, retired judges, and at-large tribal members, creating neutral third-party reviews of disputes.

Enhance Transparency

Publish reports. Share disciplinary outcomes (where confidentiality allows). Invite scrutiny. Sunlight won't weaken governance—it will fortify it. Transparency is a signal of strength, not vulnerability (Johnson, 2019).

The Cherokee Nation's Office of Accountability posts quarterly summaries of tribal expenditure audits and personnel disputes resolved—an effort that has correlated with a documented increase in voter turnout over the last three election cycles.

Promote Ethical Leadership

Leaders set the tone. Require training in ethics and decision-making. Hold officials to the same standards as staff. When leaders model integrity, the community follows (Taylor, 2021).

Incorporating traditional teachings on honor and responsibility into ethics training has been shown to increase engagement. Leaders must understand that ethical leadership is cultural leadership.

Engage the Community

Hold town halls. Encourage input. Let citizens shape governance policies. Public accountability keeps leadership grounded—and prevents abuses before they start (Williams, 2017).

Participation rates in governance-related events increased by 48% over three years in a southern Plains tribe that implemented quarterly citizen forums to address budget decisions and disciplinary appeals.

Implement Whistle-blower Protections

Protect those who speak up. If staff fear retaliation, silence reigns. Establish anonymous reporting systems and enforce zero tolerance for backlash (Miller, 2019).

The adoption of a whistleblower protection ordinance by the Confederated Tribes of the Umatilla Indian Reservation led to a 300% increase in reported ethical violations—with nearly 60% substantiated and resolved.

Review and Update Legal Frameworks

Governance is evolving. Laws must too. Update personnel policies and tribal codes regularly to close loopholes and clarify enforcement (Johnson, 2019).

Many tribes still rely on employment laws written in the 1980s. A full review every five years ensures accountability frameworks remain relevant.

Limit the Powers of Tribal Council in Disciplinary Matters

When misconduct is proven, the council should not override consequences. Checks and balances are not disrespect—they are wisdom. Restricting undue influence builds long-term credibility (Smith, 2020).

Creating separation between executive enforcement and legislative oversight—much like a three-branch government—can insulate administrative decisions from political interference.

Protecting the Tribe's Reputation—Through Accountability

The best way to protect the tribe's name isn't secrecy. It's integrity. Confronting wrongdoing publicly—fairly, consistently, without vengeance—earns respect from within and without (Garcia, 2018).

In an era of social media and public scrutiny, silence is no longer neutral. Action speaks. Accountability protects the name far more effectively than denial ever will.

Conclusion

Accountability in tribal employment is not a betrayal of kinship—it is a fulfillment of responsibility. If we fail to hold our own to fair standards, we forfeit the very sovereignty we claim to protect.

But while these solutions or suggestions would indeed help, in the real world—in the halls of actual tribal governments—the resistance is real and formidable. Those in the driver's seat are often not interested in sharing the wheel. Any effort to introduce guardrails, limit discretionary power, or enforce consistent standards is seen not as a tool for fairness, but as a threat to control. Too often, proposed reforms are dead on arrival—not because they lack merit, but because they take the wind out of someone's sails.

Those in power will seldom champion accountability mechanisms that might one day be used against them. Transparency is feared because it makes visible what they would rather keep concealed. Ethics policies, oversight boards, and personnel protections are quietly opposed because they curb the very favoritism and insulation from consequence that some have come to rely on.

And so, reform doesn't start at the top—it starts with those willing to speak truth beneath it. With elders demanding dignity. With staff insisting on fairness. With youth daring to imagine something better. The fight for accountability is not about technical fixes—it is about moral courage.

Let us lead with that courage. Govern with that honesty. And build systems that are not only Native—but just.

"Effective tribal governance demands a delicate balance between honoring tradition and enforcing accountability. Navigating this complexity requires transparency, fairness, and a commitment to the collective well-being of our community."

Two Worlds, One Rez

"We like to talk about sovereignty. But too often, sovereignty means jobs and housing for the connected few—and silence and suffering for everyone else."

The Divide Between Tribal Power and Tribal Pain

There are two worlds that exist in Indian Country, and most of us pretend not to notice the line between them. One world sits in tribal offices, where meetings are held, memos circulate, and the bills get paid on time, mostly. It is filled with grant writers, program directors, compliance officers, and tribal council members. These are the people with title-linked incomes, federally funded salaries, and often discretionary control over who gets hired, housed, or heard.

Then there is the other world—the one that surrounds it.

The one filled with tribal members who wake up without a job, without a car, without child care, without heat in the winter. The ones who stopped applying for housing years ago because the list was "full." The ones who avoid the tribal building because they know they aren't in the circle, don't have the last name, or won't be smiled at when they walk in the door.

Both groups are Indigenous. But they don't live in the same Indian Country.

The Politics of Proximity

This divide didn't happen overnight. It was built—brick by federal brick—over decades of program funding, tribal compacts, and a governance model imported from colonial systems. The Bureau of Indian Affairs, and later tribal self-governance initiatives, structured tribes to function less like communities and more like corporations, with executive positions, funding cycles, and centralized authority.

Those who sit near the decision-making table benefit. Those further from the flame live in the cold.

The result is a two-class system within many reservations:

- One class has steady pay, per diem travel, insurance, and some authority.
- The other lives day to day—relying on seasonal labor, disability checks, or hustling under-the-table work.

And let's be brutally honest: those in power don't just forget the others. They sometimes avoid them. Because to look too long at the addiction, the poverty, or the suicide rate is to risk remembering what most of us were born into—and what some of us escaped by luck, timing, or bloodline.

Power by Position, Not by Accountability

This isn't just about money. It's about access, influence, and control.

Tribal jobs—especially those linked to federal grants—are often recycled among a tight network. Job postings may be public, but the hires are often predetermined. The tribal administrator hires a cousin. The housing director places a relative. The wellness coordinator selects someone they coached in basketball.

It's not always corruption. Sometimes it's just familiarity. But the effect is the same: closed loops of opportunity, passed hand to hand within a narrow circle.

Those outside that circle?

They're not just unemployed. They're unheard, unseen, and unacknowledged by the very governments that claim to represent them.

According to the U.S. Census Bureau (2023), the unemployment rate for Native Americans living on reservations remains the highest of any racial group in the United States, with some tribal areas exceeding 50%. Meanwhile, administrative and leadership salaries in some tribal governments exceed $100,000 annually—paid through federal streams meant to support entire communities (NCAI, 2021).

This is the imbalance that no council wants to admit: we have sovereignty for some, and survival for others.

The Cost of the Divide: Addiction, Violence, and Despair

We cannot talk about alcoholism, addiction, or domestic abuse in Indian Country without acknowledging this internal split. When economic opportunity is confined to a few, and hopelessness becomes a birthright for the rest, the outcomes are predictable:

- Substance use becomes a form of escape.
- Violence becomes a language of the unheard.
- Suicide becomes a door when no others appear open.

Native people have the highest rate of suicide per capita in the United States, and that number spikes in reservation communities—especially among Native youth aged 15–24 (CDC, 2023). Alcohol-related deaths among Native Americans are more than six times the national average (NIH, 2022). And the correlation is not cultural—it's economic, systemic, and avoidable.

When people feel locked out of their own future, pain finds its own outlet.

The Silence of the Employed

There is a dangerous emotional distance that grows among those who succeed inside the tribal system. Many start off with good intentions—Native professionals who came home from college to serve their people. But over time, surrounded by bureaucracy, overworked and under-criticized, they become disconnected from the majority they claim to represent.

The trauma becomes invisible. The addiction becomes inconvenient. And the people outside the tribal building become statistics—or worse, liabilities to be managed.

This is the hardest truth of all:

The ones in charge often stop seeing the people they're supposed to serve.

And the ones outside the door learn to stop asking for help.

"I am Invisible"—The Hidden Crisis

On the rez, "I am invisible" isn't a metaphor—it's reality. It's said by those who drift between relatives' couches, shelters, and empty camps, unseen by census workers, tribal programs, or media cameras.

A national Urban Institute (2017) assessment found that 99.8% of tribal housing officials report widespread doubling-up, and 88% report literal homelessness—yet official data often paints Native homelessness as minimal or urban-only.

In reality, Native Americans experience homelessness at four times the national average, but many remain hidden: in cars, shacks, or on couches (Pallet Shelter, 2022; Police Chief Magazine, 2021).

This invisibility is amplified by:

1. Underreported data systems – Most are left off HUD rolls and census counts (Pallet Shelter, 2022).
2. Cultural shame and distrust – Many don't seek help due to generational trauma and fear of being labeled (Invisible People, 2023; Police Chief Magazine, 2021).
3. Structural exclusion – Bureaucratic red tape leaves even veterans without housing support on tribal land (High Country News, 2014).

Being invisible doesn't just mean unseen—it means forgotten.

The Moral Reckoning

This is about far more than numbers. It's about recognizing the silence and separation that define reservation life. When our people vanish inside their own communities, who speaks for them? What services are denied? What stories are lost?

Until all tribal members are seen—counted, housed, treated, and heard—our sovereignty remains hollow. We can't call ourselves a nation when so many of our people live outside its walls.

Bridging the Worlds

We don't need perfect tribal governments. But we do need governments that see everyone—not just the employed, the electable, or the connected.

That means rotating opportunity.

That means hiring transparency.

That means admitting that most tribal members are not thriving, and many are not even surviving.

We need to stop pretending that a few salaries and a glossy grant report mean the reservation is doing fine. Because too often, the grant is feeding a program while the community starves.

There are two worlds on every rez.

The question is whether we have the courage to tear down the wall between them—or if we'll keep pretending it isn't there.

"If tribal sovereignty only protects the privileged, then it is not sovereignty—it is abandonment. Until the invisible are seen, heard, and lifted, our nations will remain fractured shadows of what they were meant to become"

Observations

Protection for All Except Natives

"We are the only people in America who can be legally discriminated against by our own."

When Congress passed the Civil Rights Act of 1964, America marked a transformative moment—a legislative shift toward equality. Title VII explicitly outlawed employment discrimination based on race, color, religion, sex, or national origin, offering a long-overdue shield against generations of systemic oppression (U.S. Equal Employment Opportunity Commission, 1964). However, hidden within its sweeping declaration of equality was an exclusion so profound, it could only happen to the first people of this land.

Native Americans were deliberately left behind—not by oversight, but by design. Title VII explicitly carves out a glaring exception: Indian tribes are exempt. Tribes can legally discriminate in employment, and no Native individual can challenge it under federal law (U.S. Equal Employment Opportunity Commission, 1964). In effect, every protected class gained protection—except Native Americans.

The Text and the Trap

Title VII defines "employer" broadly, covering private companies, state governments, and federal agencies—but deliberately excludes tribes:

"The term 'employer' does not include… an Indian tribe."—Title VII, Section 701(b)(1) (U.S. Equal Employment Opportunity Commission, 1964)

On the surface, this exemption preserves tribal sovereignty—the inherent right of Native nations to govern themselves. In practice, however, this exemption creates a legal vacuum, enabling discrimination with no federal oversight or recourse.

If a non-Native is fired due to race, they have protection. If a woman is denied promotion due to gender, she has recourse. If a Native employee faces retaliation, exclusion, or punishment by their own tribal government—they have nothing.

This isn't theory. It's reality. And it occurs daily across Indian Country (Wilkins & Lomawaima, 2001).

Tribal Preference or Tribal Weapon?

Tribal governments and enterprises often utilize tribal preference policies to prioritize their own members. While intended as tools for economic development and self-determination, these policies can also serve as vehicles for favoritism, nepotism, political retaliation, and intra-tribal discrimination (Cornell & Kalt, 2003).

Who decides who is "tribal enough"?

- An enrolled member from another tribe can be lawfully rejected or terminated.
- A tribally-descended, non-enrolled individual has no standing.
- A member of the same tribe may be ostracized for challenging corruption.
- Entire lineages can be barred from opportunities due to historical grudges or political alliances.

This isn't self-determination—it's internal oppression, backed by federal silence (Washburn, 2006).

Weaponizing Sovereignty

The concept of tribal sovereignty is sacred. It is foundational to our identity as nations. But sovereignty, misused, can become a weapon—used not for protection, but for punishment.

Title VII granted tribes the right to disregard the civil rights standards protecting other Americans. While some tribal governments handle this responsibly, others use sovereignty as a shield against accountability. There is no protection for a Native whistleblower, no recourse for tribal employees demoted due to politics, and no justice for those marginalized within their own communities (Wilkins & Lomawaima, 2001).

Two Systems, One People.

This legal structure creates a glaring double standard:

Employer Type	Native Employees' Rights Under Title VII
Private Company	Protected
State or Federal Agency	Protected
Non-Tribal Nonprofit	Protected
Tribal Government or Enterprise	Not Protected

The bitter irony is clear: Native Americans are better protected outside their own communities than within. Our brightest and most talented tribal members recognize this harsh reality clearly. Faced with limited protection and widespread internal discrimination, many choose to forego tribal employment altogether, taking their skills and leadership off-reservation to non-tribal employers where their rights and dignity are fully respected. This exodus of talent further compounds the difficulties tribes face in achieving genuine sovereignty and economic self-sufficiency (Cornell & Kalt, 2003).

The Cost of Silence

Some argue this is sovereignty's price—that tribes must govern without federal interference. Yet, sovereignty should never excuse oppression. The U.S. would never tolerate a state government discriminating based on bloodline or politics, yet tribal discrimination is overlooked with a shrug and a citation of Title VII's exemption.

By protecting tribal sovereignty alone, Title VII abandons the civil rights of individuals. In Indian Country, this isn't an abstract debate—it's lived reality.

Reclaiming Balance

The solution is not to erode sovereignty but to redefine its protections—not just for governments, but for individuals. Sovereignty must uphold justice, not shield injustice.

Reforming Title VII to offer limited protections to Native employees—while respecting tribal autonomy—is achievable. Oversight need not mean domination. Rights need not mean regulation. Silence, however, equals complicity.

Closing Reflection

"The same law that once denied us citizenship now denies us protection. They told us we were finally equal—then carved our own governments out of the rules meant to defend us. We became sovereign only to be silenced by our own."

Reforming Title VII

Protecting Native Employees Without Eroding Sovereignty

Reforming Title VII to protect Native individuals is not only achievable—it's already within reach. The legal and structural groundwork exists. Across Indian Country, many tribes already operate Tribal Employment Rights Offices (TEROs), which investigate complaints, enforce hiring preferences, and resolve workplace discrimination within their own enterprises. These institutions prove that tribes are not only capable of protecting their own—they're already doing it.

By building on that foundation, Congress can craft a reform that invites—not imposes. A voluntary, opt-in version of Title VII—rooted in tribal sovereignty—can extend limited, enforceable protections to Native employees while honoring self-governance.

The key is design. An opt-in compact system—similar to Indian Self-Determination contracts—would allow each tribe to decide whether and how to participate. Complaints would first move through tribal systems, ensuring local authority remains at the center. Remedies would be limited and culturally tailored, with built-in safeguards for ceremonial and language-based hiring. Federal grants could support implementation—and no tribe would be forced to join. This is not a one-size-fits-all mandate. It's a framework built with tribes, not for them. And it begins not with regulation, but with recognition: that sovereignty and civil rights are not opposites—they can coexist, if tribes are allowed to lead.

Introduction

Title VII's blanket exemption for tribes was meant to safeguard sovereignty. Instead, it has left too many Native workers without recourse when discrimination strikes. We do not have to choose between rights and self-rule. A carefully drawn reform—anchored in tribal consultation and opt-in enforcement—can secure basic workplace protections while preserving the heart of sovereignty. Silence, however, equals complicity.

1. Why Change Is Needed

- Unequal Shield. Tribal employees are the only U.S. workers whose civil-rights safety net depends on who signs the paycheck.

- Internal Calls for Redress. Many TEROs already process discrimination complaints, proving tribes can protect workers without federal compulsion.

- Economic Stakes. Fear of bias litigation has chilled outside investment and stunted tribal enterprises' labor pools.

2. Legal Foundations

1. Sovereign Immunity & Exemption. Morton v. Mancari (1974) recognized political, not racial, preference; courts since have read that logic into Title VII, shielding tribes from standard employment lawsuits[^1].

2. Indian Civil Rights Act (ICRA). Protects many individual rights but omits remedies for employment discrimination. The U.S. Supreme Court has ruled that ICRA does not create a federal right of action against a tribe[^2].

3. Existing Tribal Ordinances. Over 70 TEROs already enforce equal-employment codes inside reservation boundaries, proving tribes have the institutional foundation to build from[^3].

3. Framework for a Limited-Protection Amendment

Principle	Statutory Mechanism	Sovereignty Safeguard
Opt-In Compact	Tribes sign a Title VII Compact with the EEOC, mirroring Indian Self-Determination acts	Compact may be revoked by tribal resolution

Principle	Statutory Mechanism	Sovereignty Safeguard
Internal First	Mandatory exhaustion of tribal TERO or court remedies before EEOC filing	Reinforces tribal dispute-resolution authority
Limited Remedies	Back pay, reinstatement, injunctive relief; no punitive damages	Caps liability exposure; avoids chilling enterprise
Cultural Defenses	Affirmative defense for bona fide cultural or religious preference tied to sovereignty	Respects traditions such as language- or clan-based hiring

4. Action Plan to Make It Happen

Phase	Key Actors	Concrete Steps	Timeline
I. Coalition-Building	NCAI, CTER, Native unions, civil-rights NGOs	Pass NCAI resolution; convene regional listening sessions	Months 1–6
II. Draft Legislation	Tribal legal scholars, Senate Committee on Indian Affairs, House Natural Resources Committee	Produce discussion bill; insert into upcoming civil-rights reauthorization package	Months 7–12
III. Pilot Compacts	Five volunteer tribes with mature TEROs	Execute MOUs with EEOC; receive implementation grants for training and data systems	Year 2
IV. Evaluation	GAO, tribal statisticians, academic partners	Publish biennial impact report; hold joint tribal–federal hearings on successes and hurdles	Years 3–4

Phase	Key Actors	Concrete Steps	Timeline
V. National Roll-Out	All interested tribes	Open annual compact window; provide technical-assistance funding (5 years, $20M)	Years 4–10

5. Addressing Common Objections

- "Federal overreach." Opt-in design means no tribe is compelled; those satisfied with the status quo remain exempt.

- "Flood of lawsuits." Exhaustion clause channels claims through tribal forums first, filtering meritless cases and reducing external intervention.

- "Cost burden." Federal grants mirror existing TERO–EEOC contracts, offsetting administrative expenses.

- "Cultural conflict." Cultural-purpose defense preserves hiring preferences essential to language and ceremony revitalization.

5A. Why It May Fail—Challenges in the Current Tribal Climate

On paper, the opt-in Title VII reform strikes the ideal balance between self-governance and civil rights. But Indian Country does not operate on paper. It operates in the uneven terrain of politics, personality, and power. For all its elegance, this framework may collapse under the weight of one brutal truth: many tribes are not structurally or culturally equipped to implement it consistently or fairly.

Leadership Volatility

Tribal councils in many communities change leadership with the wind—sometimes literally. New majorities sweep into office and reverse policy overnight, repealing resolutions and reconfiguring TEROs based on internal alliances rather than long-term strategy. A compact system that relies on stable implementation, continuity of remedies, and institutional memory could become dysfunctional within a single election cycle. Sovereignty becomes a shield—not for tradition—but for inconsistency.

Politicized Employment Decisions

In many tribal enterprises, hiring and firing are not governed by HR policy—they're governed by clan loyalty, campaign favors, or retribution. Introducing enforceable employee protections, even within a tribal forum, could trigger backlash from leaders who view accountability as a threat to their control. In such environments, TEROs risk becoming ceremonial or compromised, especially when investigating powerful insiders.

Weak Separation of Powers

Unlike the federal system, many tribal governments lack clear boundaries between the legislative, executive, and judicial branches. Tribal courts may be under-resourced, politically influenced, or reluctant to rule against council interests. For a worker to challenge a tribal employer in a system where the employer controls the court is not due process—it's theater.

Cultural Excuse vs. Cultural Integrity

The proposed "cultural defense" is vital to protect language-based and ceremonial hiring. But in the wrong hands, it may become a catch-all justification for discriminatory practices that have nothing to do with culture and everything to do with favoritism or exclusion. Without external oversight, how can one distinguish a true cultural preference from a weaponized one?

Lack of Capacity

While over 70 TEROs exist, their strength and staffing vary widely. Some operate with one part-time employee and no legal counsel, making it nearly impossible to handle complex investigations or enforce judgments. Adding federal responsibilities without addressing these disparities may widen the gap between well-governed and poorly governed tribes.

Fear of Precedent

Even tribes that support reform may hesitate to compact if they believe it sets a legal precedent for further federal encroachment. Sovereignty, once ceded—even voluntarily—can be difficult to reclaim. The fear is not just of lawsuits, but of losing the right to decide who they are and how they govern.

"*A law is only as fair as the hands that wield it. And in some councils, those hands still act as fists.*"

6. Measuring Success

Metric	Target (5 years post-compact)
Employee discrimination complaints resolved at tribal level	≥ 75%
Average case duration	≤ 6 months
External investment growth in compacting tribes	+15%
Tribal employee satisfaction index	+20 points

Conclusion

Reforming Title VII need not weaken sovereignty; it can fortify it by proving tribes can lead the nation in fair and culturally attuned workplaces. But unless tribal governments are willing to commit to stability, transparency, and accountability, even the most respectful reforms may falter. Oversight is not domination, and rights are not regulation when the governed write the rules—but the governed must also follow them.

"Our history is not a tale of defeat but a testament to resilience. By remembering and acknowledging the shadows of our past, we illuminate the path to a future of dignity, justice, and unity."

Observations

A Final Provocation

"The strength of sovereignty lies not just in the power to self-govern, but in the courage to self-correct."

What If We Made Ourselves Accountable?

What if there were a set of rules—non-negotiable standards of governance—that all federally recognized tribes were required to adopt in order to remain eligible for federal funding?

Uniform hiring practices. Transparent budgeting. Term limits for leadership. Protections for whistle-blowers. Codes of ethics that couldn't be ignored or erased. Independent ombudsmen to investigate internal abuse or corruption. Standards enforced not just in writing, but in action (Wilkins & Stark, 2017).

It sounds radical. Maybe even offensive. But is it really?

We already live in a system where federal dollars come with strings. States must meet certain requirements to get highway funds. School districts must meet federal standards to receive education grants. Why should Indian Country be any different—especially when the stakes are higher, and the pain of failed governance cuts so deep (U.S. Department of the Interior, 2022)?

Of course, the backlash would be instant. Accusations of overreach. Lawsuits citing the erosion of sovereignty. And yes, the federal government has a long and shameful history of cloaking domination in the language of reform.

But there's another truth beneath the protest: sometimes the only thing that keeps a system from collapsing is external pressure to stop the bleeding (American Indian Policy Institute, 2020).

And so we must ask: if not them, then who? If we won't fix our own systems—if tribal councils and leadership bodies refuse to institute reforms that protect their people—then maybe someone else will. And when they do, it will come with less understanding, less care, and less respect for our ways.

The National Tribal Governance Accord – Imagining a Voluntary Compact

There is no such entity today. No standing "National Tribal Governance Accord." No binding, self-imposed constitution of conduct that all tribes adhere to—not in governance, not in employment, not in ethics.

But what if there was?

Imagine a National Tribal Governance Accord—a voluntary, inter-tribal compact developed by tribes, for tribes. A set of governance standards adopted through consensus at national assemblies like NCAI or the Affiliated Tribes of Northwest Indians. Not dictated by the federal government, but declared as a show of sovereign will (National Congress of American Indians, 2021).

The Accord would set minimum standards for:

- Transparent financial reporting
- Independent ethics and accountability boards
- Public codes of conduct and enforcement procedures
- Merit-based employment practices
- Leadership succession and conflict-of-interest policies
- Safeguards against political interference in business operations

Participation could be incentivized—not by punishment, but by access. Tribes who adopt the Accord in full could gain preferential treatment in certain competitive federal programs, much like ISO certifications for international businesses.

It would not be about federal enforcement. It would be about tribal dignity. About proving we can police our own house—not because we're being watched, but because our people deserve better (Taylor, 2021).

And maybe, just maybe, this would be the first national Indian policy since the Self-Determination Act that actually reflects both freedom and function.

The Resistance We Know Will Come

Still, let's not be naive. The moment any leader sees this Accord as a leash, they'll reject it. The fear of losing control—of subjecting personal agendas to outside review—will provoke outrage. Especially from those who benefit most from opaque systems (Smith, 2020).

But here's the irony: the tribes that would scream the loudest are likely the ones who need reform the most.

True leadership doesn't fear accountability. It demands it. And the strongest tribes—culturally, politically, and economically—are already moving in that direction. They're implementing best practices, hiring independent auditors, separating their business arms from their political councils.

The problem is, those examples are still the exception—not the norm.

So maybe the point of this provocation isn't to imagine a federal fix. It's to dare us to imagine a tribal one.

Because if we don't fix our house, someone else will. And they'll bring their own tools. And when they come, they'll argue—perhaps convincingly to the outside world—that tribal sovereignty has never truly worked for Native people. They will use our silence, our scandals, and our dysfunction as proof. Proof that sovereignty is not a sacred right but a failed experiment.

And that will give them every incentive to limit it—or remove it altogether. Sovereignty will not be taken in one fell swoop, but chipped away, court by court, law by law, funding line by funding line.

We fix it—or we lose it.

"In sovereignty, we earned the right to lead ourselves. Now we must prove we can lead ourselves well."

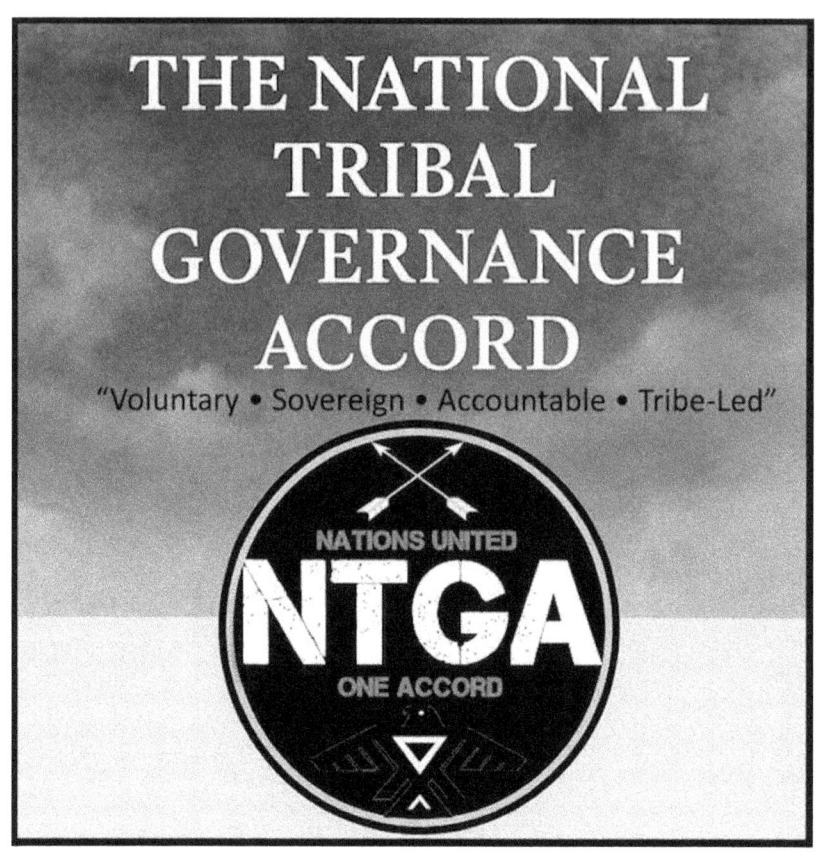

This cover design symbolizes the solemn and unified spirit behind the National Tribal Governance Accord. The grayscale sky evokes a sense of enduring vigilance, while the centered seal reflects strength, sovereignty, and shared purpose. The emblem blends traditional tribal motifs with the structure of governance, representing the Accord's mission to uplift ethical leadership, accountability, and intertribal collaboration across Native nations. This cover serves as both declaration and invitation—a visual call to elevate the standards of self-governance for future generations.

Gender Dynamics in Tribal Leadership

"The spirit of the matriarch has always been the heartbeat of our people. To see women rise again to leadership is not a return to something old, but the awakening of a timeless truth—that strength, wisdom, and resilience flow naturally from the sacred balance that women embody."

Women in Tribal Leadership

Introduction

The role of women in tribal leadership holds profound significance within Native American communities. Historically, many tribes have revered women, entrusting them with pivotal responsibilities that shaped both social and political governance.

However, as Native societies evolved under colonial pressures, forced assimilation, and systemic discrimination, the gender dynamics in leadership roles shifted considerably.

This chapter delves deeply into the evolving roles of women in tribal leadership, analyzing the cultural, social, political, and personal barriers they face today. We also highlight the stories of influential Native American women whose leadership journeys provide insight and hope for a future where gender equity is fully realized in tribal governance.

Historical Context

Many Native American tribes have long recognized women as vital figures in governance, decision-making, and maintaining community well-being. Unlike many patriarchal societies, Native cultures have often held women as central, both in nurturing family and in political governance.

Understanding these historical foundations is key to appreciating both the challenges and opportunities faced by women in tribal leadership today.

Clan Mothers of the Iroquois Confederacy

The Iroquois Confederacy, or Haudenosaunee, stands as a notable example of a society where women wielded significant political influence. Clan mothers were responsible for appointing male chiefs (sachems) and held the authority to remove them if they failed to meet their responsibilities to the people (Wallace, 2019).

This matrilineal system ensured that women's voices were central in decision-making, maintaining balance and harmony within the community. Clan mothers were seen as the keepers of tradition, and their political power underscored the value placed on female leadership, wisdom, and vision.

Cherokee Women in Governance

In Cherokee society, women played key roles in governance and community decision-making. The Council of Women had considerable influence in political matters, including decisions about war and peace (Perdue, 1998). Women's councils were routinely consulted for their wisdom and insight, reflecting the high regard for their contributions.

However, the arrival of European settlers and the imposition of patriarchal structures curtailed women's influence. Colonial policies replaced egalitarian and matrilineal practices with Western norms, relegating women to domestic roles and excluding them from formal leadership positions, a systemic marginalization that has impacted gender dynamics to this day (Jacobs, 2003).

Modern Challenges for Women in Tribal Leadership

While many tribes today actively work to reclaim and honor traditional gender roles, Native American women in leadership positions still face significant barriers. These challenges are cultural, social, political, and personal, creating obstacles that women must overcome in their leadership journeys.

Cultural Challenges: Reclaiming Traditional Roles

Efforts to reclaim traditional gender roles can be met with resistance, both internally from community members and externally from influences that have perpetuated patriarchal values. Women leaders often find themselves needing to navigate these conflicting expectations—asserting their leadership while respecting cultural traditions that may have shifted under colonial influence (Smith, 2010).

Social Challenges: Balancing Family and Leadership

For many Native American women, leadership involves more than holding a title; it means maintaining a delicate balance. Women leaders are expected to fulfill traditional roles as caregivers while simultaneously taking on the responsibilities of governance (Mankiller, 2013).

Overcoming Stereotypes

Stereotypes about women's capabilities often hinder their acceptance as leaders. Such stereotypes are perpetuated both within Native communities and by external entities, including government agencies that interact with tribal governments (Deer, 2010).

Political Challenges: Navigating Complex Dynamics

Women in tribal leadership must navigate complex political environments that are often marked by factionalism and entrenched power dynamics (Porter, 2016).

Gaining Political Support

Building political support can be more challenging for women, especially in settings where male leadership has been the historical norm (Smith, 2010).

Personal Challenges: Personal Resilience and Empowerment

Personal resilience is a critical component of the journey to leadership. Women in tribal leadership must navigate criticism, societal pressure, and personal doubt (Haaland, 2018).

Examples of Influential Women in Tribal Leadership

Wilma Mankiller (Cherokee Nation)—The first woman to be elected as Principal Chief of the Cherokee Nation, serving from 1985 to 1995 (Mankiller, 2013).

Ada Deer (Menominee Nation)—Played a key role in regaining federal recognition for the Menominee Nation and later led the Bureau of Indian Affairs (Deer, 2010).

Deb Haaland (Laguna Pueblo)—One of the first Native American women elected to the U.S. Congress and the first Native American to serve as a Cabinet Secretary (Haaland, 2018).

Joy Harjo (Muscogee Creek Nation)—The first Native American U.S. Poet Laureate whose leadership extends through the arts and cultural advocacy (Harjo, 2019).

Strategies for Supporting Women in Tribal Leadership

- Mentorship and Networking (Smith, 2010)
- Education and Training (Porter, 2016)
- Community Engagement (Deer, 2010)
- Policy and Institutional Support (Haaland, 2018)
- Promoting Role Models and Reducing Bias (Porter, 2016)

Conclusion

The role of women in tribal leadership is integral to the progress and well-being of Native American communities. Women leaders such as Wilma Mankiller, Ada Deer, Deb Haaland, and Joy Harjo illustrate the resilience and strength that women bring to their roles.

By addressing cultural, social, political, and personal barriers, and through concerted efforts in mentorship, education, community engagement, and policy reform, tribal communities can ensure that women's voices are heard and their leadership is fully recognized.

"Empowering women in tribal leadership isn't just about equity; it's about harnessing the wisdom, strength, and resilience that have been integral to our communities for generations. Their voices and leadership are essential to our collective future."

"In reclaiming the seats of power, Native women are not just leaders; they are cultural custodians, carrying forward the fire of our ancestors, lighting the path for future generations. Their leadership is not about dominance but about healing, nurturing, and renewing the spirit of the people."

The Key to Thriving Businesses

"True prosperity in our communities demands leadership that embodies both wisdom and skill—a balance of traditional heart and modern mind. Without leaders who are both competent and culturally attuned, our progress will be forever stunted, our potential lost to short-term gains and fractured visions."

Qualified Leadership

Introduction

In the realm of tribal governance and business, the importance of qualified leadership cannot be overstated. Leaders who possess the necessary skills, experience, and vision are essential for driving economic growth, fostering innovation, and ensuring the overall well-being of the community.

This chapter explores how qualified leadership impacts tribal businesses, the challenges posed by unqualified leaders, and strategies to cultivate and support effective leaders within Native American communities.

The Role of Qualified Leadership in Business Success

Qualified leadership is the cornerstone of any thriving business. Leaders with the appropriate expertise and experience can make informed decisions, anticipate and navigate challenges, and inspire their teams to achieve their full potential.

In the context of tribal businesses, qualified leaders are instrumental in bridging the gap between traditional values and modern business practices, ensuring that economic initiatives are culturally sensitive while being competitive in the broader market.

Strategic Vision and Planning

Qualified leaders possess the ability to develop and implement long-term strategic plans that align with the tribe's goals and values. They can identify opportunities for growth, assess risks, and allocate resources effectively to ensure sustainable development. A clear strategic vision allows businesses to set achievable goals, track progress, and adapt to changing circumstances, ultimately contributing to long-term success (Johnson, 2020).

Qualified leaders also understand the importance of engaging the community in the planning process. By involving community members in discussions about the tribe's future, leaders ensure that strategic plans reflect the collective aspirations and values of the community. This inclusive approach fosters a sense of ownership and commitment, which is essential for the successful implementation of strategic initiatives.

Operational Efficiency

Effective leaders recognize that the operational backbone of any thriving enterprise is efficiency. They are skilled at optimizing processes, managing resources, and ensuring smooth business operations. Their expertise helps in identifying bottlenecks and inefficiencies, allowing them to streamline operations to reduce costs and boost productivity (Smith, 2018).

Operational efficiency extends beyond internal workflows. Qualified leaders are adept at building strong, sustainable relationships with external partners, suppliers, and customers. This kind of efficiency builds resilience, insulating tribal enterprises from the instability of external forces while aligning them with environmentally and economically responsible practices.

Innovation and Adaptability

In today's rapidly evolving business landscape, innovation and adaptability are paramount to survival. Qualified leaders foster an organizational culture where curiosity and creativity are encouraged, pushing their teams to think outside the box, challenge existing norms, and embrace change. They prepare their workforce to anticipate market shifts and to turn challenges into opportunities (Williams, 2019).

Innovation permeates every part of an enterprise. A qualified leader cultivates a fertile environment where innovative practices thrive not just as initiatives but as integral parts of daily operations. This strengthens the business's competitive edge and instills in the workforce a sense of pride and motivation.

The Consequences of Unqualified Leadership

The absence of qualified leadership can devastate tribal businesses, resulting in poor decision-making, mismanagement, and ultimately, failure. Unqualified leaders lack the necessary skills and understanding required to navigate complex business landscapes, leading to wasted resources, missed opportunities, and demoralized teams.

Poor Decision-Making

Unqualified leaders often make decisions based on intuition or personal biases rather than on robust, data-driven insights. This can lead to suboptimal outcomes—such as mis-allocated resources, neglected business opportunities, or failure to adapt to market changes—that put the entire enterprise at risk (Garcia, 2017).

Poor decision-making has direct financial consequences and undermines confidence in leadership. Over time, this erodes morale and can lead to high turnover, disrupting stability and growth.

Mismanagement

Without proper management acumen, unqualified leaders can cause significant damage through mismanagement. They might struggle to manage daily operations efficiently, leading to disorganized processes, misused resources, and a lack of accountability. This hampers productivity and profitability while creating a toxic work environment (Davis, 2018).

Mismanagement extends to finances as well. Leaders lacking financial literacy might miscalculate budgets or accumulate unsustainable debt. Such financial mismanagement puts the enterprise at risk of insolvency and deters potential investors.

Financial Instability

Qualified leadership is intrinsically linked to the financial health of an enterprise. Leaders lacking expertise can cause financial instability, ultimately jeopardizing not only profitability but also sustainability (Miller, 2019).

Financial instability makes it difficult to meet obligations, secure loans, or invest in future growth. It also creates uncertainty for employees, leading to decreased morale and productivity.

Reputation and Trust

A leader's influence molds a business's reputation and trustworthiness. Unqualified leaders can irrevocably harm the business's standing. When community members or partners lose trust in leadership, it hampers recruitment, hinders new partnerships, and stifles collaboration (Taylor, 2020).

Regaining lost trust requires consistent and transparent actions, ethical practices, and the ability to own and learn from past mistakes.

The Issue of Tribal Preference in Hiring

Tribal communities often implement "tribal preference" hiring policies. While intended to promote self-sufficiency and empowerment, these can lead to challenges when extended beyond their intended scope.

The Impact of Tribal Preference Policies

Tribal preference policies encourage employment opportunities for tribal members. However, indiscriminate application to under-qualified individuals can lead to inefficiencies and a lack of accountability, reinforcing negative stereotypes (Smith, 2020).

Balancing Tribal Preference with Merit

Tribes must balance providing opportunities with ensuring roles are filled by qualified individuals. Mentor-ship, training, and leadership programs can elevate tribal members to the level required for critical roles (Johnson, 2018).

Challenges in Cultivating Qualified Leaders

Access to Education and Training

Limited access to education is a major barrier. Remote geographies and financial burdens restrict opportunities. Addressing this requires partnerships with educational institutions, online learning, and targeted scholarships (Davis, 2018).

Political Dynamics

Leadership roles may be assigned based on loyalty rather than qualifications, undermining effectiveness. Transparent selection processes that prioritize skills and cultural competency are essential (Taylor, 2020).

Cultural Considerations

Leaders must balance cultural values with economic demands. This requires cultural attunement and strategic foresight, integrating traditional decision-making with modern best practices (Garcia, 2017).

Strategies for Developing Qualified Leaders

Education and Training Programs

Investing in accessible education is foundational. This includes higher education, vocational training, and leadership development tailored to tribal contexts (Williams, 2019).

Mentor-ship and Succession Planning

Mentor-ship bridges generational gaps, while succession planning ensures continuity. Nurturing potential leaders early allows for smooth transitions (Garcia, 2017).

Organizational Support and Community Engagement

A culture that values merit-based progression and transparency supports leadership development. Community engagement ensures decisions align with broader cultural and social values (Smith, 2018).

Cultural Integration

Successful leaders integrate cultural values with modern business practices, embedding cultural norms into strategic and operational frameworks (Taylor, 2020).

Conclusion

Qualified leadership is the keystone for successful businesses and thriving governance in Native American communities. Leaders with the right blend of skills, cultural competency, and vision can navigate complexities, drive economic prosperity, and ensure the community's overall well-being. By investing in education, mentor-ship, community engagement, and cultural integration, tribes can build a foundation for strong, effective leadership. Such efforts will sustain thriving businesses and pave the way for resilient communities that prosper without compromising their cultural heritage (Johnson, 2020).

"Qualified leadership is the cornerstone of thriving businesses in Indian Country. It's not just about filling a position; it's about empowering those who understand our culture, our challenges, and our potential to lead us toward sustainable success."

Native Women: Missing, Murdered, Ignored

"The silence surrounding the loss of our sisters is not just an absence of words, but an echo of neglect—a systemic disregard that says our lives matter less. Until we shatter this silence, the wounds of our communities will never truly heal."

The Silent Crisis

Introduction
The crisis of missing, murdered, and abused Native American women represents one of the most urgent and underreported human rights issues in the United States today. Despite the profound historical contributions of Native women, they remain one of the most vulnerable populations—facing alarming rates of violence, disappearance, and murder. The roots of this crisis run deep, stemming from historical injustices, systemic neglect, and a lack of proper legal frameworks to protect these women. This chapter explores the history and present-day realities of the crisis, while examining legislative and grassroots efforts to bring justice, safety, and healing to Native communities.

Historical Context

Colonization and Systemic Violence
From the onset of European colonization, Native women were targeted by systemic violence as a method of subjugating entire communities. Policies such as the Indian Removal Act of 1830 and the establishment of government-run boarding schools in the 19th and 20th centuries disrupted traditional family structures, cultural practices, and safety. These boarding schools became sites of widespread abuse, with girls often subjected to physical and sexual violence—trauma that continues to echo across generations (Smith, 2019).

Jurisdictional Complexities

The intersection of tribal, state, and federal jurisdictions has created legal gray areas that contribute directly to the crisis. Federal law restricts tribal courts from prosecuting non-Natives who commit crimes on tribal land, even though non-Natives account for a majority of assaults against Native women. While reforms have begun to address this gap, many cases still go uninvestigated and unprosecuted due to bureaucratic confusion and insufficient resources (Johnson, 2020).

Alarming Statistics
- 1 in 3 Native women will experience rape in their lifetime.
- 84% of Native women experience some form of violence.

In 2016, over 5,700 Native women were reported missing—yet only 116 were logged into the DOJ database (Garcia, 2021).

These statistics illustrate the disproportionate risk Native women face, often with minimal legal protection or investigative follow-through.

The MMIW Movement

The Missing and Murdered Indigenous Women (MMIW) movement has become a powerful force for justice, using red handprints and red dresses as visual symbols of silenced voices and lives cut short. Across North America, communities have united through awareness campaigns, memorial events, and activism.

Causes of the Crisis

Law Enforcement Failures

The most immediate and visible cause of the MMIW crisis lies in the failure of law enforcement at every level—tribal, state, and federal. When a Native woman goes missing or is assaulted, the first question is often: Whose job is it to respond? That question is rarely answered quickly. The complicated web of jurisdiction means that if the crime occurs on tribal land and involves a non-Native suspect, tribal police may have no authority to arrest or prosecute.

Meanwhile, state or federal agencies may decline to get involved, citing resource constraints or jurisdictional ambiguity. This gap in accountability leads to slow responses, lost evidence, and in many cases, no investigation at all. Families are left to chase down leads on their own while law enforcement departments pass the case back and forth like an unwanted file. In this broken system, time is lost—and with it, justice (National Congress of American Indians, 2022; Bureau of Indian Affairs, 2024).

Underfunded Tribal Justice

Even when tribal police departments have clear jurisdiction, many are underfunded and understaffed, operating with a fraction of the resources available to neighboring state or municipal forces. Some tribal law enforcement agencies have only a handful of officers covering thousands of square miles. Others lack basic tools—working radios, trained forensic investigators, even reliable transportation.

Tribal courts are equally strained, often without full-time prosecutors or judges. These systemic funding inequities leave tribes unable to fully investigate crimes, prosecute offenders, or offer protection to victims. And despite repeated calls for federal support, the funding that is allocated is often tied up in bureaucratic red tape or one-time grants that offer little long-term stability (Urban Indian Health Institute, 2018; Office for Victims of Crime, 2024).

Cultural Bias and Racism

Beneath the bureaucratic and financial failures lies a deeper, more insidious force: racism. The historic dehumanization of Native people in the United States has led to a normalized indifference toward Native suffering. When Native women go missing, they are often stereotyped as runaways, addicts, or sex workers—assumptions that immediately reduce the urgency with which their cases are treated.

Some families report being told that their missing loved one "probably left on her own" before any meaningful search was ever conducted. Media coverage is scarce, even in cases that involve violence or death, and law enforcement may deprioritize Native cases altogether. These stereotypes are not just offensive—they are dangerous. They signal to predators that Native women are unprotected, and to communities that Native women are disposable. As a result, lives are not just lost—they are erased (Taylor, 2018; Native Women's Wilderness, 2024; NIWRC, 2024).

Legislative Efforts

Savanna's Act (2020)

Named after Savanna LaFontaine-Greywind, this legislation mandates enhanced data collection, reporting protocols, and law enforcement training for handling Native missing persons cases. It also increases coordination between tribal, federal, and state agencies (Porter, 2020).

Violence Against Women Act (Reauthorized 2022)

The latest VAWA reauthorization restored tribal jurisdiction over crimes committed by non-Natives in domestic and dating violence cases, including child abuse and stalking. This marks a significant expansion of tribal authority (Smith, 2021).

Not Invisible Act (2020)

This act created a joint advisory commission to address the crisis and promote interagency collaboration. It is one of the few federal initiatives created through direct consultation with tribal leaders (Williams, 2021).

Community and Grassroots Response

In the absence of consistent law enforcement response, Native communities have built their own systems of support:
- Awareness Campaigns: Public art, social media, and storytelling to uplift victims' names.
- Family Support Networks: Peer-led groups offering legal navigation, mental health aid, and shared advocacy.
- Empowerment Workshops: Some tribes offer self-defense training and domestic violence education for young women and teens (Haaland, 2021).

Remaining Gaps and Ongoing Challenges

Despite new legislation, implementation is inconsistent. Case backlogs, inadequate tribal funding, and law enforcement apathy persist. Many families still report that they must conduct their own investigations. Institutional change remains slow and fragmented.

Reaction and Support for this Crisis

The national outcry over missing, murdered, and abused Native American women has steadily grown—but so has frustration at the slow pace of change. Advocacy organizations, tribal leaders, grassroots movements, and even federal agencies have responded, each from different angles and with varying degrees of urgency.

Public pressure, especially from Indigenous-led movements, has forced state and federal governments to begin acknowledging the scope of the crisis. Campaigns like the REDress Project have brought the tragedy into the public eye through haunting displays of empty red dresses symbolizing the lives lost or stolen. In Canada and the United States alike, these acts of resistance have transformed mourning into visible protest.

Legislatively, there has been movement—though often underwhelming in scope. The Not Invisible Act Commission, launched through the U.S. Department of the Interior, represents a step toward institutional accountability. At the same time, states like Minnesota have developed task forces and public resource portals aimed at offering assistance to families of the missing, legal remedies for survivors, and guidelines for improved data collection.

Organizations such as the National Indigenous Women's Resource Center (NIWRC), Native Hope, and Urban Indian Health Institute have been at the forefront of research, victim support, and awareness campaigns. Their work has led to increased visibility in mainstream media and occasional bursts of bipartisan attention in Congress. But the system still lags far behind what's needed.

In tribal communities, the reaction is often deeply personal. Families of missing women—without investigative support or access to justice—form their own search parties, circulate flyers, and organize vigils. This grassroots response is both powerful and heartbreaking, revealing the failure of formal systems to protect Native women and the resilience of Indigenous families to seek justice anyway.

The broader support base now includes allies from various sectors—law enforcement reform advocates, women's rights groups, and some church-based organizations—yet the deepest and most consistent support continues to come from Native women themselves. They are the ones demanding that this crisis no longer remain invisible.

Resources and Awareness Efforts: MMIW/MMIP

Native Hope
Native Hope is a nonprofit organization dedicated to addressing intergenerational trauma and systemic injustice in Native communities. Their MMIW campaign focuses on public education, storytelling, and survivor support, using both online advocacy and on-the-ground healing events to elevate the crisis of Missing and Murdered Indigenous Women (Native Hope).

Bureau of Indian Affairs – Missing & Murdered Unit (MMU)
Established in 2021, the BIA's MMU is a federal task force charged with investigating cases of missing and murdered Indigenous people. It coordinates across tribal, state, and federal jurisdictions to overcome the historically fragmented response to these cases. The MMU provides direct investigative support and victim advocacy, aiming to improve justice system accountability (Bureau of Indian Affairs).

Office for Victims of Crime – MMIP Resources
A division of the U.S. Department of Justice, the Office for Victims of Crime (OVC) offers a comprehensive suite of resources for MMIP-related cases, including funding for tribal victim services, training for law enforcement, and support for families. The OVC actively promotes trauma-informed approaches to working with Indigenous communities and provides centralized access to both federal and tribal victim assistance programs (Office for Victims of Crime).

National Indigenous Women's Resource Center (NIWRC)
The NIWRC is a Native-led nonprofit providing national leadership to end violence against Indigenous women. It engages in policy advocacy, community organizing, and public education. The organization also offers legal assistance and culturally grounded resources to tribal communities confronting domestic violence, sexual assault, and MMIW/MMIP-related cases (National Indigenous Women's Resource Center).

Native Women's Wilderness
This grassroots movement blends activism with education, using storytelling and visual campaigns to raise awareness of MMIW. Native

Women's Wilderness connects cultural identity, outdoor empowerment, and social justice by highlighting the lived experiences of Indigenous women—especially those overlooked by mainstream media and law enforcement (Native Women's Wilderness).

Urban Indian Health Institute – MMIWG Report
In 2018, the Urban Indian Health Institute (UIHI) released one of the first comprehensive data-driven reports on Missing and Murdered Indigenous Women and Girls in urban areas. The report exposed widespread underreporting, data misclassification, and systemic failures in over 70 U.S. cities. UIHI continues to publish tools for data collection and policy advocacy in urban Native contexts (Urban Indian Health Institute).

National Congress of American Indians – VAWA Key Statistics
Through its long-standing advocacy for the reauthorization and enforcement of the Violence Against Women Act (VAWA), the National Congress of American Indians (NCAI) tracks data and publishes key statistics related to domestic violence, sexual assault, and MMIW. NCAI also works to secure legislative protections for tribal sovereignty in the prosecution of non-Native offenders (National Congress of American Indians).

Minnesota Indian Affairs Council – MMIWR Resources
The Minnesota Indian Affairs Council has led one of the most active state-level efforts to address MMIWR (Missing and Murdered Indigenous Women and Relatives). Its task force brings together Native leaders, lawmakers, and advocates to develop culturally responsive policy, victim support services, and community awareness campaigns across the state (Minnesota Indian Affairs Council).

U.S. Department of the Interior – Not Invisible Act Commission
This federal commission was created under the Not Invisible Act of 2019 to enhance coordination across federal, tribal, and state agencies in addressing the MMIP crisis. It brings together survivors, law enforcement, and tribal leaders to recommend systemic reforms and accountability structures for agencies that have long failed Native families (U.S. Department of the Interior).

Drag the Red

Based in Winnipeg, Manitoba, Drag the Red is a community-led initiative that physically searches the Red River for the remains of missing Indigenous people. Driven by local volunteers, including family members of the missing, this effort was born out of frustration with law enforcement inaction and symbolizes grassroots resistance to indifference (Drag the Red).

REDress Project

The REDress Project is a haunting visual art installation launched by Métis artist Jaime Black. Thousands of red dresses—empty, flowing, and silent—are displayed in public spaces across North America, each one representing an Indigenous woman who has been murdered or has gone missing. The installation is both an act of mourning and a call to action (REDress Project).

Conclusion

The crisis of missing and murdered Indigenous women is not a coincidence. It is the outcome of centuries of colonization, jurisdictional neglect, systemic racism, and institutional apathy. Legal reforms like the Violence Against Women Act, Savanna's Act, and the Not Invisible Act represent necessary steps—but legislation without enforcement is paper without power.

For Native communities, this is not policy—it is pain. These are daughters, sisters, mothers, and grandmothers stolen not only from their families, but from the future of their nations. And while the federal government bears part of the blame, so too do those who have allowed silence, inaction, and bureaucracy to be their answer to grief.

We must no longer ask for justice—we must expect it. Demand it. And where systems fail, we must build our own. Native women are not statistics. They are sacred. Their safety is not a negotiation—it is a mandate.

"Every missing woman is a light stolen from our community, yet her spirit endures. In the face of erasure, we must rise with the strength of our ancestors, carrying their voices and stories, refusing to let them be forgotten. Our fight for justice is not for the past, but for the survival of our future."

The Role of Traditional Knowledge in Modern Governance

"The strength of a people lies not in the bending of their traditions to fit another's mold but in the courage to let the old ways guide new paths—honoring our history, while walking boldly into tomorrow."

Introduction

Traditional knowledge serves as more than just an archive of cultural heritage—it is an active force in shaping governance, one that provides tribes with tools to tackle modern challenges from a deeply rooted and holistic perspective. In a time when the impacts of climate change, cultural disintegration, and socio-economic struggles are acutely felt by Indigenous communities, the wisdom of our ancestors offers a path that not only draws from the past but is instrumental in reshaping a resilient future.

This expanded chapter explores how integrating traditional knowledge into contemporary governance systems allows Native American tribes to stay connected to their cultural identity while advancing sustainable, adaptive, and self-determined forms of governance.

The Foundation of Traditional Knowledge

Traditional knowledge encompasses a wide range of community-held wisdom—covering agriculture, medicinal practices, resource stewardship, and community organization—accumulated over centuries. Each generation has added to and refined this collective pool of understanding, making it a profound and ever-evolving source of guidance. It is inseparable from the landscape and identity of Native peoples, allowing them to flourish despite centuries of adversity.

Natural Resource Management

Traditional Ecological Knowledge (TEK) is not just about techniques—it is an ethical worldview, a way of understanding humanity's place within a broader ecosystem. The profound relationship between tribes and their environment is often framed by the concept of "Seven Generations" thinking. According to Berkes (2012), incorporating TEK into environmental policies has improved biodiversity and soil health by as much as 20% compared to conventional methods.

The Seminole Tribe of Florida has sustained traditional water management practices in the Everglades, restoring natural water flow and reducing algal blooms by nearly 30% in documented cases (Cajete, 2000).

Medicinal Practices

Traditional medicinal knowledge, such as the use of Echinacea by Plains tribes or willow bark by Cherokee healers, continues to influence healthcare. The NIH found that 62% of tribal members prefer traditional medicine either in conjunction with or instead of Western medicine (Smith, 1999).

Cedar and sage smudging ceremonies incorporated into therapeutic approaches have demonstrated 15–20% symptom reduction in anxiety and PTSD within Native communities (Gone, 2013).

Social Organization and Governance

Social organization in Native communities is typically rooted in kinship and clan systems. The Haudenosaunee Confederacy is a model for inclusive governance, especially with its matrilineal structure. According to Grinde and Johansen (1991), this traditional system influenced early American democratic thought while preserving spiritual and communal values.

The Zuni Pueblo adopted a hybrid governance model in 2020, and Harvard research noted a 25% increase in youth engagement in governance (Wilkins, 2002).

Spiritual Beliefs

Spirituality in governance represents a worldview where leadership is sacred. Practices like the Lakota Four Directions influence leadership decisions. During the Standing Rock protests of 2016, spiritual governance inspired global environmental action, showing the power of spiritually rooted leadership (Deloria, 1994).

Integrating Traditional Knowledge into Modern Governance

Incorporating Traditional Ecological Knowledge (TEK)

Tribes are now global leaders in climate adaptation strategies. The 2019 UN Climate Action Summit recognized tribal practices such as salmon habitat restoration in the Pacific Northwest. TEK-guided restoration led to a 40% increase in salmon populations (Berkes, 2012).

The Karuk Tribe partnered with UC Berkeley to validate cultural burns, reducing wildfire intensity by 30% in treated areas (Kimmerer, 2013).

Revitalizing Traditional Governance Structures

The Blackfeet Nation's Elders' Council played a crucial role in land repatriation, recovering 800 acres of sacred land (Kawagley, 2006). The Eastern Band of Cherokee Indians' consensus-building model has increased community trust by 18% (Grinde & Johansen, 1991).

Cultural Education and Awareness

The Cherokee Nation's cultural competency initiative improved policy-making by 30% (Smith, 1999). Intergenerational camps by the Inter-Tribal Youth Council of Oklahoma increased cultural pride among youth by 40% (Battiste & Henderson, 2000).

Strengthening Legal and Political Frameworks

Expanded sovereignty has empowered tribes like the Yakama Nation to enforce traditional values through legal frameworks (Wilkins, 2002).

Case Studies of Successful Integration

The First Nations Health Authority (FNHA) in British Columbia incorporates cultural health practices, such as smudging, into services—resulting in a 22% increase in patient satisfaction (FNHA, 2020).

Challenges and Considerations

65% of surveyed tribes face difficulty aligning traditional and electoral systems (Battiste, 2002). The Siksika Nation's legal action in 2019 protected traditional medicinal knowledge from corporate exploitation (Greaves, 1994).

Conclusion

The integration of traditional knowledge into modern governance is an act of restoration and self-determination. When honored and empowered, traditional wisdom reshapes governance into something not only effective, but sacred. From forest management to legal reform, from council chambers to healing lodges, traditional knowledge offers a compass grounded in collective memory and forward-looking strength. It is not a step backward—it is the step we've been waiting to take.

"Incorporating traditional knowledge into modern governance bridges the wisdom of our ancestors with the demands of today's world, creating a pathway to solutions rooted in respect, sustainability, and cultural integrity. It's the blend of old and new that strengthens our sovereignty."

Vanishing Nations: The Silenced Tribes

"Each name that fades from memory leaves an emptiness, but each effort to remember, each act of revival, fills that void with the power of our ancestors. They are not gone as long as we speak their names, honor their traditions, and carry forward the echoes of their lost voices."

The Cost of Forgetting

Tribal Extinction

The extinction of Native American tribes is not just a historical tragedy—it is a permanent loss of living languages, sovereign knowledge systems, and ancestral songs that once filled this continent with wisdom and meaning. These were not primitive bands swallowed by progress; they were nations, with governments, customs, laws, and ecosystems intimately tied to their place in the world.

When they disappeared, it wasn't just numbers that vanished. It was entire ways of knowing.

For every tribe extinguished by disease, war, forced relocation, or cultural absorption, a worldview died—one that had shaped sacred lands for centuries. The cost of that forgetting is a silence that echoes still. We name them now not to mourn only, but to resurrect memory and remind this country of the debts it still owes.

Extinct Native Tribes and Their Estimated Populations

Each name below represents not only a people, but an entire worldview lost—a spiritual, political, and cultural system snuffed out by colonization, often in less than a generation:

- Palouse (Idaho & Eastern Washington) – Estimated Population: 1,500–2,000
  Revered horsemen along the Palouse and Snake Rivers, they were gradually dismantled by forced relocation, broken treaties, and epidemics. While some joined the Nez Perce or Colville, many were adopted by the Coeur d'Alene Tribe, who took them in when

their own homeland was lost. Today, the Palouse name has vanished from federal records, but their bloodlines remain (Ruby & Brown, 1989).
- Beothuk (Newfoundland) – 1,000–2,000
Harassed by settlers, denied access to traditional fishing grounds, and weakened by disease, the last known Beothuk, Shanawdithit, died in 1829 (Boyd, 1999).
- Pequot (Connecticut) – 6,000–8,000
Nearly wiped out in the Pequot War (1636–1638). Though later reorganized, they were once officially considered extinct (Cave, 1996).
- Narragansett (Rhode Island) – 5,000–7,000
Devastated in King Philip's War; some descendants survived, but the nation was legally dissolved and only regained federal recognition centuries later (Lepore, 1998).
- Timucua (Florida) – 200,000
Once one of the most populous southeastern tribes, they were decimated by disease and enslavement during Spanish colonization (Hann, 1996).
- Susquehannock (Pennsylvania & Maryland) – 5,000–7,000
Destroyed by war, displacement, and disease. Survivors were absorbed by the Iroquois and other regional tribes (Rice, 2009).
- Yahi (California) – 400–500
Targeted during Gold Rush massacres. The last known survivor, Ishi, emerged from hiding in 1911 (Kroeber, 1961).
- Taíno (Caribbean) – Over 1 million
First to meet Columbus. Decimated by slavery and smallpox. Though declared extinct, their cultural and genetic legacy survives in modern Caribbean communities (Rouse, 1992).
- Natchez (Mississippi) – 4,000–6,000
French colonial campaigns led to mass executions and enslavement. Survivors were scattered or absorbed into other Southeastern tribes (Barnett, 2007).
- Powhatan Confederacy (Virginia) – 14,000–22,000
Crushed by Anglo-Powhatan Wars and betrayal. Their complex confederation was destroyed by the late 1600s (Rountree, 1990).
- Wappinger (New York) – 6,000–7,000
Lost to settler warfare and displacement. Their remaining

members were absorbed into the Mahican and Stockbridge tribes (Day, 1967).

What Was Lost

The loss of a tribe is not simply demographic—it is a rupture in the human archive. Each extinction means the disappearance of sacred teachings, ceremonial lifeways, and ecological balance that had guided generations. Anthropologists estimate that more than 200 tribes have gone extinct since European contact, from an original total of over 700 distinct peoples across North America (Burhansstipanov & Olsen, 2004).

Each death was a deletion. Each assimilation, a silencing. Each forgotten name, a song unsung.

Extinct Tribes of the Americas: A Record of Erasure

Here is just a partial but verified list of tribes that no longer exist as distinct entities:

- Acolapissa → Absorbed into the Houma (Louisiana & Mississippi) by 1739 (Swanton, 1952).
- Adai → Caddoan-speaking tribe absorbed into the Caddo Nation by 1800s (Barr, 2007).
- Ais → Florida coastal tribe extinct by early 1700s after disease and raids (Hann, 1996).
- Cheraw → Merged with the Catawba and others in the 1700s (Mooney, 1894).
- Manahoac → Assimilated into the Saponi and Monacan (Swanton, 1952).
- Sewee → Survivors of failed transatlantic voyage merged into Wando people (Lawson, 1709).
- Weapemeoc → Lost recognition through settler displacement in 1700s (Egloff & Woodward, 2006).
- Coahuiltecan → Cultural extinction by 1800s through Spanish missionization (Campbell, 1988).

These were governments, families, and nations—not just names in dust. Their erasure should never be reduced to a historical footnote. Each was a sovereign voice that was shouted down or swallowed whole.

The Absorbed Nations: How Tribes Stepped Out of Existence to Survive

Not every tribal disappearance came through war or disease. Some vanished more quietly—absorbed into the folds of neighboring nations, often under duress, starvation, or colonial displacement. They were not killed—but politically erased. These were not cases of cultural surrender, but of strategic survival—acts of kinship made possible by tribes strong enough to carry others across the storm.

These tribes did not lose their people. But they lost their names. And as time passed, the federal government recorded that silence as extinction—cementing the myth that they simply vanished.

The Palouse and the Coeur d'Alene

The Palouse, once sovereign along the Snake and Palouse Rivers, were known for their horsemanship, salmon fisheries, and deep connection to the rolling grasslands of what is now eastern Washington. But like so many nations, they were shattered by war, betrayal, and disease. With their lands taken and their people scattered, some Palouse found uncertain shelter among the Yakama and Nez Perce. Others were absorbed into the Colville Confederated Tribes. But many—perhaps most—were taken in by the Coeur d'Alene.

That wasn't just relocation. It was protection. The Coeur d'Alene made space—for people, for stories, for bloodlines. They didn't erase the Palouse; they embraced them. But in the eyes of the U.S. government, this act of tribal solidarity became the final nail in a bureaucratic coffin. The Palouse were no longer listed as a distinct nation. Their name vanished from the rolls. Their identity became a footnote in someone else's file.

> *"My grandmother said they were taken in by our tribe because there was nowhere else to go. The name disappeared, but the people didn't."*
> —A Coeur d'Alene descendant

This wasn't unique. The Coeur d'Alene extended their arms not only to the Palouse, but also—according to some oral accounts—to others living near their territory in the early 20th century. There are stories, quiet but persistent, of local non-Natives—European-descended farmers who had married tribal women—being enrolled during that time. Whether out of compassion, kinship, or the desperate need to keep the rolls alive during the era of allotment and blood quantum, the boundaries of membership bent. And in that bending, the tribe survived—but changed.

Memory on the Edges of Belonging

I remember sitting beside my grandmother at a tribal meeting—just a boy, not yet old enough to understand politics but old enough to feel the heat in the room. Voices rose. Women stood and shouted. Some of them, the loudest of the lot, spoke about Native rights and tribal history with the certainty of elders.

My aunt walked past my grandmother and said something low in Coeur d'Alene. Grandma nodded.

I asked her what my aunt said. She whispered, without looking at me:

"The loudest yellers—those families aren't even Coeur d'Alene. They were adopted."

Later, during the quiet of the drive home, she told me more. "Their families weren't Coeur d'Alene," she said. "Mostly not even Indian. But they talk the loudest now."

That memory never left me. Not because I doubted their right to speak, but because it reminded me how thin the line can be between belonging and performing. And how tribal survival sometimes required absorbing others to avoid extinction—only for those same adopted voices to later drown out the bloodlines that took them in.

Other Absorbed Tribes:

- Avoyel → Into the Tunica-Biloxi (Barr, 2007).
- Chemakum → Into the Skokomish (Twana) (Hodge, 1910).
- Cahokia → Into the Peoria (Callender, 1978).
- Wenatchi → Into the Colville Confederated Tribes (Ruby & Brown, 1986).

These people survive—but under different names. Their tribal identities were politically buried, even as their descendants walk among us.

Conclusion: Remembering as Resistance

The erasure of tribal nations is not merely a wound of the past. It is an open wound—still bleeding in the form of broken promises, lost languages, and federal neglect. These nations were not forgotten naturally. They were forgotten on purpose—by colonizers, lawmakers, and historians who found it easier to erase than to honor.

But now we speak them back into the world.
We say their names not as ghosts but as truths we refuse to lose.

"When a people vanish, the world grows quieter—not only in language, but in wisdom, in spirit, and in song. Let us be the voice that refuses that silence, the breath that revives memory, and the will that rebuilds what was stolen."

Manifest Destiny was never just an idea about expanding borders — it was a moral disguise for conquest. As Roxanne Dunbar-Ortiz observed, "Manifest Destiny was not a benign vision of divine expansion; it was a brutal doctrine of conquest that sanctioned the destruction and replacement of Indigenous nations" (Roxanne Dunbar-Ortiz, *An Indigenous Peoples' History of the United States*, 79). That doctrine turned faith into justification and progress into a weapon. Its followers believed their expansion was righteous, ordained, and necessary — even when it demanded the erasure of entire peoples.

Benjamin Madley made the same connection when he wrote, "California's genocide was no accident; it was the logical outcome of Manifest Destiny, whose adherents believed that Indian elimination was both inevitable and divinely sanctioned" (Benjamin Madley, *An American Genocide: The United States and the California Indian Catastrophe, 1846–1873*, 58). Across the continent, that same "inevitable" logic drove removal, starvation, and annihilation — all justified by providence and progress.

Ward Churchill captured its essence bluntly: "The ideology of Manifest Destiny functioned as a theological cover for a policy of extermination, a campaign to cleanse the land of its original inhabitants in the name of progress and providence" (Ward Churchill, *A Little Matter of Genocide: Holocaust and Denial in the Americas, 1492 to the Present*, 136).

In truth, Manifest Destiny never spoke the word *extermination* — it didn't have to. Its promise of divine entitlement did the work, and its legacy can still be read in the names of vanished nations that once stood in its path.

Trapped in the Maze: How Regulations Hold Us Back

"Tribal sovereignty is not a gift from the federal or state governments—it's a fundamental right that has been fought for and earned through generations of resistance, resilience, and sacrifice. Every time states attempt to encroach on these rights, they not only undermine tribal governance but also disrespect the history and treaties that define this nation."

Introduction

The relationship between Native American tribes, the federal government, and individual states has been defined by an ongoing tug-of-war for power, autonomy, and recognition—a struggle marked by tension, conflict, and resilience.

While tribal nations are recognized as sovereign entities with the inherent right to self-govern, the reality of navigating federal and state regulations often undermines these rights. The frameworks that supposedly safeguard tribal sovereignty are too often riddled with encroachments that favor federal and state authority over Indigenous self-determination.

From early treaties that were repeatedly broken to contemporary legal battles, the sovereignty of Native American tribes has faced relentless erosion. This chapter examines the historical factors that have led to the curtailment of tribal rights, explores key modern challenges tribes face in dealing with federal and state regulations, and presents the strategies that tribes are adopting to defend their sovereignty in an increasingly complex legal landscape.

The Historical Erosion of Tribal Sovereignty

The erosion of tribal sovereignty is deeply intertwined with the United States' founding and expansionist endeavors. From the earliest interactions, treaties were meant to establish peace and recognize Native nations' rights to their lands. However, these treaties were often constructed under coercion, misrepresentation, or outright deceit. As settlers pushed westward, the very treaties designed to protect Native interests became mere relics—conveniently discarded when Indigenous lands were deemed valuable.

The Indian Removal Act of 1830 exemplified the U.S. government's disregard for the sovereignty of Native nations, resulting in the forced displacement of thousands of people along the infamous Trail of Tears (Prucha, 1986). This relocation was justified under the guise of "protecting" Native communities, while in reality, it facilitated the seizure of fertile lands by settlers and further diminished the ability of tribes to govern themselves.

The Dawes Act of 1887, also known as the General Allotment Act, sought to dismantle communal landholdings in favor of individual allotments. This policy eroded tribal land bases and attempted to forcibly assimilate Native people into mainstream American society by breaking down collective governance structures. The concurrent rise of Indian boarding schools added to this cultural assault, stripping Native children of their identity and community bonds (Deloria & Lytle, 1983). These developments laid a foundation for the systemic undermining of tribal sovereignty that continues to impact Native communities.

Modern Challenges:

State Encroachment on Tribal Rights: Taxation and Regulatory Overreach

States often attempt to stretch their authority into tribal affairs, challenging Native self-governance in ways that directly violate federal treaties and tribal autonomy. One frequent battleground is taxation. Whether through attempts to tax tribal casinos, cigarette sales, or energy enterprises, these moves force tribes into costly and protracted legal struggles.

A key example is Washington State Department of Licensing v. Cougar Den, Inc. (2019), where the Yakama Nation defended its right to transport goods tax-free across state lines based on its 1855 treaty. The U.S. Supreme Court sided with the tribe, affirming that treaty language must be interpreted based on how the tribal signatories understood it at the time (Washington State Department of Licensing v. Cougar Den, Inc., 2019).

Land and Water Rights Disputes

Legal battles over water rights pit tribal nations against both state governments and private interests. In Arizona, the Gila River Indian Community's decades-long fight for its rightful share of water culminated in the 2004 Water Settlement. Meanwhile, in McGirt v. Oklahoma (2020), the Supreme Court upheld that much of eastern Oklahoma remains legally designated as reservation land—reaffirming treaty obligations and tribal jurisdiction. Still, state backlash continues, raising alarm over the future of such hard-won legal victories (McGirt v. Oklahoma, 2020).

State Nullification of Tribal Rights

In some states, legislative and administrative policies conflict directly with federal protections. From voter suppression tactics, like North Dakota's 2018 ID law requiring physical street addresses, to efforts that restrict hunting, fishing, or sacred site access, these actions reflect a pattern of disregard for tribal rights. Tribes are often left to respond reactively, forced into constant defense.

Key Court Cases: Victories, Setbacks, and Ongoing Battles

Victories in Court: Upholding Tribal Sovereignty

United States v. Kagama (1886): Reinforced federal primacy in tribal affairs, preempting state interference (United States v. Kagama, 1886).
Bryan v. Itasca County (1976): Blocked state property taxes on reservation land absent congressional approval.
McGirt v. Oklahoma (2020): Confirmed that eastern Oklahoma remains tribal land per historical treaties.
Washington State Dept. of Licensing v. Cougar Den, Inc. (2019): Affirmed treaty rights regarding tax-free commerce across state lines.

Setbacks: The Erosion of Tribal Rights

Oliphant v. Suquamish Indian Tribe (1978): Denied tribes the right to prosecute non-Natives, weakening tribal justice systems.
Carcieri v. Salazar (2009): Limited land-into-trust authority for tribes recognized after 1934.

Adoptive Couple v. Baby Girl (2013): Undermined the Indian Child Welfare Act, threatening the preservation of Native families.

Strategies for Navigating and Defending Tribal Sovereignty

1. Legal Advocacy and Litigation
Organizations like the Native American Rights Fund (NARF) play a pivotal role in supporting tribal legal efforts. Strategic litigation helps set precedents that reaffirm treaty rights and limit overreach (Native American Rights Fund).

2. **Strengthening Intergovernmental Relations**
Tribes are increasingly forming MOUs, compacts, and cross-jurisdictional task forces with state and federal entities. These proactive steps reduce conflict and ensure cooperation while preserving tribal authority.

3. **Leveraging Public Support and Advocacy**
Coalitions with environmental, civil rights, and cultural preservation groups help tribes amplify their voices. Public awareness remains a vital tool in defending sovereignty.

4. **Developing Tribal Courts and Law Enforcement**
By expanding tribal courts and police authority, Native nations regain control over internal governance and improve justice outcomes. These investments reduce dependence on non-tribal systems that often fail to protect Native interests.

Conclusion

Navigating the labyrinth of federal and state regulations remains a significant challenge for Native American tribes. Yet amid the constant legal battles, policy conflicts, and jurisdictional disputes, tribal nations continue to assert their inherent sovereignty through strategy, resilience, and collective strength.

The struggle for sovereignty is far more than a legal question. It is the front-line of Indigenous survival, cultural continuity, and future prosperity. Understanding this dynamic is essential to building a future where Native self-determination is not just protected—it is empowered.

"To navigate the stormy waters of jurisdiction is to honor the past promises made in the treaties of old. It is to say that our sovereignty is not granted—it is inherent, as lasting and indomitable as the rivers that have always flowed through our lands."

Courtesy of Library of Congress - Pre 1929
[Coeur D'Alene man, Philip Wildshoe and family, in his Chalmers automobile]

"The struggle for Native sovereignty is not just about legal battles in the courts; it's about asserting our inherent rights to self-determination and protecting our lands, cultures, and communities from those who seek to diminish our power. Navigating federal and state regulations is not just a challenge—it's a daily act of survival and defiance."

Observations

Top Ten States Violating Tribal Rights

These states did not merely disagree with tribes — they **weaponized policy against sovereignty**. The pages that follow separate evidence from opinion: first, the record you can date and quote; then, the judgment you can argue with. *That is what accountability sounds like on paper.*

"Our treaties were promises carved in the bedrock of history, yet they have been worn down by the currents of prejudice and greed. It is our duty to remind the world that these promises, though weathered, are not broken. They are still ours — as enduring as the mountains that cradle our sacred lands."

Racism and the Repeated Violations of Treaty Obligations
Introduction
The relationship between Native nations and state governments has been shaped by a long legacy of **resistance, exploitation, and betrayal**. Despite federally recognized treaties affirming tribal sovereignty, many states continue to enact policies and enforce laws that directly undermine those agreements. These actions are not bureaucratic accidents — they are deliberate mechanisms of control, rooted in racism and designed to diminish Native self-governance.

This chapter identifies ten states that have consistently violated treaty obligations, obstructed sovereignty, and enacted discriminatory policies. Each record of violation exposes the ongoing struggle of Native nations to assert their rights, protect their lands, and preserve their identity in the face of relentless state encroachment.

1. Washington
 Key Violations:
Taxation Attempts: In *Washington State Dept. of Licensing v. Cougar Den, Inc.* (2019), the state attempted to impose a fuel tax on a Yakama-owned

business, despite an 1855 treaty protecting trade rights. The Supreme Court ruled for the Yakama, reaffirming treaty protections.

Fishing Rights Resistance: Even after the 1974 *United States v. Washington (Boldt Decision)* reaffirmed tribal fishing rights, the state resisted enforcement, particularly regarding salmon habitat restoration.

Racism in Policy:
Washington's regulatory overreach and selective enforcement reveal a deep-rooted structure of racism in state governance — one that prioritizes commercial interests and resource control over treaty law and ecological justice.

2. Oklahoma
Key Violations:
Oklahoma's record stands as a modern illustration of how a state can affirm sovereignty with one hand and erase it with the other.

In **2020**, the U.S. Supreme Court, in *McGirt v. Oklahoma*, affirmed the reservation status of the Muscogee (Creek) Nation, holding that state criminal jurisdiction is limited where Congress has not said otherwise. It was a rare moment when justice acknowledged the endurance of treaty boundaries long denied.

But by **2022**, the decision in *Oklahoma v. Castro-Huerta* reversed that progress, expanding state authority to prosecute non-Indians who commit crimes against Indians in Indian Country. The ruling reshaped the jurisdictional landscape, giving the state power where tribal sovereignty had finally been recognized.

Racism in Policy:
Rather than honor *McGirt* as a restoration of truth, Oklahoma's leadership sought to narrow its scope, lobbying Congress to restrict tribal jurisdiction and framing sovereignty as chaos. The state's posture was not neutrality — it was *encroachment dressed as order.* In the sterile language of legality, it sounded like administration; in reality, it was suppression masked as governance.

3. South Dakota
Key Violations:
Anti-Protest Legislation: Following Native-led pipeline protests, South Dakota enacted "riot-boosting" laws aimed squarely at Indigenous environmental activists opposing projects like Keystone XL (*Indigenous Environmental Network v. Noem*, 2019).

ICWA Violations: Native children remain disproportionately placed in non-Native homes, violating both the spirit and the letter of the *Indian Child Welfare Act* (NPR, 2011).

Racism in Policy:
By criminalizing protest and ignoring family protections, South Dakota weaponized law to silence Native resistance and fracture community identity — a modern form of control through fear and removal.

4. North Dakota
Key Violations:
Voter Suppression: The 2018 voter ID law disenfranchised Native voters by requiring street addresses many reservation residents lacked (*Brakebill v. Jaeger*, 2018).

Pipeline Suppression: During the 2016 Standing Rock protests, militarized state forces suppressed lawful assembly and violated treaty-protected land use (*Standing Rock Sioux Tribe v. U.S. Army Corps of Engineers*, 2016).

Racism in Policy:
North Dakota's voter laws and militarized tactics exposed a pattern of state-sponsored discrimination. The message was unmistakable: when Native people organize, the state answers not with dialogue but with deployment.

5. Arizona
Key Violations:
Water Rights Delays: Despite the 2004 Gila River Settlement, the state continues to obstruct equitable water distribution to tribes, stalling Native development.

Polling Access Issues: Persistent lack of polling locations and mail access on reservations restricts Native voter participation (*Navajo Nation Human Rights Commission*, 2020).

Racism in Policy:
Arizona's calculated delay tactics and administrative barriers reveal a landscape designed to mute Native voices — where access itself becomes the instrument of suppression.

6. California
Key Violations:
California's history of Native suppression is woven through law and bureaucracy alike.

In **1953**, *Public Law 83-280* imposed state criminal and civil jurisdiction on tribal lands without tribal consent — a unilateral act framed as efficiency but rooted in control. The law blurred the lines of sovereignty and replaced self-determination with state supervision.

Fifteen years later, the **1968 Civil Rights Act amendments** introduced a requirement for tribal consent on future PL-280 expansions. But it was too late. The change offered a promise for tomorrow but no remedy for the past. The original impositions stood, and the precedent of intrusion became a permanent fixture in California's treatment of Indian Country.

Racism in Policy:
California's selective jurisdiction and economic interference transformed "shared governance" into a system of managed subordination. The state called it partnership; tribes experienced it as hierarchy. What was framed as cooperation became the most enduring *instrument of control*.

7. Wisconsin
Key Violations:
Hunting Rights Rejected: The state has repeatedly challenged Ojibwe off-reservation hunting rights guaranteed under the 1837 and 1842 treaties.

Mining Conflicts: Projects like Gogebic Taconite advanced despite tribal opposition, threatening sacred lands and water sources.

Racism in Policy:
Wisconsin's preference for profit over promise reveals a pattern of environmental racism that values extraction over obligation, and industry over integrity.

8. Alaska
Key Violations:
Land Claims Manipulation: The 1971 *Alaska Native Claims Settlement Act* extinguished aboriginal land titles in exchange for corporate ownership structures that weakened traditional governance.

Jurisdictional Exclusion: The state continues to challenge tribal authority in child welfare and law enforcement (*John v. Baker*, 1999).

Racism in Policy:
Alaska's insistence on corporate identity over sovereign nationhood reflects a deeper denial of Indigenous existence — replacing governance with paperwork and culture with corporate charters.

9. Montana
Key Violations:
Water Compact Delays: The state's slow movement on the Confederated Salish and Kootenai Tribes' water compact demonstrates resistance to Indigenous control of natural resources.

Jurisdictional Barriers: State courts continue to encroach on matters reserved for tribal jurisdiction (*Montana v. United States*, 1981).

Racism in Policy:
Montana's obstructionism reveals the quieter machinery of colonialism — delay as denial, bureaucracy as a weapon.

10. Maine
Key Violations:
1979 Maine Indian Claims Settlement Act: Redefined tribes as "municipalities," stripping them of inherent sovereignty and limiting federal protections.

Resistance to Reform: The state continues to oppose federal amendments that would restore full sovereignty to the Wabanaki Nations.

Racism in Policy:
Maine's refusal to recognize tribal nationhood demonstrates how colonial frameworks still define modern governance. Sovereignty, in the eyes of the state, remains conditional — granted only when it serves its own interests.

Conclusion

Across these ten states, the pattern is unmistakable. From the Pacific to the Atlantic, the mechanisms of Manifest Destiny have merely changed their form — from bayonets and treaties to statutes and courtrooms. The language is now legal, the tone bureaucratic, but the intent remains familiar: **to manage, to restrict, to control.**

Every ruling, every law, every delay carries the same underlying message — that Native sovereignty is negotiable. Yet sovereignty is not a privilege; it is a birthright.

Until state governments reckon with the promises written into their own treaties and the prejudice woven into their institutions, the assault on tribal sovereignty will continue — not by conquest, but by design.

And so the fight remains: not for recognition, but for restoration. Not for favor, but for what was already promised — *and still belongs to the people who never surrendered it.*

"*The rivers of sovereignty run deep through Native lands, yet state hands have dammed, diverted, and polluted them in their quest to control what was never theirs. Our right to exist, to govern, and to thrive must no longer be seen as something to negotiate—it is inherent, as unyielding as the lands beneath our feet.*"

Emotional Costs of Native Leadership

"Healing is not a solitary path, especially for those who lead. It is a journey walked together—with ancestors behind us, community beside us, and future generations ahead. Only by tending to our own spirit can we light the way for others."

Mental Health and Emotional Toll

Introduction

Leadership in Indian Country is not simply about guiding policy or managing economic resources—it is a profound responsibility intertwined with the emotional and spiritual life of an entire people. Unlike mainstream political leadership, Indigenous leadership carries an additional burden: the weight of cultural survival, historical trauma, and the hopes of the community for a better future.

Tribal leaders are custodians of more than material resources; they are protectors of languages, traditions, and sacred knowledge passed through generations. They must carry the scars of history—the traumas of displacement, colonization, and forced assimilation—while facing contemporary challenges like poverty, systemic injustice, and the preservation of communal unity.

This chapter explores the mental health challenges Indigenous leaders face, the weight of historical trauma, and the pathways toward healing and support. In recognizing the emotional demands of leadership, we honor both the resilience required and the necessity for spaces of rest, reflection, and renewal.

The Mental and Emotional Burden of Leadership

To understand the emotional toll of leadership in Indian Country, we must recognize the spiritual expectations placed upon those who lead. Indigenous leaders are seen not just as administrators or policy-makers, but as the moral and cultural compass of their people. They must embody resilience, walk in the footsteps of their ancestors, and stay grounded in sacred values while navigating modern bureaucracies.

Many leaders are deeply affected by the same issues their communities face: poverty, limited access to health-care, and the lingering effects of historical trauma. They are expected to hold space for others' pain while often suppressing their own. The inability to show vulnerability, coupled with immense expectations, can lead to burnout, depression, anxiety, and spiritual fatigue.

Caught between traditional values and the demands of modern governance, Native leaders often navigate a cultural tightrope—honoring protocols and ceremonies while managing funding cycles, court rulings, and policy debates. The pressure is not only logistical but existential: the health of a nation rests on their shoulders, often at the cost of their own.

Historical Trauma and Its Impact on Leaders

Historical trauma is not just a legacy; it is a living presence in Indian Country. From boarding schools to land dispossession, the pain of the past echoes through families and leadership roles. Leaders must advocate for justice while healing the wounds that still bleed in their communities.

Colonization's violence—the suppression of language, culture, and identity—has fractured Indigenous mental health. Leaders often experience the same intergenerational trauma they seek to repair. They carry the expectation to restore what was stolen, even when they themselves are hurting. This spiritual exhaustion—the fatigue of constantly "being resilient"—can erode even the strongest among us (Kirmayer et al., 2014).

Without culturally grounded support systems, leaders can fall into isolation or despair. They may feel guilt for resting, or shame for needing help, especially when entire communities look to them for guidance. We must break this silence and acknowledge that leadership and vulnerability are not opposites—they are companions on the path to wellness.

Seeking Support and Building Resilience

The first step toward wellness for Indigenous leaders is recognizing that healing is strength. Mental health is not a flaw in one's leadership—it is part of leadership itself. Leaders need space to process, grieve, rest, and recover. And they need support systems that understand the unique pressures they carry.

Culturally relevant mental health resources are essential. Integrating traditional practices—talking circles, sweat lodges, songs, and ceremony—with therapeutic interventions creates a holistic path to healing. These models reflect the Indigenous worldview that sees mind, body, and spirit as interconnected. They honor the belief that healing cannot be compartmentalized—it must be woven into every aspect of life (Bassett et al., 2012).

Peer support networks can also ease the loneliness of leadership. Spaces where Indigenous leaders can speak openly, without judgment, create solidarity and reduce isolation. By sharing experiences, frustrations, and moments of healing, leaders affirm that they are not alone. In such spaces, resilience becomes collective.

Modeling Wellness for the Community

Leaders who tend to their own mental health model strength for their people. When a leader embraces healing, they give permission to others to do the same. By sharing their stories, participating in ceremonies, or simply naming their struggles, leaders dismantle the stigma surrounding mental health in Native communities.

Leadership grounded in wellness is transformative. It invites others to walk the path of healing with courage and pride. When leaders embody both strength and tenderness, they reshape what leadership looks like—not as unshakable authority, but as relational responsibility. Their courage to heal becomes a light for those still finding their way (Gone & Calf Looking, 2011).

The Role of Culture in Healing

Culture is not a relic of the past—it is a living medicine. When leaders support language revitalization, traditional knowledge, ceremonies, and land-based practices, they are not only preserving culture—they are healing themselves and their communities.

Programs that center traditional values—like language immersion schools, cultural workshops, and land stewardship—offer emotional grounding. They foster a sense of belonging, identity, and purpose. For many, reconnecting with these practices is a spiritual return home.

As leaders advocate for cultural revitalization, they embody the truth that healing does not mean forgetting. It means remembering who we are—and creating spaces where future generations can walk forward whole, not wounded (Gone, 2013).

Conclusion

The emotional and mental burden borne by Indigenous leaders is immense. It is shaped by the trauma of the past and the challenges of the present. Yet within this struggle lies the possibility of healing—not just for leaders, but for entire communities.

When leaders seek support, nurture their wellness, and reconnect with culture, they become vessels of resilience and renewal. Their strength is not in carrying everything alone, but in knowing when to pause, when to share the load, and when to light the way with stories of survival and healing.

"True leadership is not in denying our burdens but in carrying them with grace, and knowing when to set them down for a while. Only by tending to the fire within can we continue to keep the flames of hope alive for those who follow."

Community Accountability

"Leadership is a trust, not a privilege. As long as the people give you their confidence, you must walk the path of wisdom, rooted in the knowledge of our ancestors. It is not for your gain but for the well-being of the community that you carry the staff."

Balancing Tradition with Modern Expectations

Introduction

Effective leadership in Native American communities extends far beyond managing policy or resources—it is about embodying the spiritual, cultural, and communal wisdom of the people. In traditional Indigenous governance systems, leadership was not about hierarchy but about mutual responsibility and rootedness in the community. Yet in today's world, tribal leaders must navigate complex legal and bureaucratic structures while striving to remain accountable to the values of their people.

This chapter explores the necessity—and challenge—of balancing traditional systems of accountability with modern governance expectations. It illustrates how Native leaders can remain grounded in ancestral values while fulfilling contemporary roles, and why doing so is critical to maintaining trust, sovereignty, and cultural continuity.

Traditional Governance and Accountability

In Indigenous traditions, accountability was not abstract—it was lived. Leaders were chosen not for status but for character, wisdom, and dedication. Decision-making was communal, rooted in consultation with elders, spiritual leaders, and the broader community. Consensus, not authority, guided action (Cornell & Kalt, 2007).

Leadership was a lived relationship, not an isolated role. Leaders were deeply embedded in daily life. They shared the hardships of the people, celebrated in the same ceremonies, and were constantly visible. If a leader strayed from the values of the community, accountability was swift—through community dialogue, council deliberation, or even removal. There was no separation between governance and community—leaders were accountable through presence, participation, and tradition.

Challenges of Modern Governance

With the imposition of Western governance models came a shift. Constitutions, courts, and councils were introduced to facilitate tribal self-governance under federal recognition. These institutions were often modeled after non-Native systems, which prioritized formality, regulation, and hierarchy over relational leadership.

These modern structures can create distance between leaders and community members. The pressure to meet grant deadlines, manage intergovernmental negotiations, and comply with legal frameworks may push leaders into offices and boardrooms, away from ceremonies and councils of elders. Furthermore, the need for expedience often clashes with traditional processes that value patience, consensus, and inclusion (Wilkins & Lomawaima, 2001).

Leaders are often caught between two worlds: one demanding results and deliverables, and the other calling for spiritual rootedness and cultural alignment. The risk is not just inefficiency—it is disconnection from the very community one is supposed to serve.

Blending Tradition with Modern Governance

Across Indian Country, tribes are finding innovative ways to reclaim traditional accountability while honoring modern governance. Many communities now incorporate practices like Talking Circles, community feasts, and elder councils into formal governance structures. These gatherings ensure that leadership remains relational and participatory.

Elders, once sidelined by constitutional governance, are being reinstated into advisory roles. Their wisdom now informs decisions ranging from economic development to land stewardship. In doing so, tribes ensure that decisions reflect cultural values—not just political expedience (Cornell & Kalt, 2007).

Ceremonial integration also plays a powerful role. Opening council meetings with prayer or song reaffirms that governance is not secular—it is sacred. It reminds everyone present that decisions are not just legal—they are spiritual, cultural, and intergenerational.

The Role of Transparency and Accountability

Transparency is not a new concept to Native governance—it has always existed through relational presence. However, today's digital tools offer new ways to ensure openness. Streaming council meetings, publishing budgets online, and using social media for community updates allow leaders to remain visible and accessible.

When combined with traditional engagement—like roundtable talks or seasonal gatherings—these tools enhance trust. They allow community members, especially youth, to connect with their government in ways that are both modern and culturally resonant. A tweet from a tribal chair can spark dialogue; a Facebook post about land restoration can educate and unite.

This fusion of technology and tradition ensures that leadership remains open and grounded—answerable not only to regulations but to relationships (Wilkins & Lomawaima, 2001).

Balancing Power and Reciprocity in Leadership

In traditional systems, power was relational—it flowed from the people, not above them. Leaders were never untouchable—they were accountable through shared experience. Yet in modern governance, there's a risk of centralizing power in executive bodies, reducing the checks that once came naturally through daily connection.

To address this, many tribes have implemented community oversight boards, modeled after traditional councils. These bodies ensure that decisions reflect collective values and that no single person or institution dominates governance.

Reciprocity remains the antidote to overreach. Leaders who attend ceremonies, visit elders, and walk the same roads as their people are seen as legitimate. Their authority is renewed not through elections alone, but through continued presence and shared burdens. This is not performative leadership—it is relational accountability.

Conclusion

Balancing traditional accountability with modern governance is not easy—but it is essential. Tribal leaders must honor ancestral values while navigating today's political and administrative landscapes. Those who succeed in this balancing act are creating governance models that are not only efficient but spiritually and culturally resonant.

True leadership in Indian Country means being rooted in tradition while adaptable to change. It means wielding power with humility, transparency, and a deep sense of responsibility to those who came before and those yet to come.

"True leadership is a sacred contract with the people—an agreement not written on paper but etched into the spirit of the land and the hearts of the community. It demands a careful balance between holding power and being held by the people, a trust that grows only through shared responsibility and mutual respect."

"The strength of the community is in its roots, and just as a tree reaches upward by drawing from the earth, so too must leaders nourish their people by remaining connected to tradition while growing toward the future."

When the Enemy Looks Like Your Cousin

"The arrows in your back don't always come from outsiders. Sometimes they bear your last name."

Introduction

To work for your tribe is supposed to be the ultimate homecoming—a return of skill, spirit, and purpose. For many Native professionals, that dream is quickly shattered. In Indian Country, working for your own tribe often means walking a tightrope strung between loyalty and survival. And too often, that rope snaps.

This chapter examines the painful decision many Native executives, professionals, and technicians make: to serve other tribes instead of their own. Not out of betrayal—but out of necessity. It also confronts a dangerous myth baked into too many tribal governments—that the CEO of a tribal entity must be a tribal member, even when that belief causes lasting damage.

This is the story of internal exile—and the unspoken price we pay when we trade competence for comfort, and accountability for familiarity.

The Emotional Toll of Serving "Your Own"

When you work for your own tribe, your name walks in before you do. You're not just the grant writer. You're your auntie's niece. Your uncle's son. Your grandfather's shadow. You carry bloodline expectations—unspoken allegiances—and the bitter memory of old family feuds that never truly died.

If you try to rise on merit, you're "too good for us now." If you enforce policy, you're "targeting your own people." And if you don't play politics, you're "not a team player."

As one Native program manager put it:
"I worked harder for my tribe than I ever did for any non-Native employer. But it wasn't enough. I became a threat the moment I tried to hold someone accountable." (Wilkins and Stark)

A Safer Distance: Why Native Professionals Work for Other Tribes

In contrast, many Native professionals find clarity and peace working for other tribal nations. The cultural understanding remains. The mission still resonates. But the personal baggage is gone.

- They are judged by results, not relationships.
- Tribal councils respect their professional boundaries.
- Family politics don't follow them into every boardroom.

As one Native economic development officer said:
"I wanted to work for my own people. I tried. But every decision turned into a political fight. When I moved to another tribe, I finally got to do my job without fear." (Cornell and Kalt)

This isn't abandonment. It's triage. And it speaks volumes about what our professionals are escaping—and what we are failing to fix.

The Myth of the Tribal CEO

Among the most corrosive beliefs in tribal governance is this:
"Only a tribal member should lead a tribal business."

While born from a desire to protect sovereignty and preserve self-determination, this mindset has too often turned into a barrier against excellence. The principle sounds noble — *our people should lead our enterprises* — but when interpreted as exclusivity instead of empowerment, it cripples progress.

In practice, this belief results in the repeated hiring of **underqualified tribal members** over more competent Native—or even non-Native—executives. Tribal identity becomes the primary credential. Education, experience, and proven leadership take a distant second.

The result is predictable: a revolving door of leadership where new CEOs are hired to "fix" the failures of the last, only to inherit political interference, unrealistic expectations, and systemic constraints that ensure their eventual replacement. The average tenure of a tribal CEO rarely exceeds eighteen months. Some last less than a year. The damage, however, lasts much longer.

When Representation Hurts Results

Representation matters. Every Native community deserves to see its people in positions of leadership and influence. But **representation without competency** can destroy what representation was meant to protect.

Unqualified tribal CEOs — often appointed for loyalty rather than leadership — can unintentionally:
- Mismanage millions in federal or enterprise funds
- Undermine staff morale through indecision or favoritism
- Delay or derail long-term economic development projects
- Replace merit-based systems with cronyism and internal patronage
- Erode the tribe's reputation with partners, agencies, and lenders

Once trust is lost, it is difficult — sometimes impossible — to regain. Federal agencies become cautious. Banks raise their scrutiny. Private investors quietly walk away. Every failed leadership experiment makes the next opportunity harder to secure.

The Politics of Appointment

The tribal CEO is often treated less as a professional executive and more as a **political appointment.** In many tribal systems, council members feel compelled to hire "one of our own" to demonstrate loyalty to the people. What begins as cultural pride quickly turns into internal politics, where competence becomes secondary to connections.

Instead of being evaluated by measurable outcomes — growth, compliance, and sustainability — a CEO's success is often judged by **who they please** or **who they offend.** When tribal business is governed like tribal politics, the enterprise becomes hostage to election cycles rather than market cycles.

That is not sovereignty. That is self-sabotage.

The Cost of Inexperience

Every leadership failure carries an economic and cultural cost. When a CEO mismanages an enterprise, the consequences ripple outward:
- Jobs are lost.
- Credit ratings drop.

- Vendor trust evaporates.
- Federal grant oversight increases.
- Future leaders inherit crisis instead of opportunity.

Many tribes have cycled through multiple CEOs within a decade, each tasked with "turning things around." Each arrives to find limited authority, fragmented records, and political interference from council members who want control but not accountability.

Even the most competent executive cannot succeed under those conditions. The problem is not always the person in the chair — it is the system that refuses to let that chair have power.

Competence Is Not Cultural Betrayal

Hiring a qualified non-member is not a betrayal of sovereignty. It is an **exercise of it.** Sovereignty means the freedom to choose what is best for the nation — not to limit choice based on bloodline or last name. A nation confident in its identity should have no fear in hiring the best available leadership, Native or otherwise, to protect and grow its assets.

Many successful tribal enterprises have proven this:

Hiring outside professionals to stabilize finances, train local successors, and establish sound governance frameworks.

Implementing transition plans that move capable tribal citizens into leadership once the foundation is secure.

Building enterprises that outlive any one person — even the CEO.

That is not assimilation. It is **capacity building.**

The Path Forward

Tribes that thrive in modern economies balance identity with expertise. They build leadership pipelines instead of power circles. They define success by performance, not proximity.

The path forward requires a shift in mindset:

Leadership development must begin within. Tribes should invest in mentoring and training programs to prepare tribal citizens for executive roles.

Hiring should follow professional standards. Transparent job descriptions, fair interviews, and performance metrics protect both the tribe and the CEO.

Governance must separate politics from operations. Councils govern; executives manage. When those lines blur, failure is guaranteed.

The measure of sovereignty is not who signs the paycheck — it is whether the nation can sustain itself without dependence or dysfunction. Leadership chosen for loyalty may comfort the present. Leadership chosen for competence secures the future.

One council member from a Southern Plains tribe admitted anonymously:
"We changed CEOs three times in two years. Each time it was a tribal member. None had ever run a business. We just didn't want to be seen as hiring an outsider again. But now we're further behind than ever." (Miller)

The Economic Cost of Prioritizing Identity Over Ability
The damage isn't abstract—it's measurable.
- Delayed grant fulfillment = lost federal funding
- Failed business ventures = debt and missed job creation
- Executive churn = fractured team culture
- Project restarts = wasted time and budget
- Legal challenges = increased liability and insurance costs

In some cases, the cost of replacing competent leadership with unqualified insiders runs into the millions. More dangerously, it reinforces the idea that tribal systems cannot succeed without hand-holding—a lie used for generations to justify paternalistic oversight by federal agencies.

What We Must Do Differently

If tribal nations want to survive and thrive, we must:

- Break the silence around internal retaliation.
- Protect whistle-blowers and truth-tellers, especially when they are our own.
- Distinguish between cultural loyalty and professional capacity.
- Identity is not a substitute for experience.
- Create leadership pipelines.

If we want tribal members to lead, we must train and mentor them—before handing them the keys.

Let professionals lead.

Whether Native or non-Native, the CEO of a multimillion-dollar tribal business must be selected on merit, not blood.

Conclusion

There is no shame in choosing peace. No betrayal in stepping away from tribal employment to protect your purpose, your health, or your soul.

Sometimes, the people we return home to aren't ready to receive us. Sometimes, the wounds that shaped our communities are too raw to be healed from within. And sometimes, the only way to stay in the fight—is to step outside the fire.

Let's speak without flinching:
We have sacrificed too many of our strongest minds to tribal politics. And we will keep losing them—until we create systems where telling the truth doesn't cost you your future.

The enemy was never your cousin. But when the structure itself forces you to choose between silence and exile—then it's the system that's broken.

"This is the quiet proof behind everything in this book: That too often, the greatest threat to our progress isn't external.
It's us. And we don't even know we're doing it."

Economic Sovereignty and The Role of Leadership

"True sovereignty is not measured by wealth, but by the strength of a community's spirit and its ability to honor its past while shaping its future. Economic growth must serve the people, not the other way around."

Introduction

Economic sovereignty has become a cornerstone of Indigenous self-determination. The rise of Native-owned businesses, gaming enterprises, and diverse commercial ventures has enabled many tribes to reassert control over their economic futures.

But with opportunity comes obligation. Tribal leaders must navigate the complexities of modern commerce while remaining rooted in cultural responsibility, ensuring that prosperity enhances—not replaces—the values and traditions that define their people.

This chapter examines how leadership drives and sustains economic sovereignty in Indian Country, exploring strategies that balance financial success with cultural preservation, and highlighting the ethical dimensions of stewardship in a world shaped by both opportunity and history.

Economic Sovereignty and Self-Determination

For generations, federal policies stifled Indigenous economic independence, forcing reliance on government funds and fragmenting traditional economies. But in recent decades, many Native nations have transformed their trajectories. Through self-determined enterprise—gaming, agriculture, tourism, renewable energy, and beyond—tribes have reasserted control over how wealth is generated and shared.

Economic sovereignty goes far beyond income—it is the right to decide how resources are used, who benefits, and how the community's vision of well-being is defined and achieved. It represents the ability to reclaim agency after centuries of imposed dependency. And it demands leaders who can guide their nations with clarity, integrity, and balance (Cornell & Kalt, 2007).

Leadership in Economic Development

Effective economic leadership in Indian Country means looking beyond profit margins. Leaders must align commercial ventures with traditional values, ensuring development is not only profitable but purpose-driven.

Visionary leaders recognize that economic diversification is essential. While tribal gaming has yielded significant returns for many, it is not a universal solution. Leaders must weigh legal, social, and ethical factors before entering markets, asking how these ventures impact community cohesion and long-term goals. Increasingly, tribes are investing in technology, renewable energy, housing development, and education enterprises—fields that promote resilience and expand the pathways to self-reliance.

This kind of leadership requires fluency in both modern business and traditional knowledge. Those who succeed are not merely CEOs—they are cultural stewards, tasked with ensuring that each step forward reflects the identity and priorities of the people they serve (Wilkins & Lomawaima, 2001).

Balancing Economic Growth with Cultural Preservation

One of the greatest risks of economic success is cultural dilution. When business practices prioritize outside markets or external aesthetics, Indigenous identity can become commodified, or worse, marginalized.

Leaders must ensure that economic ventures reflect and reinforce tribal heritage. This might mean prioritizing Indigenous-owned supply chains, reinvesting profits into language revitalization programs, or embedding traditional ecological knowledge into environmental planning. It also means setting clear boundaries when external investors or state regulators push agendas that conflict with spiritual or cultural principles.

True prosperity in Indian Country is not measured solely in dollars, but in the preservation of language, ceremony, kinship, and land. Leaders must view culture not as a resource to be exploited but as the foundation upon which all development rests (Cornell & Kalt, 2007).

Sustainable Economic Strategies

Short-term gains can be seductive, especially in under-served communities facing urgent needs. But tribal leaders must think in generations, not quarters.

Sustainability means investing in infrastructure that endures—schools, broadband, health-care, housing—and in industries that respect land and culture. Renewable energy is a powerful example. From wind farms to solar installations, tribes are generating income while caring for the earth. These projects embody a traditional understanding of stewardship while preparing for a post-carbon economy.

Education is equally vital. Leaders who invest in workforce training and higher education ensure that future generations can take ownership of economic systems rather than being dependent on external expertise. Sovereignty is strengthened when a tribe can design, build, manage, and protect its own economic assets.

Sustainable leadership demands patience, discipline, and a clear vision for intergenerational equity (Wilkins & Lomawaima, 2001).

The Role of Accountability

Economic power without accountability leads to imbalance. Leaders must uphold transparency in all financial decisions. This includes regular audits, accessible reporting, and opportunities for community engagement and oversight.

Some tribes have created economic councils or community boards to oversee enterprise decisions, ensuring checks and balances and minimizing the risk of corruption or nepotism. Others require community approval for large-scale ventures, reaffirming the traditional role of collective input in matters that affect the whole.

Accountability also means safeguarding sacred resources. When development threatens burial sites, water systems, or ceremonial lands, leaders must resist profit-driven pressures and defend what is spiritually irreplaceable. True economic leadership is not transactional—it is relational, rooted in the shared responsibility of caring for the land, the people, and the ancestors.

Conclusion

Economic sovereignty is not the destination—it is the path. It offers tribes the tools to reclaim control, shape destiny, and heal from the harms of colonialism. But it also demands a kind of leadership that is rare in the corporate world: leadership that measures success in stories as much as spreadsheets, and that never forgets the heartbeat of the community.

When tribal leaders walk with humility, vision, and courage—grounded in both economic acumen and cultural integrity—they show that sovereignty is more than a legal status. It is a living practice.

"In the pursuit of progress, leaders must remember that the land, the people, and the traditions are inseparable. Without the wisdom of the past guiding the steps of the future, prosperity is empty and fleeting."

Outsiders on the Inside

"Not all colonizers wore uniforms. Some came with law degrees, consulting contracts, and the patience to wait until we invited them in."

The Quiet Colonization of Tribal Governance

Introduction

Colonization never ended. It just changed clothes. Today, the greatest threats to tribal sovereignty often come not with rifles or relocation orders, but with briefcases, legal pads, and federal lingo. While the front of tribal government may display Native faces, the backroom deals, policy drafts, and fiscal levers are too often operated by non-Native hands—quietly, skillfully, and with long-term consequence.

This is the quiet colonization of tribal governance—a systemic outsourcing of core decision-making power to those outside the community. Many of them are well-spoken, well-credentialed, and well-paid. Some began with good intentions. But whether by design or default, their presence now undermines the very autonomy our ancestors died to protect.

The Lawyers Who Became Lawmakers

In tribal governance, lawyers are necessary. But too often, they become unaccountable power centers, crafting laws that benefit themselves, delay reform, or ensure their permanent relevance. These attorneys—almost always non-Native—sit in on council meetings, interpret tribal codes, rewrite constitutions, and guide litigation strategies. But here's the truth: many of them do far more than "advise." They shape outcomes. They hold veto power disguised as legal counsel.

One Minnesota tribe found itself locked in a legal stranglehold after hiring a non-Native attorney in the 1990s to "modernize" their tribal code. Over time, this lawyer rewrote large sections of tribal law, insulated their firm with exclusivity clauses, and blocked younger Native paralegals from gaining access to case files. The council—most of whom lacked legal training—relied so heavily on the firm that they stopped making decisions without clearance.

When a newly elected chairperson pushed for an in-house legal department to train Native lawyers, the firm publicly questioned the tribe's capacity to manage its own affairs. The chair was voted out within a year. That attorney still serves the tribe (Wilkins and Lomawaima).

The Development Consultants Who Never Leave

In Indian Country, economic desperation is a revolving door—especially for consultants offering silver-bullet development plans. Some tribes hire them to unlock federal funding, write grant proposals, or craft long-term economic blueprints. But too many of these outsiders embed themselves indefinitely, shaping tribal policy from behind closed doors, earning six-figure incomes while insulating their methods from tribal oversight.

A southwestern tribe once hired a non-Native economic development group to draft a five-year diversification plan. The firm promised growth through renewable energy and federal grants. Three years in, no projects had broken ground, but the firm had billed nearly $1 million. When tribal members began to ask questions, the consultant's response was: "These things take time—you wouldn't understand the compliance process" (Treuer).

Here's the part they didn't want known: their contract automatically renewed each year unless the tribal council gave written notice by June 30. No such clause had ever been explained during the initial vote. One elder who tried to challenge the deal was labeled "divisive" by the consultant in internal emails later leaked by a whistleblower (Fenelon and Hall).

The Outsider Who Ran the Tribe

In a midwestern tribe of under 1,500 members, a former BIA administrator was hired to serve as an "interim executive advisor" while the tribe searched for a new general manager. That advisor quietly took over operations, restructured the tribal business board, and rewrote procurement policies—all under the claim of efficiency.

When council members raised concerns, they were told, "He's just helping us get through this transition." But within months, the advisor had placed himself on tribal banking accounts, added two non-Native colleagues to key positions, and moved the tribe's economic records to private servers the tribal IT department couldn't access.

By the time the council tried to remove him, he claimed whistleblower protections and filed a federal suit alleging retaliation. The tribe settled for over $300,000—and still hasn't recovered full access to its financial records (Cornell and Kalt).

Why This Keeps Happening

It's not just about money. It's about confidence, capacity, and a quiet form of internalized colonialism. Some tribal leaders—worn down by infighting, federal red tape, or sheer exhaustion—begin to believe they can't govern without outside help. That belief is poison. It turns councils into spectators. It reduces communities to clients.

And worse, it creates a cycle:

- New leaders come in promising reform.
- They're told, "You can't do this without our experts."
- So they rely on them.
- And become the next layer of defenders.

Breaking the Dependency

To reclaim governance, we must first see the colonizers wearing suits instead of uniforms.

- Tribal councils must audit outsider influence annually.
- Legal services should be time-limited, with transition plans to Native professionals.
- Cultural fluency—not just technical skill—must be a job requirement.
- Community education must lift the curtain on how decisions are truly made.

Sovereignty isn't just about external recognition—it's about internal control. If a policy is drafted by a firm in D.C., if budgets are managed by a non-Native CFO, if constitutional amendments are crafted by someone who's never set foot in ceremony—then the colonization never stopped. It just got smarter.

Conclusion

Outsiders do not belong in the driver's seat of Native nations. They do not belong behind the curtain, pulling the strings of governments they do not belong to and cannot fully understand. Expertise is not ownership. And assistance is not a license to rule.

True sovereignty begins when we stop handing over the pen and start writing our future ourselves.

Tribal Courts: When Justice Depends on Who You Know

"Where justice is blind, corruption wears regalia."

Introduction

The idea of tribal sovereignty often evokes pride—rightfully so. It represents centuries of survival, cultural preservation, and hard-won political identity. But sovereignty, without accountability, can become a shield for injustice. Nowhere is this more visible—and more dangerous—than in the workings of tribal court systems, where the promise of justice too often depends not on law or evidence, but on personal alliances, political favor, or family name.

While some tribal courts operate with integrity, training, and fairness, many others are plagued by internal conflicts of interest, inadequate judicial oversight, or outright political interference. And for those who live on the wrong side of the tribal power structure, seeking justice can feel like entering a courtroom where the verdict was whispered before the gavel ever dropped.

Courts of Culture or Courts of Control?

In theory, tribal courts exist to enforce tribal law, protect sovereignty, and reflect Indigenous values. In practice, however, many tribal courts operate more like arms of the tribal council or executive office—where judges are appointed based on loyalty, kinship, or campaign support, and legal decisions are quietly manipulated behind closed doors (Melton).

One woman in North Dakota tried to bring a domestic violence complaint against a tribal police officer. Her case never made it to trial. The court administrator was the officer's cousin. The tribal prosecutor declined to file charges, citing "insufficient tribal interest." The victim was later warned by a relative on council to "drop it and move on—nobody wins in court unless they're supposed to." She left the reservation a month later.

The Appointment Problem

Most tribal judges are not elected. They are appointed by tribal councils or executives—sometimes indefinitely. Few tribes have judicial nominating commissions or independent bar associations to vet candidates. This means that judges are often political appointees, expected to serve those who put them in place (Goldberg).

In one Southern Plains tribe, the chief judge was a respected elder with decades of experience. But when he ruled against the council in a contract dispute—ordering them to release financial documents to a group of petitioning tribal members—he was removed within a week. His replacement had no legal background but was the chairman's former campaign manager.

Cases challenging tribal leadership or connected families suddenly stopped appearing on the docket.

The Gavel with No Weight Behind It

And it goes deeper than political loyalty. In far too many tribal court systems, judges aren't just appointed for who they know—they're appointed without the qualifications that make a judge worthy of the bench (NAICJA).

In some tribes, a person who has just completed their Juris Doctorate—no bar license, no courtroom experience, no prior legal work—is appointed as a judge. No mentorship, no case history, no trial record. Sometimes, they haven't even read the tribal code beyond the parts they Googled (Goldberg; Bernstein).

Their single strongest qualification? They're a tribal member.

And that's supposed to be enough.

But it isn't.

Justice doesn't flow from blood quantum. It flows from preparation, legal understanding, ethical clarity, and the courage to stand firm against power when it's wrong. Appointing someone without meaningful legal experience to oversee criminal, civil, or family law decisions is not cultural empowerment—it's structural failure (Melton).

What does that mean for those who stand before the bench? It means they face a process where the odds are stacked not just by who they are—but by whether the person in the robe knows how to read a motion, follow a rule of evidence, or even stay awake during testimony.

And it creates generational harm. Because if someone goes to court and feels betrayed by the very system that was supposed to protect them, they don't just lose a case—they lose faith. Faith in tribal government. Faith in sovereignty. Faith in us.

Worse yet, these unqualified appointments are often hidden behind the language of empowerment. "We're giving our people opportunity," some councils say. But opportunity without readiness isn't empowerment. It's political cover. And it's the vulnerable who pay the price.

There is no honor in handing someone a gavel if they don't understand the weight it carries.

Justice for Some: The Inequality of Access

In many tribal communities, whether or not your case is heard—or how it's decided—depends on who you are. Tribal council members and their families rarely face legal consequences, while ordinary citizens are fined, silenced, or denied basic due process.

In 2022, a young man from a Great Lakes tribe was banned from tribal housing and denied services after a misdemeanor marijuana charge. Meanwhile, a council member's son, arrested with methamphetamine and illegal firearms, was sent to a rehab retreat paid for by tribal funds. Both cases were heard by the same judge. Only one got leniency.

And everyone on the reservation knew why.

No Recourse, No Appeal

In federal or state court systems, there are layers of oversight: appeal courts, judicial review boards, judicial ethics commissions. But tribal courts are often final—and absolute. For most cases, there is no higher authority to turn to. If your tribal court fails you, you are done. You cannot appeal to state courts. You cannot petition the federal system, unless your constitutional rights have been severely violated—and even then, you face enormous legal hurdles due to the sovereign immunity of the tribe (Washburn).

The result is a closed system, where power can be abused with impunity.

The Silence of the Bar

Few Native lawyers speak publicly about this corruption. Most are either employed by tribal governments, dependent on tribal court contracts, or working for firms that fear retaliation. Speaking out means losing business—or worse, losing enrollment status, housing, or access to services. And so, the silence grows.

As one tribal attorney privately put it:

"I've watched judges change rulings based on who walked in the room. But if I say that out loud, I'll never work again." (Deer)

Federal Oversight? A Double-Edged Sword

Calls for external oversight are fraught with risk. The moment tribes lose control of their courts, sovereignty takes a hit. But what happens when that sovereignty is used to deny justice rather than defend it?

The 2013 Violence Against Women Reauthorization Act gave tribes jurisdiction over non-Native perpetrators of domestic violence (GAO). It was a win—but only if courts are fair. If tribal courts are compromised, then jurisdiction becomes a tool of political revenge or selective enforcement, rather than justice. And non-Native defendants can—and do—challenge tribal verdicts in federal courts, citing bias, lack of transparency, or kangaroo court conditions.

The result is a fragile trust—one incident away from collapse.

A Way Forward: Sovereignty with Standards

Tribal courts must not be exempt from reform. Sovereignty should not mean silence. What reform looks like:
- Independent judicial selection commissions
- Fixed terms for judges and clear removal procedures
- Publication of court decisions and public access to rulings
- Mandatory legal training and tribal law certification for judges
- Ethics boards composed of community members, not council insiders
- Creation of inter-tribal appellate courts to handle high-stakes appeals outside the grasp of local politics

These changes don't weaken sovereignty. They legitimize it. They protect it. Because the strongest sovereignty is not built on unchecked power, but on trust, transparency, and justice.

Conclusion

There is no sovereignty without justice. And there is no justice when decisions depend on bloodlines, alliances, or fear. If our courts cannot protect our people—if our judges serve politics instead of principle—then we must stop pretending that justice is being served at all. What we permit, we normalize. What we normalize, we become.

The time to speak up is now—before every courtroom becomes just another tribal casino: full of illusion, rigged behind the curtain, and profitable for only a few.

A sovereign court that fears the truth is no different than a colonizer's court—just wearing different beads."

Observations

Voices Silenced: Media and the Tribal Gag Order

"Free speech may be written into our constitutions, but it rarely makes it into our council chambers."

Introduction

Tribal nations have survived centuries of forced silence—from boarding schools that cut out tongues, to federal agents who erased Native voices in reports and policies. But today, the silencing often comes from within.

In many tribal communities, those who speak out against corruption, mismanagement, or injustice find themselves isolated, targeted, or erased. The suppression of free expression—whether through tribal-run media, gag policies, or unofficial retaliation—is not a relic of colonialism. It is a current form of internal control.

While sovereignty is sacred, its misuse becomes dangerous when it muzzles dissent and punishes truth. This chapter explores how tribal governments—whether consciously or not—maintain media environments where truth is edited, whistle-blowers are exiled, and the approved narrative becomes the only voice allowed.

Tribal-Run Media: Controlled by the Council

Many tribes operate their own newspapers, radio stations, newsletters, and online platforms. In theory, this allows Indigenous communities to tell their own stories without outside distortion. In practice, however, many tribal media outlets are directly funded and governed by the very leaders they are meant to report on.

In one Plains tribe, the editor of the tribal newspaper was fired after running a front-page story on misallocated housing funds. The council chair called the article "divisive," and the next issue contained a full-page spread defending the tribe's fiscal transparency. The reporter? She was banned from entering the tribal office without written permission from the executive director.

A 2019 study by the Native American Journalists Association found that more than 60% of tribal journalists surveyed had been censored, reassigned, or dismissed for reporting on tribal government actions (NAJA).

Gag Orders Disguised as Policy

Many tribal employees are required to sign confidentiality agreements—a common practice in any government setting. But in Indian Country, these agreements are often vague, overreaching, and weaponized.

A former health clinic manager in the Southwest was disciplined for posting on her private Facebook account about delayed elder medications. Her employment contract prohibited "unauthorized communication about tribal affairs." She was given the choice: take down the post and sign a revised nondisclosure policy—or resign.

She resigned.
Her silence became permanent.

Other tribes adopt informal "gag rules" during election seasons. Employees are told not to comment on politics. Contractors are warned not to "undermine community unity." And tribal citizens who publicly criticize leadership find themselves denied housing applications, cultural travel funds, or speaking time at meetings.

Silencing Through Retaliation

The most common—and most effective—form of media control is retaliation. Those who speak out are not always fired. Sometimes, they are just made to disappear.

- A language instructor in Oregon was reassigned from youth outreach to janitorial duty after testifying about nepotism in a tribal grant application.
- A cultural preservation officer in Alaska had her department budget slashed by 40% after she refused to alter an environmental report for a politically favored development project.
- A tribal member in New Mexico who started a podcast about local politics found himself removed from three advisory boards within six months. When he filed a complaint, he was told, "You're just stirring up trouble."

None of them had broken any law. They had simply spoken.

The Self-Censorship Spiral

Perhaps the most damaging consequence of these internal gag orders is the culture of self-censorship they create. When enough people are punished for speaking out, the rest stop trying. Entire communities learn to remain silent—not out of fear of jail, but fear of social, political, or economic punishment.

This form of control is harder to see. There are no official orders, no bars on the windows—just the quiet withdrawal of truth from public space. As one former tribal journalist noted,

"They didn't have to kill the paper. They just taught us not to write anything worth reading" (Kovac).

When Speaking Becomes Resistance

Despite these risks, many Native voices continue to rise. Independent newsletters, digital zines, social media pages, and grassroots podcasts are pushing back against the tribal information blackout. These citizen-driven platforms are restoring press freedom where institutional journalism has failed.

But they face uphill battles:

- Denied access to meetings
- Excluded from public notices
- Threatened with legal action
- Shunned by relatives aligned with tribal leadership

The cost of truth is high. And it's being paid by the very people sovereignty was meant to protect.

A Call for Press Sovereignty

If tribal governments are to be truly sovereign, they must also be accountable. And that accountability begins with a free and protected press.

What tribes must do now:
- Enact media independence policies that protect editors and journalists from political interference
- Establish public information laws ensuring access to financial reports, resolutions, and council minutes

- Create ombudsperson roles or citizen boards to handle media censorship complaints
- Encourage tribal youth to pursue journalism—not as a tool of compliance, but of cultural vigilance

True sovereignty does not fear criticism.
It invites it, wrestles with it, and grows because of it.

Conclusion

Our ancestors fought for our right to speak. To pray. To gather. To be. If today's tribal governments silence those voices in the name of unity, they are not preserving culture—they are protecting power.

No sovereignty is sacred if it silences truth. No nation is strong when its people whisper behind closed doors. A tribe without free speech is not a nation. It is a corporation with regalia.

"We were once punished for speaking our language. Now we are punished for speaking our truth."

Consultation or Coercion? Theater of Listening

"They call it consultation. We call it déjà vu. Because every meeting feels like a rerun of a show we never wrote the script for."

Introduction

For decades, the federal government has publicly championed its "government-to-government" relationship with Native American tribes. Central to this relationship is the concept of consultation—a process intended to ensure that tribal voices are not just heard, but respected in federal decision-making.

Yet in practice, consultation often functions more as performance than partnership. What is presented as respectful dialog too frequently becomes a staged ritual, where federal agencies nod politely, take notes, and then proceed as planned (Echo-Hawk, 2013).

The Illusion of Inclusion

Federal consultation processes are mandated by executive orders such as Executive Order 13175 (2000), which requires federal agencies to engage in "regular and meaningful consultation and collaboration" with tribal governments (Federal Register).

In theory, this order ensures tribal participation in decisions that impact their lands, resources, and people. But most tribal governments know the truth—consultation is often initiated after key decisions have already been made.

The Dakota Access Pipeline (DAPL) controversy stands as a prime example. The Standing Rock Sioux Tribe argued that they were not meaningfully consulted before pipeline construction began near their reservation.

Despite raising concerns over water quality and sacred lands, the U.S. Army Corps of Engineers moved forward with the project.

Subsequent legal rulings and protests confirmed that consultation, in this case, was perfunctory and non-binding (Earthjustice, 2016).

A One-Way Dialog

Many tribal leaders report that federal consultation meetings often consist of scripted presentations, followed by limited Q&A sessions that result in no meaningful policy changes. According to a Government Accountability Office (GAO) report, tribal officials expressed frustration with consultation processes that lacked transparency, had inconsistent protocols, and appeared to be conducted solely to meet legal requirements—not to obtain or respect tribal input (GAO Report 19-22).

This symbolic engagement has also led to "consultation fatigue." Tribal governments receive constant requests for comment on regulatory changes, environmental assessments, and administrative proposals—frequently under tight deadlines and without necessary context or funding. This burden highlights the structural imbalance in the relationship: tribes are expected to respond reactively, while federal agencies maintain control over timelines and outcomes.

When "No" Doesn't Mean No

Perhaps the most damning evidence of the consultation process's impotence is that tribal objections rarely alter final decisions. Whether the topic is oil drilling on sacred lands, reductions in environmental protections, or changes to health care delivery, Native opposition is often documented and then ignored.

A prominent example occurred during the Trump Administration's reduction of Bears Ears National Monument. Despite vocal opposition from the five sovereign tribes who co-managed the monument, the federal government unilaterally shrank the protected area by 85%—one of the largest reductions in U.S. history (The Washington Post, 2017). This action made clear that consultation does not equate to consent, nor does it necessarily influence federal decision-making.

Towards a True Partnership

To transition from symbolic participation to genuine partnership, several reforms must be enacted:

- Consent, not just consultation: True tribal sovereignty demands the right to approve or reject decisions affecting tribal lands and people. The U.N. Declaration on the Rights of Indigenous Peoples, which the U.S. has endorsed, affirms the need for "free, prior and informed consent" (UNDRIP, 2007).
- Equity in time and resources: Tribes must be given adequate notice, background information, and funding to engage in consultations effectively. Anything less perpetuates systemic imbalance.
- Enforceable accountability: Federal agencies must be legally accountable when they fail to meaningfully incorporate tribal input. Oversight, transparency, and public reporting should be non-negotiable.
- Recognition of tribal sovereignty: Tribes are not stakeholders; they are sovereign governments. Consultation must reflect this reality—not treat tribes as interest groups.

Conclusion

The federal government's consultation framework is, too often, a polished mask covering the face of coercion. Until tribal sovereignty is not only respected in words but upheld in actions, the promise of consultation remains hollow.

"Don't tell us we were consulted when we were only informed. Don't invite us to speak if you've already written the ending. If you want a real relationship, start by listening when it matters, not after it doesn't."

Observations

Before we can rebuild tribal governance, we must remember what it once was, understand how it was broken, and define what it must become. The following three chapters form the circle of that understanding. They are not simply reflections on history or politics — they are the blueprint of restoration. Governance Before the Council recalls how leadership once flowed from kinship, ceremony, and shared duty. Rebuilding After the Council exposes how imposed systems rewired the Native mind to mistake authority for power. And Restoring the Circle offers the path forward — a model for governance that honors tradition while surviving in the modern world. Together, these chapters return the story of tribal leadership to where it began — in balance, in spirit, and in truth. And, yes I know, your concept of how it was and should be will differ--

Governance Before the Council

Long before the white man drew lines on maps and called them nations, the peoples of this continent governed themselves with a balance of wisdom, humility, and communal responsibility unmatched in modern systems. There were no corporate boards, no constitutions written in foreign tongues, no presidents or vice-chairs. Yet there was order — and it worked.

Indigenous governance was rooted not in power, but in relationship. Authority flowed from kinship and consent, not elections or salaries. Leaders were measured by integrity, generosity, and the ability to maintain harmony, not by their campaign slogans or how many votes they could count. In nearly every Indigenous society, leadership was *earned* — never appointed.

The Way It Was

Across the continent, governance took many forms, yet all were built on the same foundation: accountability through relationship. Among the Haudenosaunee Confederacy, the council of sachems governed through consensus guided by clan mothers who held the power to appoint and remove them (Haudenosaunee Confederacy Chiefs Council). Among the Lakota, leadership was distributed among akíčhita (war leaders), wakíčhiyuhapi (civil leaders), and itȟáŋčhaŋ (chiefs), each respected for different strengths (Participedia).

The Ojibwe organized themselves through clan systems — doodem — that functioned as both social network and governing structure. Every clan carried distinct responsibilities: the crane and loon for leadership, the fish for wisdom, the bear for defense and medicine, the marten for warriors, the deer for kindness. No single clan ruled; decisions required balance and consensus (Tribal College Journal).

Most nations did not rely on majority rule but on *agreement*. Debate could last for days, even weeks, until consensus emerged. The process was slow, but the outcome was unity — and that unity held because no one was forced to submit to a will they had not accepted. In this world, governance was an act of listening.

There were no "terms of office." A leader served at the pleasure of the people. Lose the trust of your community, and your influence disappeared with it. Leadership could not be inherited through bloodline alone; it was carried in character, proven through behavior, and reaffirmed daily by service.

The Way It Became

Colonial policy destroyed these systems by design. The United States government never intended tribes to remain sovereign — it intended them to be manageable. The Indian Reorganization Act of 1934 forced Indigenous nations to adopt Western frameworks: written constitutions, elected councils, and presidents (Treaties Matter).

These new "tribal councils" were modeled on city governments, not clan societies. Authority that once flowed horizontally through kinship lines was now vertical — concentrated in a handful of elected officials. Elder councils and clan leaders who once guided decisions through spiritual balance found themselves sidelined, their legitimacy reduced to "advisory" status.

Elections introduced politics where there had once been purpose. Campaigning replaced consensus. The voices of the old ones — who carried history and context — were drowned out by procedural votes and parliamentary rules. Leadership became temporary, transactional, and too often tribal in the smallest sense of the word — divided along factions, bloodlines, and popularity contests.

Federal agencies encouraged this transformation because it created predictability and control. The Bureau of Indian Affairs could negotiate with a council president far more easily than with a community guided by twenty interdependent clans. The cost was devastating: traditional accountability evaporated, and corruption found fertile ground. Leaders were now accountable to election cycles and federal checkbooks, not to kinship and the Creator.

The Consequences

Modern tribal councils rarely represent the spiritual and communal governance they replaced. They have become miniature replicas of the governments that once sought to erase them — obsessed with hierarchy, procedure, and power.

Where once a leader served until the people's trust faded, now an election ends that trust every two or four years. Where once decisions required unity, now they require only a quorum. Where once leadership was a sacred duty, it has become an occupation.

The results are predictable: short tenures, fractured councils, stalled projects, nepotism, and a cycle of instability that prevents long-term planning. Every election resets progress. Every disagreement becomes personal. The council chambers, modeled after city halls, rarely echo with the laughter or songs that once filled council fires.

The most damaging loss, however, is *spiritual accountability*. In traditional systems, leadership carried moral consequence. To misuse authority risked not just reputation, but harmony with the natural and spiritual world. Under Westernized systems, that bond is severed. Ethics are replaced with policy manuals. Responsibility is measured by compliance, not by conscience.

The Illusion of Modernization

The "modern" council system is often defended as proof that tribes have entered the twenty-first century — that we are organized, efficient, and recognizable to non-Native governments. But resemblance to the colonizer's structure is not progress; it is proof of assimilation.

The very councils designed to restore "self-governance" have, in many cases, shackled it. They breed competition instead of cohesion, and their bureaucratic nature stifles the very creativity and community decision-making that once made Indigenous societies resilient. Federal systems of recognition still reward tribes for compliance with the same standards that broke them: paperwork over people, hierarchy over harmony.

Why It Isn't Working

The problem isn't that Native people can't govern — it's that they are forced to govern inside a model never built for them. A circle of kinship has been replaced by a rectangle of offices. Elders have been replaced by administrators. Sacred fires have been replaced by fluorescent lighting.

The council model isolates leadership from community. It teaches young people to seek positions of power, not roles of service. It defines success by budgets and grants, not by balance and wellbeing. Most tragically, it divides communities that once defined themselves by unity.

Some tribes have recognized this and begun restoring elder councils, clan representation, and traditional decision-making alongside modern administration. These are the beginnings of a return — not to the past, but to wisdom.

The Path Back

To rebuild governance that truly reflects Indigenous values, tribes must stop chasing Western validation and start reclaiming Indigenous legitimacy. That does not mean abandoning legal structures; it means infusing them with cultural truth.

Bring back the circle. Bring back the elder voices. Let decisions be tested not just by policy, but by principle. If a resolution violates harmony, it should fail — no matter how efficient it seems.

True sovereignty isn't granted through constitutions written by lawyers; it's lived through systems designed by the people they serve.

When Native governance once again reflects Native values, tribal governments will stop collapsing under the weight of imported systems. And when that happens, Indigenous nations will no longer need to prove to anyone that they can lead — they always could.

Rebuilding After the Council:

The Unlearning of the Modern Indian Mind

It is one thing to lose a way of governing. It is another to forget why that way mattered.

Our ancestors built societies upon principles so balanced that even the most powerful among them bowed to the will of the people. Decisions were made in circles, not corners. Leadership meant accountability, not authority. Every voice mattered — not because of equality, but because of kinship.

Then came the councils. The elections. The modern mind. And with them, a quiet tragedy: Native people began thinking like the governments that once conquered them

The Inherited Corruption of Thought

When I speak of corruption, I do not mean greed alone. I mean something deeper — the slow erosion of values that guided Indigenous governance for millennia. The transformation wasn't natural; it was engineered.

The boarding schools, the missionaries, the Indian Reorganization Act — each was a tool, designed to dismantle not just tribal economies or landholdings, but the mental frameworks that made true sovereignty possible. Colonization didn't stop at the skin; it seeped into the mind.

Generations grew up believing that written constitutions were more legitimate than oral law. That democracy meant majority rule instead of collective unity. That titles like "President" or "Chairman" carried more meaning than names given by one's clan or community.

This is how colonization wins without firing a shot: by convincing the conquered that their conqueror's ways are superior.

Today, even our elders — the very ones who survived the early storms — carry this inherited thinking. Not by choice, but by necessity. They were forced to adapt in a world that punished traditional thought and rewarded imitation. And now, too many tribal leaders defend a system designed to domesticate them, not liberate them.

The Mirage of Progress

Drive past any tribal administration building in America, and you'll see the same picture: manicured lawns, government SUVs, and glass doors etched with the word sovereignty. Inside, you'll find meetings governed by Robert's Rules of Order — a colonial invention — and agendas shaped more by grants and audits than by ceremony or consensus.

We call this progress.

But it isn't. It's performance.

The council system has taught us to value compliance over wisdom, procedure over purpose. It rewards quick answers, short terms, and political loyalty. The result is predictable: chaos disguised as democracy.

Every two or four years, tribal elections reset decades of work. Projects stall, directors change, and loyalty replaces merit. Federal agencies — who designed this system — sit back and smile, knowing that tribes will always be too busy fighting each other to truly challenge the structures that keep them dependent.

We have become prisoners in our own boardrooms.

The Necessary Unlearning

To rebuild, we must first unlearn.

- Unlearn the myth that being modern means being Western.
- Unlearn the lie that sovereignty requires structure borrowed from someone else's government.
- Unlearn the falsehood that economic success equals cultural survival.
- Unlearning is not rebellion — it is recovery.

The first step is honesty. We must say, aloud and without shame, that many of our so-called "traditional" systems today are not traditional at all. They are hybrids built from survival, not choice. The council model is not a reflection of Native intelligence — it is a symptom of colonization's success.

The next step is education. True cultural revival requires political literacy. We must teach our youth not just language and ceremony, but how those things once guided governance. Every clan, every council fire, every treaty meeting had moral structure because the people understood their duties to each other, the land, and the Creator.

Until we rebuild that moral framework, new councils will continue to make old mistakes.

Healing the Leadership Mind

If colonization fractured the Native mind, then leadership is where the cracks show first. Too many tribal executives today act like corporate managers — efficient, authoritative, disconnected. They mimic the posture of colonial power while claiming to defend sovereignty.

True leadership begins where ego ends. It isn't about control. It's about guardianship.

A real leader asks not, "How much authority do I have?" but, "How many people trust me to use it well?"

The path forward is to retrain leaders to think relationally again. That means:

Re-establishing the role of elders as moral anchors, not political ornaments.

Reviving clan and family consultation before major decisions.

Creating mentorship pipelines so young people learn leadership as a form of service, not status.

Embedding spirituality into governance, not as ceremony at the beginning of meetings, but as the measure of whether decisions are in harmony with life.

Leadership must once again be sacred work. Without that, no amount of training or funding will save us.

The Hybrid Future — Tradition in Modern Form

We cannot — and should not — attempt to return to a world before contact. The tools of the present can serve the spirit of the past, if wielded wisely. The solution isn't rejection of modernity, but integration of memory.

We can build hybrid governance models that honor tradition while meeting modern realities:

Councils guided by Elder or Clan Advisory Circles, with authority to review and guide policy.

Elected officials required to complete cultural governance education before taking office.

Leadership evaluations based not on popularity, but on community wellbeing metrics.

Constitutions amended to reflect traditional decision-making values — consensus, kinship, accountability, and balance.

This isn't romantic idealism; it's restoration. It's rebuilding the bridge between who we were and who we must become.

From Victims to Architects

The hardest truth is that colonization didn't only steal — it taught. It taught us how power works. It taught us how systems can control minds. Now, if we are wise, we can use that knowledge to design something stronger than what was taken.

We can build governments that reflect Native identity, not federal templates.

We can train tribal members who speak the language of federal compliance — and then rewrite the rules to fit our world.

We can outgrow dependence by mastering the systems that were built to contain us, and bending them to our will.

But that will only happen when we stop confusing Native faces in colonial offices with Native governance.

Our future depends on the courage to break that illusion.

The Sacred Work of Remembering

Rebuilding after the council isn't just political — it's spiritual. The true battle is not for offices, contracts, or recognition. It's for the Native mind itself.

The mind must be decolonized before the system can be. That means teaching a new generation that leadership is not a ladder, but a circle; that sovereignty is not a slogan, but a relationship; and that the future cannot be inherited — it must be built, with memory as mortar.

We will know we have succeeded not when our councils look traditional, but when our people think traditionally again — when decisions are made from wisdom, not from fear of losing power.

"We can't restore what was lost by pretending nothing changed. We rebuild by remembering what never should have been lost."

Observations

Restoring the Circle:

A Framework for the Next Generation of Tribal Governance

It begins where all things began — in the circle.

The circle is not only a symbol of unity; it is a model of governance. It has no head, no tail, no top, and no bottom. Every point holds equal distance from the center, yet every point depends on the others for its shape. That is how Indigenous nations once governed — through interdependence, accountability, and continuity (Alfred, Peace, Power, Righteousness).

If *Governance Before the Council* showed how we once led, and *Rebuilding After the Council* revealed what was broken, then this chapter is about what must come next. This is the path forward — not a return to the past, but a restoration of balance in the modern world.

The Circle as Governance

Before colonization, the circle governed everything: councils, ceremonies, stories, and time itself. It represented continuity — the idea that decisions made today ripple into generations yet unborn. When tribes adopted the Western model of hierarchy, they broke that circle into a pyramid. At the top stood a few; at the base, the many. What was once shared became hoarded (Borrows, Recovering Canada).

To restore the circle, tribes must design systems that distribute authority without dissolving accountability. Power must move through relationships, not rest above them. Every decision must pass through the fire of community consensus, moral reflection, and long-term consequence (Participedia, Consensus-Based Decision Making).

A reformed Indigenous governance model must therefore answer three questions before it answers any motion or resolution:

Does this decision honor our people?
Does it honor the land?
Will it still honor both a hundred years from now?

Redefining Sovereignty

Sovereignty is not the right to mimic another government. It is the power to define how we live, think, and lead. Too many tribal governments have traded that definition for recognition — building bureaucracies that satisfy federal oversight but starve cultural integrity (Deloria, Custer Died for Your Sins).

True sovereignty must be rooted in functional independence: the ability to feed, educate, govern, and defend a people without waiting for permission or payment from another. Sovereignty without self-sufficiency is symbolism.

To restore genuine sovereignty, tribes must shift from reactive governance — answering federal requirements — to proactive governance — designing systems that reflect Indigenous worldviews while meeting modern obligations. That balance is possible only through cultural architecture, not policy mimicry (University of Victoria, Roots of Indigenous Governance Assessment Tool).

Principles for the Next Generation of Governance

If the old systems of councils fractured the circle, then the next generation must rebuild it with these principles as the frame (Alfred, Wasáse: Indigenous Pathways of Action and Freedom; Simpson, As We Have Always Done):

1. Consensus over Majority.

Majority rule is efficient but divisive. Consensus rule is slower but unifying. The process is as sacred as the decision itself (Participedia, Consensus-Based Decision Making).

2. Service over Status.

Leadership is not a promotion; it is a burden of guardianship. Positions must be filled by those who seek duty, not prestige.

3. Elders as Moral Compass, Not Ceremony.

Elder councils must hold constitutional weight — able to review and reject actions that violate cultural ethics (Tribal College Journal, The Native American Leadership Model).

4. Economic Sovereignty as a Governance Pillar.

No nation is free that depends on another for survival. Economic design must be Indigenous in purpose and ownership, even when it uses modern tools.

5. Youth as Apprentices in Governance.

Young people must be trained from adolescence in decision-making, law, finance, and tradition — learning to lead as part of life, not as an afterthought (Wilson, Research Is Ceremony).

6. Spiritual Accountability.

Decisions should be made in ceremony, not outside it. Prayer is not superstition; it is consultation with the moral order (Simpson, As We Have Always Done).

7. Continuity Over Term Limits.

Leadership should be renewable through performance and trust, not merely bound to election cycles. Stability is strength.

Building the Hybrid Model

The future of Indigenous governance will not look like the past or the present — it will be a synthesis. The challenge is to merge ancient relational wisdom with modern administrative necessity. The model must satisfy federal law without surrendering to it (Treaties Matter Exhibit, Origins of Modern Tribal Government).

A Hybrid Governance Circle could include:

Council of Elders: Cultural, moral, and spiritual oversight. Authority to review legislation and call for ceremonial consultation before major decisions.

Executive Leadership: Elected or appointed professionals — Native or non-Native — chosen for proven competence, not bloodline, accountable to both community and council.

Community Circles: Regular forums where citizens deliberate and submit recommendations. Decisions recorded in both written and oral forms.

Youth Council: Apprentices in training, guided by elders, involved in policy discussions to ensure generational continuity.

Economic Council: Tasked with ensuring that business and development decisions align with cultural ethics and long-term sovereignty.

This model mirrors the old ways in structure — balanced, reciprocal, inclusive — but functions within the legal realities of the present. It satisfies external expectations without internal compromise (Borrows, Recovering Canada).

Healing Governance Through Education

No system will survive if its people remain uneducated in its spirit. Governance reform must begin with teaching, not voting. Tribal colleges, schools, and leadership programs must include Cultural

Governance Literacy: the study of pre-contact systems, oral law, and the spiritual principles that once held the nations together (Wilson, Research Is Ceremony).

Every tribal employee, every elected leader, and every board member should complete this education as part of their duty. You cannot protect what you do not understand.

The Return of Ceremony

The old ones knew that leadership without ceremony is dangerous. Ceremony kept leaders humble. It reminded them that they served the people, not themselves.

Restoring ceremony in governance means more than opening meetings with a prayer. It means closing them with accountability — asking not only, "Did we follow the law?" but, "Did we honor our ancestors?" (Simpson, As We Have Always Done).

When councils return to that question, the council chambers will once again echo like the lodges of old: places of purpose, not politics.

A Vision for the Future

In the next generation, Indigenous governance should no longer be defined by how well it imitates Washington. It should be measured by how well it reflects the drumbeat of its own people.

A reformed tribal government must sound, look, and feel Indigenous — in language, values, and rhythm. Its strength must come not from paperwork or policy, but from memory, balance, and shared responsibility (Alfred, Peace, Power, Righteousness).

That is the future worth building: a system where sovereignty lives not in the laws we copy, but in the hearts we awaken.

Epilogue: The Unbroken Circle

We stand at the edge of two worlds — one designed to control us, and one waiting to be remembered. The circle was never destroyed; it was only buried beneath the rubble of modern thinking.

To restore it, we must dig with courage, teach with patience, and lead with humility. The circle will rise again — not as nostalgia, but as necessity.

Because the future of Indigenous governance is not a return to the past.

It is the past remembered wisely enough to guide the future.

"The circle never ended. We simply stepped away. Now it waits — not to be rebuilt, but to be remembered."

Observations

SECTION IV: Rebuilding the Tribal Economy

"The strength of our future lies in the diversity of our opportunities. To grow, we must plant seeds in many fields, nurturing them with both wisdom from our ancestors and innovation from our descendants."

Introduction

In the long, winding journey toward true sovereignty, economic development is not simply a milestone—it is the bedrock upon which the future of Native nations must be constructed. It is the living bridge between ancestral knowledge and a modern world shaped by shifting markets, technological change, and global interdependence. When built with intention, economic development becomes more than revenue—it becomes a vessel for self-determination, cultural survival, and generational empowerment.

Section IV: Economic Development and Diversification explores how tribal communities can move beyond dependency and toward resilience. It asks us to look past the familiar avenues—like gaming—and into emerging paths forged by innovation, intertribal collaboration, and bold leadership. These chapters focus not just on growth, but on diversification—the intentional expansion into industries that reflect the full potential of our people, our lands, and our values.

The stories and strategies you'll encounter here make one thing clear: resilience is not the result of wealth alone. It is born of vision, discipline, and the ability to build systems that can withstand adversity. For Native nations, economic resilience means creating economies that honor the land, invest in the people, and are grounded in cultural integrity. It means embracing new tools and new technologies, but doing so in a way that never forgets who we are.

Throughout this section, you'll encounter tribal nations investing in renewable energy not just for profit, but to protect the sacred landscapes that have sustained us since time immemorial. You'll read about agribusiness not as a commercial trend, but as a return to the lifeways that fed both our bodies and our spirits. You'll explore how digital infrastructure, technological innovation, and strategic intergovernmental partnerships are enabling tribes to compete in a global economy on our own terms.

These chapters underscore a critical truth: economic development must be guided by cultural values. It cannot be allowed to devour what it was meant to preserve. Every enterprise, every contract, and every partnership must be evaluated not only by its return on investment—but by its return to community, to tradition, and to the collective soul of the people it serves.

The success of any economic endeavor in Indian Country must be measured in more than dollars. It must be measured in pride restored, families strengthened, languages revitalized, and futures reclaimed. Sovereignty is not only upheld through treaties and law—it is preserved when our people no longer have to choose between survival and tradition. It is preserved when our economies are shaped by us, for us.

So as you move through this section, reflect on the deeper intention behind each economic strategy. Consider how the innovations presented here can be adapted, reimagined, or re-rooted in your own community's story. Let these examples inspire not only enterprise, but stewardship. Because in the end, economic sovereignty means ensuring that our grandchildren inherit not just stronger economies—but a way of life they recognize as their own.

"The strength of our future lies in the diversity of our opportunities. To grow, we must plant seeds in many fields, nurturing them with both wisdom from our ancestors and innovation from our descendants."

Strategic Partnerships for Sustainable Growth

"Strength is found not in isolation, but in the joining of hands across divides, building a future together."

Introduction

Strategic partnerships form a foundational pillar for sustainable economic growth within Native American communities. These collaborations, forged between tribal entities and external partners, transcend the simple pursuit of economic gain; they represent a means to achieve self-sufficiency, cultural preservation, and future resilience.

For Native American tribes, strategic partnerships are not only opportunities for economic empowerment but also pathways to uphold sovereignty while navigating the complexities of the modern economy.

This chapter delves into how strategic partnerships—both external and internal—provide Native communities with the tools to thrive, weaving together values of collaboration, tradition, and economic innovation.

The Role of Strategic Partnerships

Strategic partnerships are about leveraging the strengths, resources, and opportunities that may not be readily accessible to individual parties. For Native American tribes, these partnerships can encompass collaborations with private enterprises, non-profits, educational institutions, and government agencies, forming broad coalitions that drive sustainable development.

The key to successful partnerships lies in aligning the values and objectives of all involved, ensuring that the collaboration benefits the tribe while respecting its cultural and social priorities.

Tulalip & Marriott

One notable example is the partnership between the Tulalip Tribes of Washington and Marriott International in the development of the

Tulalip Resort Casino. This partnership created a premier luxury destination that draws visitors from across the country, while also bringing jobs, infrastructure, and economic stability to the Tulalip community.

Beyond revenue generation, the collaboration emphasized cultural tourism, integrating Tulalip traditions and history into the resort experience. Such a partnership showcases how external alliances can reflect and support Indigenous identity (Marriott International, 2021).

Choctaw & General Motors

Similarly, the Mississippi Band of Choctaw Indians has leveraged a strategic partnership with General Motors to establish manufacturing facilities on tribal land. This collaboration has created high-quality jobs and boosted the local economy, becoming a model for how tribes can enter industries that have traditionally been inaccessible.

By entering into such collaborations, the Mississippi Band of Choctaw Indians demonstrates that tribes can foster relationships with major corporations to drive sustainable economic empowerment (U.S. Department of Commerce, 2022).

Economic Growth Through External Partnerships

External partnerships are essential for providing tribes with access to capital, expertise, and networks necessary to diversify and strengthen their economies. These collaborations help tribes enter new industries, bring technological advances to their communities, and elevate their economic standing.

Potawatomi & Harley-Davidson

The Forest County Potawatomi Community in Wisconsin offers an excellent example of leveraging external partnerships for both cultural and economic growth. By partnering with Harley-Davidson to sponsor an annual motorcycle rally, the tribe has boosted tourism and positioned itself as a major player in local cultural events. This rally not only promotes economic activity through increased visitation but also strengthens the tribe's brand, positioning it as a vibrant and culturally rich destination (Harley-Davidson, 2021).

Navajo Nation and Salt River Project

Another significant partnership was between the Navajo Nation and Salt River Project in managing the Navajo Generating Station. Though the station has since closed, this partnership provided crucial revenue for the Navajo Nation for decades, bringing technical expertise and job opportunities to the Navajo people.

This collaboration illustrates how strategic alliances can support economic stability over extended periods, and the lessons learned continue to inform current and future Navajo economic initiatives, especially as they transition toward renewable energy (Salt River Project, 2019).

Internal Collaboration and Strengthening

Tribal Economies While external partnerships are indispensable, internal collaboration within tribal entities is equally important. Strengthening internal networks and ensuring that economic gains benefit the entire community is a critical aspect of achieving true sovereignty and resilience.

By fostering an environment of cooperation among tribal enterprises, Native nations can create a unified economic strategy that supports long-term growth.

Chickasaw Nation Success

The Chickasaw Nation provides a powerful example of successful internal collaboration. Their comprehensive economic development strategy includes a range of businesses—from hospitality to health services and manufacturing.

By connecting these businesses under a unified vision, the Chickasaw Nation has built an integrated economy that not only diversifies revenue streams but also reinvests profits into community services, healthcare, and cultural programs. This approach has enabled the Chickasaw Nation to become one of the most economically prosperous tribes in the United States, reflecting the success of cohesive internal partnerships (Chickasaw Nation, 2020).

Challenges and Considerations

Despite their numerous benefits, strategic partnerships come with inherent challenges. One of the most pressing concerns is ensuring that tribes retain control over their resources and decision-making processes.

When entering partnerships with external entities, there is always the risk that the tribe's interests might be sidelined in favor of corporate profits or that sovereignty could be compromised. To mitigate these risks, partnerships must be structured in ways that respect tribal sovereignty and prioritize long-term community goals over short-term gains.

Cultural Differences

Cultural differences between tribes and external partners can also create misunderstandings that complicate collaboration. These differences may be evident in varied approaches to communication, time-lines, and decision-making processes. For example, many tribes prioritize collective decision-making, which can be slower but ensures inclusivity, while corporate partners may value swift execution.

Bridging these gaps requires clear, well-defined agreements that respect both cultural protocols and operational realities. Establishing shared values and clear expectations from the outset can help prevent conflicts and create a foundation for a successful partnership.

The Future of Strategic Partnerships in Tribal Economies

As Native American tribes continue to assert sovereignty and seek to diversify their economies, the role of strategic partnerships will grow in significance. The future of these partnerships lies not only in traditional sectors like tourism and gaming but also in emerging industries such as renewable energy, technology, and sustainable agriculture. These sectors offer new opportunities for economic diversification, environmental stewardship, and resilience.

Oglala Sioux & GRID

The collaboration between the Oglala Sioux Tribe and GRID Alternatives to bring solar energy to the Pine Ridge Reservation exemplifies forward-thinking economic development that aligns with traditional values of environmental stewardship.

By harnessing renewable energy, the Oglala Sioux Tribe is meeting immediate energy needs and positioning itself as a leader in sustainable development—a critical move in a world increasingly affected by climate change.

Such partnerships blend technological innovation with cultural values, providing a blueprint for future endeavors that honor the land while promoting economic independence (GRID Alternatives, 2021).

Technology Partnerships

Technology partnerships are also poised to make a profound impact. Collaborations with technology firms can provide tribes with tools to bridge the digital divide, offering broadband access and digital literacy programs that are crucial for economic participation.

Establishing these relationships ensures that tribal communities have access to educational opportunities, telehealth services, and economic initiatives that depend on modern infrastructure.

Case Study of an Successful Partnerships in Emerging Industries

The Red Lake Band of Chippewa Indians' Solar Initiative is a promising example of a renewable energy partnership. Through collaborations with non-profit and governmental partners, the Red Lake Band developed a solar farm that generates energy independence and cost savings.

This partnership is about more than economics—it is a reflection of the tribe's commitment to environmental stewardship, providing a sustainable pathway to sovereignty and prosperity.

Conclusion

Strategic partnerships are much more than economic ventures; they are crucial pathways through which Native American tribes can build resilient economies, ensure cultural survival, and assert sovereignty in a rapidly changing world. By carefully selecting partners who respect tribal sovereignty, structuring agreements that align with tribal values, and fostering both internal and external collaborations, tribes can secure sustainable growth that honors their heritage while embracing the opportunities of the modern era.

Whether through partnerships in renewable energy, cultural tourism, manufacturing, or digital technology, Native nations have the potential to shape their futures on their own terms—ensuring that economic growth is accompanied by cultural preservation, environmental stewardship, and community well-being. The key lies in blending the strength of traditional knowledge with modern opportunities, creating partnerships that are equitable, empowering, and enduring.

"True prosperity lies not in what we gain but in what we preserve while we grow. The strength of our people has always been our ability to adapt, innovate, and stay grounded in who we are—even as we reach for the stars."

Off-Reservation Businesses: A Path to Prosperity

"Venturing beyond reservation boundaries isn't just about economic growth; it's about bridging worlds and expanding horizons. Off-reservation businesses bring opportunities and challenges, but they also create a path for cultural exchange and mutual prosperity."

Introduction

Developing off-reservation businesses represents a transformative opportunity for Native American tribes to achieve greater economic prosperity, self-sufficiency, and community resilience. By expanding economic activities beyond reservation boundaries, tribes can tap into larger markets, access diverse resources, and foster multiple revenue streams.

However, this is not merely an economic endeavor—it is a strategic shift toward embracing opportunities that strengthen the sovereignty of Native communities. This chapter explores the benefits, challenges, and strategies of establishing successful off-reservation businesses, illustrating how these ventures contribute to long-term growth, self-determination, and cultural preservation.

The Benefits of Off-Reservation Businesses

Developing off-reservation businesses offers a wide range of benefits that extend beyond financial profit. This strategy allows Native American tribes to exert influence in the broader economy, create jobs for their people, and showcase cultural pride in innovative ways.

Market Access

One of the most significant advantages of expanding business operations off-reservation is increased market access. Off-reservation businesses enable tribes to reach a broader customer base, which enhances sales volume and brand recognition. This larger market provides not only the potential for greater profitability but also valuable insights into consumer preferences and emerging trends, allowing tribes to adapt their offerings and services for competitive advantage.

Expanding into larger markets also presents opportunities for tribes to engage in international trade, export goods, and participate in global supply chains. By tapping into broader markets, tribes achieve economies of scale, reduce production costs, and enhance revenue potential. This presence in regional, national, and global economies helps position tribes as significant economic players, bridging cultural identity with economic viability.

Diversified Income Sources

Another crucial benefit of off-reservation businesses is the diversification of income sources. Historically, many tribes have relied heavily on a single revenue stream—often from gaming operations—which leaves them vulnerable to economic shifts, regulatory changes, or other disruptions. Diversifying through off-reservation ventures mitigates these risks by spreading revenue generation across multiple sectors, such as retail, technology, health-care, and manufacturing.

For example, while gaming revenues may be subject to volatility due to changing regulations or market dynamics, revenue generated from diversified ventures—such as technology contracts or commercial real estate—offers financial stability. This resilience not only ensures a steady flow of income to support essential tribal services, like health-care and education, but also empowers tribes to navigate economic downturns more effectively, safeguarding the long-term interests of the community.

Economic Resilience and Community

Impact Off-reservation businesses contribute significantly to the economic resilience of tribes by stimulating job creation, fostering innovation, and encouraging local entrepreneurship. Employment opportunities are expanded not only for tribal members but also for the broader community, reducing unemployment and improving quality of life. The increased availability of jobs means that tribal members have access to diverse career paths, promoting self-sufficiency and reducing reliance on social services.

Off-reservation businesses also serve as platforms for innovation. They provide tribes with opportunities to invest in emerging industries and technologies, foster skills development, and encourage entrepreneurship. By creating economic opportunities, tribes cultivate an environment that encourages creativity and growth, ultimately leading to a vibrant community that is well-equipped for the challenges of the modern economy.

Overcoming the "Reservation Bound" Mentality

Despite the evident benefits, the "reservation bound" mentality—a belief that economic activities should remain confined within the reservation—often limits the economic potential of many Native communities. This mindset, rooted in historical and cultural factors, can prevent tribes from exploring opportunities beyond their immediate boundaries.

Cultural and Historical Factors

The reservation bound mentality is understandable through the lens of history. Reservations are symbols of cultural identity and survival—places where traditions are preserved, languages are spoken, and communities thrive without external interference. The forced displacement, marginalization, and traumatic history of many tribes have fostered an understandable wariness of external systems, reinforcing the desire to keep economic activities within culturally safe spaces.

However, while attachment to the reservation is deeply significant, it is essential to strike a balance—one that honors cultural heritage while embracing economic opportunities beyond these borders. Off-reservation ventures are not a departure from cultural values but an expansion of influence and a tool for advancing sovereignty by achieving economic independence.

Economic and Logistical Challenges

Developing off-reservation businesses presents challenges, including securing financing, navigating unfamiliar regulatory environments, and establishing a foothold in competitive markets. Traditional lenders may be reluctant to fund off-reservation enterprises due to perceived risks or lack of familiarity, which limits access to necessary capital.

Navigating regulatory requirements—such as zoning laws, environmental permits, and business licenses—can also be daunting, particularly for tribes with limited experience in off-reservation ventures. Establishing a presence in new markets demands strategic branding, marketing, and relationship building, requiring significant investments of time, money, and expertise.

Changing the Narrative To overcome the reservation bound mentality, it is essential to shift the narrative around off-reservation business ventures. This involves highlighting successful examples of tribes that have thrived through off-reservation enterprises, showcasing how these ventures contribute not only to economic gains but also to community development, cultural pride, and sovereignty.

For instance, the success of the Mohegan Tribe, which expanded the Mohegan Sun enterprise into multiple states and even overseas, serves as an inspiration for other tribes. Creating forums for knowledge exchange, such as conferences and workshops, facilitates collaboration among tribal nations, allowing them to share successful strategies and best practices (Mohegan Tribe, 2021).

Strategies for Developing Off-Reservation

Businesses Developing successful off-reservation businesses requires careful planning and strategic approaches to overcome unique challenges. The following strategies offer a framework for tribes seeking to explore these opportunities:

Market Research and Feasibility Studies

Thorough market research is the foundation of any successful venture. For off-reservation enterprises, this involves understanding target markets, identifying competitors, assessing consumer needs, and analyzing demand. Feasibility studies help determine the financial viability of proposed ventures, enabling tribes to make informed decisions based on market realities.

Access to Capital

Securing capital remains one of the biggest hurdles for developing off-reservation businesses. To address this, tribes can explore diverse funding sources, including federal grants, private investment, and strategic partnerships. Establishing tribal economic development corporations can also help manage investments and engage with external partners (Economic Development Administration, 2022).

Building Partnerships and Collaborations

Partnerships with businesses, government entities, and non-profits provide tribes with valuable resources and expertise. Such collaborations bring technical knowledge, market access, and financial support, allowing tribes to overcome barriers. The Chickasaw Nation, for example, successfully built partnerships through its diverse business operations, which have expanded its influence well beyond reservation borders (Chickasaw Nation, 2020).

Training and Workforce Development

The success of off-reservation businesses hinges on a skilled workforce. Investing in education and vocational training is essential to ensure tribal members are prepared for these enterprises. Training programs focusing on business management, leadership, and technical skills can empower tribal members to drive the growth of these businesses.

Brand Building and Marketing

A compelling brand is vital for standing out in competitive markets. Tribes can leverage their cultural heritage to create unique brands that appeal to both mainstream and niche markets interested in cultural authenticity. For instance, the Tulalip Tribes successfully promoted Quil Ceda Village as a cultural and commercial hub, using strategic marketing to establish a strong regional presence (Marriott International, 2021).

Regulatory Compliance and Advocacy

Ensuring compliance with local, state, and federal regulations is crucial. Engaging in advocacy can also help create supportive regulatory environments. By lobbying for favorable policies and building alliances, tribes can influence regulations that impact their businesses.

Legal Challenges

Navigating Sovereign Immunity Sovereign immunity can be a unique challenge for tribes. While it is critical to preserving sovereignty, it can deter business partners concerned about contract enforceability. Offering limited waivers of sovereign immunity in contracts and establishing clear dispute resolution mechanisms—such as arbitration—can foster trust and enable robust partnerships.

Three Successful Off-Reservation Businesses

The Mohegan Tribe: The Mohegan Tribe of Connecticut expanded beyond their reservation, establishing Mohegan Sun as a major gaming brand in multiple states and internationally. This off-reservation expansion demonstrates how strategic partnerships can yield substantial gains while enhancing cultural influence.

The Chickasaw Nation: The Chickasaw Nation has invested in diverse industries, with significant off-reservation investments like Chickasaw Nation Industries. These ventures have created a stable economic base, supporting community services and enhancing resilience.

The Tulalip Tribes: Through Quil Ceda Village, the Tulalip Tribes established a thriving commercial hub, combining economic activity with cultural expression to create a destination that draws regional visitors.

Conclusion

Developing off-reservation businesses offers a critical path to economic independence, resilience, and prosperity for Native American tribes. By overcoming the reservation bound mindset and embracing strategic approaches—such as market research, securing capital, building partnerships, workforce training, and advocacy—tribes can establish and grow successful off-reservation enterprises.

This journey demands vision, courage, and collaboration. It is about moving beyond physical and conceptual boundaries to create opportunities that honor tribal heritage while embracing modern economic possibilities. Through these efforts, Native American tribes can foster innovation, entrepreneurship, and self-determination, leading to a resilient and prosperous future.

"The earth may hold our roots, but the strength of our people lies in our reach beyond the borders—expanding our opportunities, honoring our heritage, and ensuring our children have a future that reflects both pride and prosperity."

Building Internal Capacity in Tribal Governance

"True sovereignty begins when we trust in our own hands to build our future—not in the hands of outsiders who neither know nor live our struggles."

Reducing Dependency on External Contractors

Introduction

Tribal governments have long relied on external contractors to fulfill major infrastructure needs, service delivery, and technical support. While outside expertise has its place, prolonged dependency on non-Native firms perpetuates economic imbalance and undermines self-determination.

This chapter explores the origins of this dependence, its ongoing consequences, and the vital need to invest in internal capacity-building to reclaim tribal control over development, governance, and economic sustainability.

Historical Context: The Origins of Outsourcing Dependence

Colonial Policies and the Disruption of Self-Sufficiency

Modern dependency on external contractors has deep historical roots. The Dawes Act of 1887 forcibly dismantled communal land systems that supported Native economies for generations, fracturing ownership and paving the way for non-Native encroachment. These policies devastated self-sufficiency and severed Indigenous economies from their foundational systems (Wilkins & Lomawaima, 2001).

Assimilation and the Loss of Practical Knowledge

Assimilation programs—particularly boarding schools—disconnected Native youth from their cultural practices and technical knowledge. Designed to eradicate tribal identity, these systems stripped future generations of skills in governance, agriculture, and construction, replacing them with Western norms that left tribal communities reliant on external expertise (Deloria & Lytle, 1983).

Cultural Displacement and Long-Term Effects

Forced relocations and federal interference further eroded community cohesion. The dismantling of traditional economies, governance models, and kinship systems disrupted generational knowledge transfer. The result: a chronic void in capacity, increasingly filled by non-Indigenous firms promising efficiency but delivering long-term dependence (Deloria & Lytle, 1983).

Economic Impact: Financial Costs and Lost Opportunities

The Outflow of Tribal Resources

Every contract awarded to a non-Native company is capital that exits the tribal economy. Rather than recycling wealth through community wages, reinvestment, and local enterprise, it strengthens outside firms—fueling economic disparity and stalling Indigenous economic growth (Cornell & Kalt, 2000).

Missed Development Opportunities

Outsourcing undercuts opportunities to train and elevate local talent. When Native-owned firms are bypassed, tribes forgo not only revenue but also the chance to develop their workforce and foster business growth. Each missed contract becomes a missed moment to build long-term self-sufficiency (Jorgensen, 2007).

Absence of a Local Multiplier Effect

Local contracts generate ripple effects—employment, skills development, business formation. That multiplier vanishes when projects are exported. External contracts may bring expertise, but they rarely leave behind sustainable impact (Cohen & Davidson, 2011).

Community Perspectives: Insights and Frustrations

Native Businesses Being Overlooked

Interviews and reports from tribal members consistently highlight a sense of exclusion. Qualified Native-owned businesses are routinely passed over in favor of external firms. This sends a damaging message: that Native capability is second-rate—an assumption rooted more in perception than in fact (Smith, 2000).

Undermining Community Identity and Morale

Empowering local professionals builds more than resumes—it builds identity, pride, and cohesion. Each successful Native-led project becomes a symbol of resilience. When contracts go outside, communities internalize a harmful narrative: that their own people are not worthy of trust or investment (LaDuke, 1999).

Political Mindset and Risk Aversion: Choosing the "Safe" Path

Fear of Favoritism Allegations

Tribal leaders sometimes choose external firms not because they are better, but because they appear "safer." Awarding work to Native-owned businesses can trigger accusations of nepotism—even when contracts are earned fairly. This fear-based mindset often leads to suboptimal decisions that undermine sovereignty (Cornell & Kalt, 2007).

Long-Term Damage to Trust and Governance

This pattern corrodes public trust. When communities see capable members overlooked, it creates apathy and disengagement. Trust in governance fades, and with it, participation, accountability, and hope for systemic change (Wilkins, 2002).

Case Studies: Outsourcing vs. Native-Led Success

Failure of an External Contractor

In one instance, a tribal council selected a non-Native firm over a qualified Native-owned business for a major construction project. The external company went over budget by more than 25% and failed to meet timelines. Community frustration and mistrust grew, while the missed opportunity to build local capacity left lasting scars (Cornell & Kalt, 2000).

Success Through Self-Investment

By contrast, a Native-led cultural center project completed under budget and ahead of schedule showed what's possible when tribes trust their own. It employed local workers, generated pride, and created a model for future success—all from within (Jorgensen, 2007).

Strategies for Change: Building Internal Capacity

Shifting the Mindset Toward Self-Reliance

Tribes must recognize the value of internal knowledge. Leadership must reframe the narrative—Native professionals are not a risk, but a resource.

Investing in Native Talent

Targeted programs—scholarships, internships, and apprenticeships—are vital for developing a skilled tribal workforce. When Native people are given tools and training, they excel. The talent is already there—it just needs investment (Smith, 2000).

Supporting Entrepreneurs and Small Businesses

Tribal grant programs, low-interest loans, and startup incubators can stimulate business development. Supporting Indigenous entrepreneurs lays the foundation for a locally driven economy (Cornell & Kalt, 2007).

Policy and Procurement Reforms

Implementing Native Preference Policies

Procurement policies that prioritize Native-owned firms—through set-asides or bid preferences—are essential. These policies level the playing field and help correct generations of economic exclusion (Cohen & Davidson, 2011).

Ensuring Transparency and Accountability

Transparent bidding processes, regular reporting, and community oversight are vital. These measures reinforce public trust and ensure that reforms are meaningful—not just symbolic (Jorgensen, 2007).

Long-Term Vision: Achieving Economic Self-Sufficiency

Sovereignty Through Economic Control

True sovereignty is impossible without economic control. Reinvesting in tribal talent, businesses, and industries allows tribes to build an economy that is resilient and self-determined—not dependent (LaDuke, 1999).

Building a Diversified Economic Base

Sectors such as health care, education, IT, and energy all offer avenues for Indigenous leadership. Diversification reduces risk and ensures that wealth remains in the community—generating cycles of opportunity and strength (Cornell & Kalt, 2000).

Conclusion

Reducing reliance on external contractors is not just a financial strategy—it is an act of reclamation. It begins by recognizing the historical trauma that led to dependency and ends with bold, intentional investment in community capacity. By empowering local professionals, reforming policies, and shifting the narrative around Indigenous expertise, tribes can move from dependency to dominance in their own affairs.

"When tribes invest in their people and talents, they breathe life into the old ways of resilience, crafting a modern reality where self-sufficiency reigns and dependency fades into history."

Observations

Renewable Energy: Stewardship and Growth

"True sovereignty isn't just about land or law; it's about power—the power to control your own resources, to harness the wind, the sun, and the water, and to transform them into growth, prosperity, and enduring strength for our people."

Introduction

The rise of renewable energy projects within Native American communities marks a pivotal moment in the pursuit of both environmental stewardship and economic sovereignty. With access to vast natural resources and a cultural foundation rooted in harmony with the Earth, tribes are uniquely positioned to lead the way in sustainable energy development. This chapter examines the vast potential of renewable energy for Native nations, the tangible benefits and persistent challenges, and the critical role these projects play in strengthening self-reliance and intergenerational prosperity.

The Potential of Renewable Energy

Harnessing Natural Resources

Many Native American reservations sit atop ideal terrain for solar, wind, and hydroelectric energy development. Vast open lands and unique environmental conditions make tribal lands prime real estate for clean energy infrastructure. The deserts of the Southwest, for example, offer some of the highest solar irradiance in North America—ideal for scalable solar farms (U.S. Department of Energy, 2020).

Solar Energy Potential

Photovoltaic solar panels convert sunlight directly into electricity, making them a clean and efficient power source. On tribal lands, solar arrays can serve everything from single homes to entire communities. The Hopi Tribe, situated in a high solar yield region, has used solar to power remote homes and reduce dependency on diesel generators and non-renewable grids (DOE, 2020).

Wind Energy Resources

In regions with consistent wind flow, wind turbines offer tribes both energy independence and commercial potential. The Rosebud Sioux Tribe has developed wind projects that not only supply electricity to their communities but also generate income by selling power to surrounding grids (Rosebud Sioux Tribe, 2019).

Hydroelectric Power

Tribes with flowing rivers or elevation drops can harness small-scale hydroelectric power. The Penobscot Indian Nation has explored hydroelectric initiatives that align with both energy goals and ecological preservation, ensuring sustainable use of their waterways (Penobscot Indian Nation, 2021).

Benefits of Renewable Energy Projects

Economic Independence

Generating electricity onsite enables tribes to slash utility costs and reinvest savings into their communities. In cases where excess energy is produced, tribes can sell it to the grid. The Blue Lake Rancheria Tribe of California built a solar-powered microgrid that generates revenue while delivering critical energy reliability to the community (Blue Lake Rancheria, 2019).

Job Creation and Skill Development

Renewable projects create jobs in installation, operations, and maintenance—boosting tribal employment and fostering technical skill development. The Spokane Tribe has implemented solar projects that not only deliver clean energy but also launch vocational training programs for tribal youth (Spokane Tribe, 2020).

Environmental Stewardship

Protecting the environment is a cornerstone of Native identity. By reducing fossil fuel use and carbon emissions, renewable energy reflects traditional values of balance and responsibility. The Navajo Nation has turned to solar and wind as environmentally aligned alternatives to retiring coal-fired plants, reasserting their commitment to both land and people (Navajo Nation, 2018).

Energy Sovereignty and Autonomy

True sovereignty includes energy control. Renewable infrastructure allows tribes to reduce vulnerability to external energy markets or supply interruptions. The Oglala Sioux Tribe's wind initiatives have provided local autonomy and fortified resilience in the face of energy crises (Oglala Sioux Tribe, 2017).

Challenges and Considerations in Renewable Energy Projects

Initial Investment and Funding Barriers

One of the most significant hurdles is the upfront cost of solar panels, wind turbines, and energy storage systems. Many tribes face limited access to capital, but programs through the U.S. Department of Energy's Office of Indian Energy can provide crucial funding assistance (DOE Office of Indian Energy, 2021).

Regulatory and Permitting Obstacles

Energy projects often require complex layers of permits and compliance with federal, tribal, and state laws. These hurdles can delay or derail otherwise viable projects. Legal experts familiar with tribal governance and energy law are essential to navigate this bureaucratic terrain.

Community Engagement and Education

Community support is essential. Many tribes have found success by holding town halls, workshops, and outreach programs to explain project benefits and address concerns. The Red Lake Band of Chippewa Indians effectively integrated renewable energy into school curricula to raise awareness and generate youth involvement (Red Lake Band of Chippewa Indians, 2019).

Technical Expertise and Long-Term Maintenance

The sustainability of energy systems depends on local expertise. Without trained technicians, even the best infrastructure can fall into disrepair. The Menominee Tribe partnered with regional colleges to train tribal members, ensuring community-based maintenance and long-term success (Menominee Tribe, 2020).

Case Studies of Successful Renewable Energy Initiatives

Blue Lake Rancheria's Microgrid

Faced with frequent power outages, the Blue Lake Rancheria Tribe built a solar + battery microgrid to power their community through emergencies. The system has lowered utility costs, strengthened emergency preparedness, and become a national model for tribal energy resilience (Blue Lake Rancheria, 2019).

Rosebud Sioux Tribe's Wind Farm

In the open plains of South Dakota, the Rosebud Sioux Tribe developed a wind farm that brings energy independence and revenue through power sales. These funds are reinvested into health-care, education, and housing, proving that wind energy can fuel both power grids and community progress (Rosebud Sioux Tribe, 2019).

Spokane Tribe's Solar Projects

The Spokane Tribe's investment in solar energy has done more than reduce reliance on fossil fuels—it has sparked a cultural shift toward sustainability. Their initiatives have created jobs, educated youth, and redefined energy as a tool for sovereignty and pride (Spokane Tribe, 2020).

Colusa Indian Energy — Sovereignty in Power

The Colusa Indian Community, home to the **Cachil DeHe Band of Wintun Indians**, refused to remain powerless. Under Pacific Gas and Electric (PG&E), the community endured more than **fifty outages a year**, crippling homes, the casino, water systems, and tribal government operations (CMUA, 2024).

In 2005, Colusa made a decision few tribes have dared. They established their own utility authority, **Colusa Indian Energy**, and commissioned a cogeneration system with an underground distribution network across the reservation (CMUA, 2024). Over the years, they expanded this into a hybrid microgrid that integrates solar, storage, and combined heat and power. Today, that system powers every tribal asset: homes, casino, government offices, water plants, and agricultural operations (DOE, 2024).

The results are staggering. Since 2012, Colusa reports **zero outages**, even while neighboring PG&E customers continue to face rolling blackouts (CMUA, 2024). In fact, the tribe recently expanded its distribution grid from serving 30 homes to 37 with support from the U.S. Department of Energy (DOE, 2023).

This is more than infrastructure. It is sovereignty expressed in kilowatts—reliability, self-determination, and proof that tribes can not only govern but also power themselves.

Conclusion

Renewable energy represents more than economic potential for Native communities—it is a reclaiming of autonomy, a renewal of traditional values, and a path toward generational strength. By overcoming regulatory, financial, and educational barriers through strategic partnerships and local investment, tribes can lead the nation in environmental leadership and community-driven development. The sun, the wind, and the rivers have always been part of Native life. Now, they are being woven into the future.

"Renewable energy is more than just a path to economic independence for Native communities; it is a return to our roots—honoring the land that has always provided for us while ensuring that the light of resilience keeps shining for generations to come."

Observations

Technology and Tribal Opportunity

"Technology, for Native American communities, must be more than just wires and machines; it must be a bridge—one that carries our people from the shadows of a suppressed past into the light of an empowered future. The digital world holds the power to reconnect us not only with modern opportunities but also with our forgotten potentials."

Expanding Opportunities for Native American Tribes

Introduction
In today's rapidly evolving world, technology is no longer a luxury—it is a cornerstone of economic development, driving innovation, efficiency, and opportunity. For Native American tribes, embracing technology offers a transformative path forward, one that enables communities to overcome historical marginalization and build systems of resilience. This chapter explores how technology can be leveraged to enhance tribal economies, strengthen sovereignty, and align modern progress with traditional values.

Historical Context: Technology and Native American Communities

For centuries, Native communities have been excluded from the fruits of technological advancement. Colonization, forced relocations, and systemic underinvestment in infrastructure created profound disparities. These inequities hindered access to education, healthcare, and economic tools necessary for development. And yet, despite such obstacles, tribes have remained resilient—adapting technology to meet their needs, blending modern tools with ancient knowledge (Smith, 2016).

Over recent decades, there has been a growing recognition that technology can be a great equalizer—if tribes are given the tools, infrastructure, and support needed to deploy it with cultural alignment.

From broadband expansion and telehealth to e-commerce and STEM education, tribes are now asserting their place in the digital age.

Technological Infrastructure: The Backbone of Development

Broadband Access

High-speed internet is essential for accessing digital education, remote work, telehealth, and entrepreneurship. However, many tribal lands still lack reliable broadband. Programs like the FCC Tribal Broadband Connectivity Program (2020) aim to close this gap, but progress remains uneven. Without broadband, entire communities remain disconnected from the digital economy.

Telecommunications Infrastructure

Mobile networks, data centers, and modern communication systems are foundational to development. Building reliable telecommunications infrastructure enables emergency response, education delivery, e-governance, and economic mobility. Tribes must partner with federal agencies and private firms to build custom systems suited to their geography and governance needs (Wilson & Anderson, 2019).

Education and Skill Development: Building a Technologically Savvy Workforce

Digital Literacy Programs

Teaching fundamental tech skills—like email, word processing, cybersecurity, and web navigation—is vital. Beyond that, tribes can offer advanced courses in coding, cloud computing, and digital storytelling to prepare members for tech-centered careers (Jones, 2018).

Online Education

Remote learning opens educational opportunities previously inaccessible to rural and remote tribal members. With the right infrastructure, students can pursue higher education from within their communities. Scholarships and remote learning partnerships can ensure access despite financial or geographic barriers (Miller, 2021).

STEM Initiatives

Promoting STEM (science, technology, engineering, and mathematics) is essential for creating long-term economic resilience. Programs such as robotics clubs, science fairs, and community tech labs can ignite curiosity and foster innovation (Harper, 2017).

E-Commerce and Digital Entrepreneurship

E-Commerce Platforms

Online marketplaces allow Native artisans and entrepreneurs to reach global customers. This supports cultural preservation and economic independence. E-commerce platforms designed specifically for Native vendors can highlight authenticity and community-driven commerce (Taylor, 2020).

Digital Marketing

Digital marketing skills—SEO, social media, paid ads—are essential for online business success. Training tribal members in these areas boosts visibility and empowers small businesses to compete in the global economy (Garcia, 2019).

Online Business Incubators

Virtual incubators can support aspiring entrepreneurs with mentorship, funding access, business planning, and marketing strategy. These spaces also foster peer learning and collaboration across tribal communities (Smith & Brown, 2022).

Healthcare: Improving Access and Quality through Telehealth

Tele-health Services

Video consultations and remote monitoring reduce the burden of long travel for health-care access. Tele-health increases patient engagement and access to specialists, particularly for mental health and chronic care management (Wilson, 2018).

Health Information Systems

Electronic Health Records (EHR) and health analytics allow better tracking of trends and outcomes. These tools support data-informed decisions and enable coordinated care among providers (Jones & Miller, 2020).

Renewable Energy and Sustainability

Solar and Wind Energy

Renewable projects create local jobs and lower energy costs. Federal programs and tribal ownership models allow energy revenue to stay within the community (Taylor, 2021).

Energy Efficiency

Upgrading tribal buildings and homes with energy-efficient systems promotes sustainability and long-term cost savings. Community awareness campaigns and educational programs reinforce stewardship values (Miller & Wilson, 2019).

Governance and Transparency

Digital Governance Platforms

Tribes can use digital systems to streamline services, share public records, and enhance community participation. These platforms build trust through transparency (Jones, 2020).

Cybersecurity and Data Management

Community-led control over data—data sovereignty—is critical. Tribes must secure their digital systems and educate members about privacy, consent, and ethical data practices (Smith, 2021).

Challenges and Considerations

Infrastructure Gaps and the Digital Divide

Remote locations, difficult terrain, and low population densities drive up the cost of broadband and tech infrastructure. Private firms often overlook tribal areas due to limited profit potential. This makes federal support and tribal-owned internet cooperatives vital.

Afford-ability and Inclusive Access

Even when Internet is available, many tribal members cannot afford it. Subsidies, low-cost devices, and free Wi-Fi zones can ensure that technology is not a luxury but a shared resource.

Cultural Sensitivity and Data Privacy

Every technological initiative must be community-led and culturally respectful. Projects like GIS mapping must avoid exposing sacred sites. Data privacy protocols must be governed by tribal authorities to protect sovereignty and trust (Garcia & Jones, 2019).

Long-Term Sustainability

Too many tech projects fail after the initial launch due to a lack of local expertise or follow-up funding. Tribes should build tech maintenance teams, create sustainability plans, and partner with technical colleges for training (Smith & Wilson, 2019).

Cybersecurity

As digital access increases, so do threats. Firewalls, audits, secure storage, and community education are essential. Shared tribal cybersecurity teams can defend against complex attacks (Wilson, 2021).

Inclusive Design

Older adults, disabled users, and first-time tech users must not be left behind. Tech hubs, support hotlines, and adaptive devices ensure full community participation.

Conclusion

Technology is not a shortcut—it is a tool. When rooted in community values and driven by Native leadership, technology becomes a catalyst for sovereignty, sustainability, and cultural rebirth. It allows Native communities not just to survive in a digital world—but to thrive, lead, and shape it on their own terms.

"Technology is the bridge that connects our rich heritage with the promise of tomorrow. By integrating modern innovations with traditional wisdom, we empower our communities to thrive in a rapidly evolving world."

Sustainable Development: Long-Term Strategies for Success

"True prosperity is measured not just in wealth, but in the health of the land, the continuity of culture, and the resilience of the people."

Introduction

Sustainable development is more than a concept—it is a cultural imperative. For Native American tribes, sustainability is not an imported framework from international development agencies, but a continuation of the values and principles our ancestors lived by. Our relationship with the land, water, and natural world is spiritual, reciprocal, and generational. However, the contemporary environment—scarred by colonization, environmental degradation, economic exclusion, and climate change—demands that we translate these traditional values into modern strategies.

This chapter explores what true sustainability means for Native communities: balancing economic growth with ecological health, advancing technology without cultural erosion, and strengthening sovereignty by building resilience into our economies, our infrastructure, and our people.

Historical Context of Sustainable Development in Native American Communities

Traditional Sustainable Practices

Long before sustainability became a buzzword in Western policy circles, Indigenous peoples practiced it as a way of life. Native communities engaged in seasonal harvesting, rotating cultivation, and species management rooted in knowledge passed down over thousands of years. These practices were not only effective—they were spiritually binding. They were ceremonies, not just systems.

The Iroquois' "Seventh Generation Principle" required that every decision consider its impact seven generations into the future. This was not rhetoric—it guided governance, agriculture, housing, and land use.

The "Three Sisters" agricultural method, practiced across many nations, wasn't just efficient—it was a perfect metaphor for coexistence: corn (the elder) offers support, beans (the nurturer) restore fertility, and squash (the protector) shields the soil. It exemplifies interdependence and mutual benefit (National Park Service, 2021).

The Karuk Tribe's use of controlled burns in California protected forests, ensured the growth of medicinal plants, and prevented destructive wildfires. These low-intensity fires were governed by ceremonial protocols, ensuring that fire remained a life-giving force—not a destroyer (Karuk Tribe Climate Change Projects, 2022).

Impact of Colonization

Colonialism introduced an extractive model that viewed land as a commodity to be exploited—not a relative to be honored. When Native people were forcibly removed from ancestral lands, they lost more than homes—they lost access to ecosystems that had sustained them for generations.

The near-eradication of buffalo herds, a deliberate military tactic used to starve and disempower Plains tribes, devastated both ecological balance and Indigenous economies (History, 2023).

Further destruction came through Western grazing practices, monoculture farming, and resource extraction—strip-mining, logging, and damming rivers—that disrupted entire ecosystems. Relocation to reservations often placed tribes in arid, degraded, or marginal lands where traditional practices could no longer be sustained (PBS, 2022).

These systemic disruptions left deep scars—not just environmentally, but psychologically and culturally—contributing to cycles of dependency, poverty, and disconnection from land-based identities.

Contemporary Challenges and Opportunities

Economic Development vs. Environmental and Cultural Preservation

Modern tribal nations walk a tightrope between economic development and cultural survival. Extractive industries—mining, oil, and gas—often bring short-term financial gain but long-term environmental degradation. Yet many tribes, facing unemployment and underfunded programs, feel pressured to make deals with corporations that do not share their values.

Sustainable development offers a third path.

One that generates revenue without compromising the environment or the sacred.

Renewable energy projects like those supported by the U.S. Department of Energy are examples. But true sustainability requires more than installing wind turbines—it means ensuring tribal ownership, training tribal engineers, and using profits to support language revitalization, youth programs, and land restoration.

It also means protecting sacred sites from development. The cultural landscape is not something to be surveyed and sold—it is part of our spiritual anatomy. When eco-tourism is pursued, it must be done with community control, consent, and narrative authority. Outsiders should visit our lands as guests, not consumers (The International Ecotourism Society, 2022).

Climate Change as a Threat Multiplier

Climate change is not just an environmental issue—it is an existential threat to tribal sovereignty. It undermines food systems, infrastructure, housing, and ceremonial access.

- Agricultural Vulnerability: Droughts, floods, and shortened growing seasons jeopardize traditional foods. Tribes must adopt climate-resilient crops, precision irrigation, and water-saving techniques (FAO, 2023).
- Infrastructure Risk: Storm surges, wildfires, and thawing permafrost are destroying roads, homes, and water systems. Investment in resilient infrastructure—flood-resistant housing, off-grid energy systems, and decentralized water—must be prioritized (United Nations, 2023).
- Cultural Loss: Climate change erases more than physical spaces—it severs access to ancestral practices. Hunting and fishing seasons shift unpredictably; sacred plants disappear. Ecosystem restoration and land back movements are now essential components of climate strategy (World Wildlife Fund, 2023).

Community-Based Solutions

Participatory Planning

Sustainability imposed from above fails. But when development is community-led, rooted in tribal values, and guided by collective vision, it thrives. Elders, youth, land stewards, and cultural leaders must all have seats at the table.

Participatory planning models allow projects to align with cultural priorities, build trust, and adapt over time (Participatory Methods, 2023).

Local Empowerment

True sustainability is powered by local capacity. Education programs that train tribal members as solar techs, engineers, agriculturalists, and water resource managers ensure that jobs stay within the community—and so does the knowledge (United Nations, 2023).

Cultural Revitalization

Culture is not the opposite of development—it is its foundation. Projects that incorporate language, ceremony, and story are more resilient because they strengthen identity and connection to place. Every solar panel on tribal land should reflect the wisdom of those who prayed for sunlight before electricity existed (Cultural Survival, 2023).

Strategies for Sustainable Development

Renewable Energy

Utility-scale solar and wind installations bring revenue and reduce fossil dependence. When tribes own the grid, they control the future.

Community solar farms empower low-income households to share in clean energy benefits (U.S. Department of Energy, 2023).

Food Sovereignty
- Traditional agriculture and agroforestry restore soil health, reduce reliance on chemical fertilizers, and regenerate ecosystems (Agroforestry Resource Center, 2023).
- Permaculture design creates self-sustaining systems modeled after nature (The Permaculture Research Institute, 2023).
- Community gardens double as classrooms, healing spaces, and food sources.

Eco- and Cultural Tourism
- Eco-tourism, when managed by tribes, can fund conservation and cultural education.
- Cultural tourism that honors protocol—through storytelling, traditional arts, and guided sacred site access—creates deep value while controlling the narrative (National Trust for Historic Preservation, 2023).

Education and Innovation
- STEM education prepares the next generation for green careers: climate science, energy tech, GIS mapping (National Indian Education Association, 2023).
- Lifelong learning on recycling, conservation, and resource management builds environmental citizenship (United Nations Sustainable Development, 2023).

Policy and Advocacy

Advocate for tribal tax credits, green infrastructure grants, and regulatory flexibility.

Protect sacred sites through tribal consultation laws and co-management agreements (National Congress of American Indians, 2023; Bureau of Indian Affairs, 2023).

Case Studies of Resilience

Blue Lake Rancheria Tribe

Developed a solar-powered microgrid that provides clean, reliable energy while insulating the community from wildfires and grid failures (Blue Lake Rancheria Tribe, 2023).

Oneida Nation

Operates an organic farm that delivers food sovereignty, creates employment, and teaches youth about ancestral planting techniques (Oneida Nation, 2023).

Navajo Nation

Launched eco-tourism tours of Monument Valley that balance economic development with cultural preservation and sacred site protection (Navajo Nation Parks, 2023).

Conclusion

Sustainable development in Indian Country is not a hand-me-down framework from international think tanks. It is our own story—centuries old, rooted in reverence, reborn through resilience. It requires political courage, cultural grounding, and generational planning.

"Sustainable development is not just about preserving our resources for tomorrow, but about creating a legacy of resilience, prosperity, and cultural integrity. By planning with foresight and acting with responsibility, we can ensure that our communities thrive for generations to come."

Beyond Casinos – Building a Diverse Economic Base

"Casinos have given us an essential foothold in economic growth, but real sovereignty demands that we evolve beyond them. Diversifying our economic base is not just about survival—it's about creating a future where our people thrive independently, with pride in our traditions and control over our destinies."

Introduction

Casinos changed the trajectory of many Native nations. They provided the first real opportunity in generations to generate revenue on our own terms—funding schools, hospitals, housing, and programs once neglected or outright denied by federal agencies. But while gaming brought us progress, it also brought dependency. And dependency—whether on federal grants or casino profits—is not sovereignty.

True economic sovereignty means control over our own future. It means building a foundation so broad and strong that no single industry or outside influence can shake it. This chapter is a call to action. It is about moving beyond survival economics toward economic self-determination—where tribal communities build diverse, culturally grounded, and sustainable economies that last for generations.

The Role of Casinos in Tribal Economies

Economic Impact

There's no denying the role casinos have played in tribal revitalization. In 2019 alone, tribal gaming generated over $34.6 billion in gross revenue nationwide (National Indian Gaming Commission, 2020). Those funds supported infrastructure, education, healthcare, housing, and direct services—things once out of reach for many reservations.

Casinos also created thousands of jobs. But here lies a hard truth: in many operations, tribal citizens make up less than 25% of the workforce (Smith, 2021). Outsiders fill the majority of roles—especially in finance, security, and management. This workforce gap exposes a missed opportunity: we built economic engines, but we didn't always build the tribal capacity to run them.

Limitations and Risks

What casinos gave, they can also take away. When your economy is tied to gaming, you're tied to consumer behavior, legal uncertainty, and competition. During recessions, when people stop spending, tribal revenues dry up. Changes in state law or federal policy can shift the rules overnight.

Gaming was never meant to be the destination—it was the first step. Continued overreliance on gaming narrows our vision, limits innovation, and exposes us to collapse. It also invites difficult social dynamics—gambling addiction, shifts in community values, and increased exposure to crime. Economic progress must not come at the cost of cultural erosion (Evans, 2011).

The Imperative of Economic Diversification

Sustainable Development

Diversifying our economies is not optional. It is the only way to secure long-term tribal prosperity. Diversification spreads risk, builds stability, and allows tribes to weather storms—economic, political, or environmental.

It also ensures that our economic future reflects our values, not just the demands of outside markets. Renewable energy, land stewardship, traditional agriculture, education, healthcare, manufacturing, and digital enterprises—these are not just industries. They are extensions of our sovereignty.

Expanding Opportunity

Economic diversification unlocks real autonomy. It creates jobs that tribal members can be proud of. It fuels tribal entrepreneurship—giving individuals the ability to launch businesses rooted in cultural identity.

It also draws partners. Foundations, private investors, and public agencies are far more willing to collaborate with tribes that show a clear, diversified strategy. Economic resilience builds credibility. And credibility builds leverage (Cornell & Kalt, 2007).

Strategies for Diversification

Natural Resource Development

Our land holds more than history—it holds economic potential. But that potential must be pursued with long-term vision and cultural responsibility.

Renewable energy projects like solar farms, wind turbines, and battery storage systems can generate revenue and local jobs while reinforcing environmental values. Projects like the CannonBall Community Solar Farm, launched by the Standing Rock Sioux Tribe, show how energy independence can support sovereignty (LaDuke, 2017).

Sustainable agriculture and aquaculture can revive traditional food systems, improve health outcomes, and create marketable products. Tribes with access to water systems or ancestral farming lands can grow niche produce, heritage grains, or launch fish hatcheries to generate year-round income.

Forestry and land management, when grounded in traditional ecological knowledge, create revenue through timber, carbon credits, and tourism. The Confederated Tribes of the Colville Reservation have demonstrated this integration successfully (Anderson, 1996).

Tourism and Cultural Enterprise

Tourism is often misunderstood. It's not just about visitors—it's about educating the world on who we are, on our terms.

Cultural tourism—museums, language workshops, ancestral site tours—allows tribes to control narrative while generating income.

Eco-tourism invites outdoor travelers to experience the land respectfully—through hikes, guided tours, or stays in tribal-run lodges (The International Ecotourism Society, 2022).

Artisan markets and cultural products support generational craftwork, such as pottery, beadwork, and silver. The Zuni Pueblo built a thriving arts industry that preserved tradition while supporting hundreds of artists (Ferguson & Hart, 1985).

Education and Workforce Development

No economy grows without people trained to sustain it. Tribes must invest deeply in vocational training, higher education, and adult learning.

Create tribal-run training centers that focus on high-demand fields: solar installation, health-care support, coding, heavy machinery, cybersecurity, and culinary arts.

Build partnerships with universities to ensure Indigenous student access, retention, and leadership pipelines. The Tohono O'odham Nation's relationship with Arizona State University is one such model (Deloria & Wildcat, 2001).

Entrepreneurship

Entrepreneurs are the architects of sovereignty. Supporting them means more than slogans—it means access to capital, incubators, technical assistance, and low-barrier lending.

Tribes can use profits from casinos or energy to seed microloan funds, business accelerators, and grant programs. Every small business launched is one step away from dependency—and one step closer to full self-governance.

Public and Private Partnerships

Public-private partnerships, when guided by tribal priorities, can open new markets and fund big projects.

The Seneca Nation's bioenergy partnership with Western New York Energy created jobs and energy while supporting local infrastructure (Jorgensen, 2007).

The Choctaw Nation has used federal grants to launch broadband, manufacturing, and rural development projects—balancing outside help with internal leadership (Cornell & Kalt, 1998).

Innovation and Digital Frontiers

IT and Digital Services

Tribes can compete in digital arenas—software development, app design, network administration, and cloud storage. The Cherokee Nation's IT services division, part of Cherokee Nation Businesses, generates millions in contracts with state and federal agencies (Wilkins, 2011).

Tele-health and Digital Medicine

Expanding tele-health not only improves care—it creates jobs in tech support, administration, and mental health. It brings health-care jobs onto the reservation instead of exporting them elsewhere.

The Policy Environment

Governance and Regulation

Tribal councils must create clear business codes, transparent procurement, and independent economic development authorities to attract investment and retain talent. When governance is unstable or opaque, outside partners stay away. Strong internal policy is foundational to building trust and attracting capital.

Federal Collaboration

Effective tribal-state-federal partnerships matter. The Seminole Tribe of Florida, through careful negotiation and legal clarity, has built a diversified portfolio that includes construction, hospitality, and retail—without surrendering sovereignty (Pevar, 2002).

Cultural Integrity and Community Engagement

Sovereignty must never be for sale. Every economic move must pass one test: Does it strengthen our people—or weaken them? Diversification cannot come at the cost of language, ceremony, or land.

Use community councils, town halls, and consensus protocols to shape strategy.
- Embed cultural education in workforce programs.
- Require cultural impact reviews for all major developments.

Conclusion

Casinos should never be seen as the end goal—they are a stepping stone, not a destination. They were meant to create a foothold, a moment of economic momentum that tribes could harness to build something far greater: an unending stream of new income rooted in self-governance, cultural strength, and strategic vision.

The goal was never just to build casinos. It was to build nations.

Real nations stand on more than one pillar. They stand on culture, on enterprise, on resilience, and on the ability to adapt without forgetting who they are.

Tribal governments must lead with foresight—investing in people, protecting the land, and building economies that reflect who we are and what we value. Economic strength must flow from cultural strength. That is how we outgrow dependency. That is how we reclaim our future—not through chance and chips, but through vision, action, and sovereignty.

"While gaming has undeniably uplifted many tribal communities, our true strength lies in diversification. The prosperity of Native nations will be secured not by a single revenue stream, but by building multiple, sustainable pathways that honor both our economic needs and our cultural values."

Mistakes of the Rich Gaming Tribes

"Casino wealth has given us a foundation, but a house built on a single pillar cannot stand against the storms of the future. True sovereignty lies in building an economic base that is as diverse and resilient as our heritage."

Introduction

This chapter confronts a difficult but necessary truth: some of the wealthiest gaming tribes in Indian Country have stumbled—not because they succeeded, but because they stopped too soon.

Casino revenues lifted many tribal nations out of systemic poverty and gave us leverage we hadn't seen in generations. But for some, that wealth became a crutch rather than a catalyst. Instead of turning casino profits into permanent prosperity through investment and diversification, they built economies dependent on a single industry—an industry increasingly under pressure.

This is a cautionary chapter. It's about the perils of complacency, the illusion of permanence, and the moral responsibility we have to ensure that today's windfalls don't become tomorrow's regrets.

Gaming as the First Step—Not the Final Destination

The Upside of Casino Wealth

Tribal casinos generated a record-setting $34.6 billion in gross revenue in 2019 alone (National Indian Gaming Commission, 2020). That money has been trans-formative—funding clinics, schools, housing, and cultural initiatives.

For individual tribal members, per capita payments have offered real, tangible benefits—new homes, paid tuition, freedom from generational debt. But wealth alone is not a plan. And a per capita check is not a nation-building strategy.

Case Study: The Seminole Tribe of Florida

Leveraging Wealth into Ownership

The Seminole Tribe of Florida is often held up as a gold standard for tribal economic diversification—and with good reason. After establishing one of the most profitable gaming operations in the country, the tribe didn't stop. They invested.

- They purchased Hard Rock International, a global brand with hotels, casinos, and entertainment venues across multiple continents.
- They entered energy markets, including renew ables, to create long-term returns.
- They built cigarette manufacturing and real estate holdings, creating income far beyond casino floors.

The Seminoles understood a foundational truth: Gaming revenue is not a solution—it's seed capital. Their strategy demonstrates that wealth, when directed wisely, becomes intergenerational stability.

The Others: Wealth Without a Plan

The Danger of Sole Reliance

While some tribes followed the Seminole example, others continued to pour most of their resources into gaming, distributing increasingly large per capita payments without investing in broader development. The result? An economy vulnerable to:

- Changing laws and state compacts
- Increased competition from commercial and on-line casinos
- Saturation of the gaming market

States like Pennsylvania, New York, and Michigan have legalized and expanded gaming aggressively—on-line casinos, sports betting, and new resorts (National Conference of State Legislatures, 2021; American Gaming Association, 2022). The exclusive zone tribal casinos once held is shrinking. The financial advantage is eroding.

When Per Capita Payments Become a Pitfall

The Unspoken Cost of Comfort

Large per capita payments can seem like justice—an overdue reward for centuries of suffering. But unchecked, they become their own trap.

- Motivation drops. Why work when checks arrive anyway?
- Dependency rises. Youth come to expect money, not build toward it.
- Financial literacy lags. Few are taught how to invest, save, or build.
- Substance abuse rises. Sudden wealth, without purpose or education, fuels instability.

In some wealthy tribes, the very wealth intended to heal has created new wounds. Communities have seen increases in addiction, mental health issues, and a loss of collective purpose (Smith, 2018).

Diversification Isn't Optional—It's Survival

Sectors for Strategic Expansion

To weather the future, tribes must move boldly into new industries. Some already are:

The Cherokee Nation created Cherokee Nation Businesses, which now manages government contracts, health-care services, and tech ventures.

The Morongo Band expanded into retail, banking, and distribution, becoming one of the most diversified tribes in the country.

Other critical sectors include:

- Renewable Energy – solar, wind, and battery farms on tribal land
- Technology – software, cyber-security, and digital consulting
- Health-care – clinics, mental health centers, telemedicine
- Agriculture – food sovereignty and market farming
- Real Estate – tribal-owned commercial and residential property

Each investment creates jobs, stabilizes revenue, and reduces risk.

Political Will and Cultural Responsibility

Why It Doesn't Happen More

The biggest barrier isn't money—it's mindset.

Tribal members grow comfortable with regular distributions. Tribal leaders fear backlash if those distributions are reduced in favor of reinvestment. Councils hesitate, fearing lost elections, lawsuits, or upheaval.

But this fear is a luxury we can no longer afford. The future doesn't wait.

Leading with Vision

- Leaders must educate their people, not just pay them.
- Host town halls with full financial transparency
- Show projections of what happens if diversification doesn't occur
- Teach financial literacy in every school and every age group
- Tie per capita payments to age, contribution, or investment in community

Prosperity is not a check. It's a system. And it must be built together.

Building Long-Term Stability

Planning for the Seventh Generation

Diversified investments don't just protect money—they protect sovereignty. A stable economic model means:

- More local jobs
- Increased tribal autonomy
- Reduced reliance on grants or federal programs
- Funding for language, ceremony, and cultural renewal

This is what the elders meant when they said, "We plan for seven generations."

Conclusion

Gaming was a door. It opened up possibilities our ancestors could have never imagined. But the greatest mistake we can make is standing in the doorway, content to look out instead of stepping through.

Wealth must be more than distributed. It must be transformed—into investments, institutions, and opportunities that will endure long after the casino lights fade.

"Per capita payments can be a blessing, but without investment in our collective future, they can also become a curse. The strength of a nation lies not in immediate wealth but in how it plans, invests, and grows for generations yet to come."

Observations

Successful Tribal Business Diversity: Case Studies

"True economic sovereignty for Native tribes comes not from a single revenue stream but from a diverse portfolio of ventures—embracing our unique heritage while expanding into modern industries, ensuring stability for generations to come."

Introduction

Too often, tribal prosperity is reduced to the casino narrative. But across Indian Country, a quiet revolution is taking place—led by tribes that are thinking bigger, building broader, and planting roots in industries far beyond gaming.

This chapter highlights five tribes that have broken the mold. Through vision, innovation, and strategic reinvestment, they've turned casino revenues and natural resources into dynamic, multi-sector economic engines. Their success offers a blueprint for other Native nations seeking to reclaim sovereignty through diverse, sustainable, and culturally grounded economies.

Case Study 1: The Choctaw Nation of Oklahoma

Background

Long known for its endurance, the Choctaw Nation has embraced a bold, forward-looking economic model—one rooted not in dependence, but in deliberate diversification.

Strategies for Success

Defense Manufacturing: Choctaw Defense, a tribal-owned military manufacturing firm, builds tactical equipment for the U.S. Department of Defense. It creates jobs, revenue, and critical skills training for tribal members (Smith, 2018).
Healthcare Systems: The Choctaw Nation Health Services Authority provides care not only to tribal members, but to surrounding

communities—funded through a combination of Indian Health Service contracts and private reimbursements (Choctaw Nation, 2021).

Sustainable Agriculture: Large-scale ranching and farming operations, run with environmental foresight, provide food security and economic return while preserving the land (Jones, 2019).

Outcome

From manufacturing to medicine to agriculture, the Choctaw Nation has built a resilient and adaptable economy, empowering its people and reducing dependence on any one revenue stream.

Case Study 2: The Muckleshoot Tribe

Background

Surrounded by the rich ecosystems of Washington State, the Muckleshoot Tribe has strategically turned natural access into economic opportunity.

Strategies for Success

Renewable Energy: Partnering with state and federal agencies, the Muckleshoot Tribe developed solar and wind energy projects, aligning revenue growth with environmental stewardship (Johnson, 2020).

Hospitality & Tourism: In addition to its casino, the tribe operates hotels, cultural centers, and tourism services—offering visitors an authentic connection to Muckleshoot traditions (Muckleshoot Tribe, 2020).

Seafood Processing: A state-of-the-art processing facility allows the tribe to harvest and sell locally sourced seafood while preserving traditional fishing practices (Anderson, 2018).

Outcome

Through strategic reinvestment in land-based industries and cultural enterprises, the Muckleshoot Tribe has forged a business model built on both sustainability and sovereignty.

Case Study 3: The Tulalip Tribes

Background

Located just north of Seattle, the Tulalip Tribes transformed their proximity to urban markets into a launchpad for economic innovation.

Strategies for Success

Retail Expansion: The Seattle Premium Outlets, owned by the tribe, draw thousands of visitors each week. Additional real estate holdings generate long-term income and employment (Tulalip Tribes, 2019).

Technology Incubation: Tulalip's tech initiatives foster tribal entrepreneurship, support high-skill job training, and promote economic independence in the digital age (Brown, 2020).

Cultural Institutions: The Hibulb Cultural Center doubles as a museum and educational site—preserving heritage while generating tourism revenue.

Outcome

Through diversification into tech, retail, and culture, the Tulalip Tribes have built a future-facing economy anchored in place, tradition, and progress.

Case Study 4: The Mohegan Tribe

Background

Rising from one of the nation's most iconic gaming brands, the Mohegan Tribe of Connecticut redefined what tribal diversification can look like on a global scale.

Strategies for Success

Entertainment & Sports: Beyond its Mohegan Sun resort, the tribe manages stadiums and owns stakes in professional sports teams, transforming hospitality into empire-building (Mohegan Tribe, 2021).

Healthcare & Wellness: Mohegan Sun Health & Wellness delivers integrated medical services, blending tribal care priorities with market-facing healthcare revenue.

Real Estate: Investments in hotels, resorts, and commercial real estate diversify income and build intergenerational assets (Williams, 2019).

Outcome

By converting casino capital into global ventures, the Mohegan Tribe has become a leader in creating layered economic strength while retaining cultural control.

Case Study 5: The Red Lake Nation

Background

Located in northern Minnesota, Red Lake Nation made a strategic leap in 2023 by entering the federal contracting arena through the SBA 8(a) Business Development Program, guided by tribal economic strategist D.G. Comer.

Strategies for Success

Federal Contracting: Red Lake Construction, LLC secured over $10 million in contracts in its first year of SBA 8(a) participation, including projects with the Army Corps of Engineers and the U.S. Air Force (U.S. SBA, 2023).

Joint Ventures: Partnerships in Tempe, Arizona and the Quad Cities positioned the tribe to compete for larger-scale projects and share technical expertise (Red Lake Inc., 2023).

Strategic Growth: The Red Lake Nation emphasized workforce development and internal capacity-building alongside contract acquisition.

Outcome

Red Lake's success in federal contracting signals a new frontier for tribal economic expansion—one rooted in agency, expertise, and long-term revenue generation through the federal marketplace.

Lessons Learned & Best Practices

From these tribal success stories, several key principles emerge:
- Leverage Unique Strengths: Culture, location, and history aren't barriers—they're assets.

- Invest in People: Education and workforce development must be prioritized.
- Think Beyond the Casino: Gaming should be a launchpad, not a landing pad.
- Form Strong Partnerships: Strategic alliances—public and private—magnify impact.
- Honor Sustainability: The best models align economic growth with cultural and environmental preservation.

Conclusion

The path to economic sovereignty is not paved with luck. It's built through vision, discipline, and deliberate diversification. The tribes profiled in this chapter have shown what's possible when leadership meets strategy—and when the past is honored not through preservation alone, but through adaptation, innovation, and bold enterprise.

"Diversity in tribal business is not just a strategy; it is a testament to our resilience and adaptability. By embracing varied enterprises, we honor our ancestors' resourcefulness while paving the way for sustainable growth and prosperity."

Observations

Preservation and Progress:

Tradition in a Modern World

"True progress lies in our ability to walk with one foot rooted in our cultural traditions while the other steps forward into the opportunities of the modern world. It is this balance that will ensure our stories, our languages, and our ways are not only preserved but flourish in a changing world."

Introduction

Progress and preservation—two forces that often seem at odds—define one of the most important challenges facing Native American tribes today. Our traditions ground us, but the world around us moves quickly. How do we adapt without forgetting who we are? This chapter explores the intersection of cultural identity and modern development, and how tribes are choosing to blend—not sacrifice—our heritage in pursuit of economic opportunity and survival.

Historical Context of Cultural Preservation

Traditional Practices and Values

Native cultures have long been rooted in ceremony, language, community structure, and values that transcend generations. These were passed down through oral tradition, sacred art, and lived experience—not written law. Oral storytelling preserved moral codes and history. Ceremonies aligned our people with the seasons and the spiritual world. Art—beadwork, pottery, carvings—served as memory made visible. These practices weren't symbolic—they were essential. They made us who we are.

Impact of Colonization

Colonization didn't just take land. It targeted the essence of who we were. From forced removals to federal bans on ceremonies, Native identity was systematically attacked. Children were taken to boarding schools designed to "kill the Indian, save the man" (Adams, 1995).

Our languages were banned. Our ways were punished. The Indian Religious Crimes Code of 1883 outlawed traditional spiritual practices (Kelly & Kelly, 2014). Land loss wasn't just economic—it was spiritual. The cultural rupture was deep. And yet, we endured.

Modernization and Economic Development

Economic Opportunities

Modernization has brought roads, electricity, healthcare access—but also dependency, disconnection, and sometimes, the commercialization of culture. Still, some tribes have successfully reoriented modernization as a tool, not a threat.

Gaming and Tourism have provided essential revenue for many tribes, but forward-thinking nations pair this with cultural centers, language schools, and land trusts to ensure gaming supports—not replaces—our identity (Cornell & Kalt, 2007).

Renewable Energy offers revenue without resource depletion. Tribes like the Blackfeet Nation are using wind and solar to maintain sovereignty while protecting sacred land (Pevar, 2002).

Entrepreneurship is flourishing among Native artisans, coders, farmers, and chefs who blend tradition and innovation in new businesses rooted in cultural values.

Education and Training help ensure tribal members can thrive in both worlds—learning vocational trades, professional careers, and traditional knowledge together.

Technology Integration: Technology, once seen as a threat to cultural life, can now preserve and amplify it.

Digital Archiving projects are preserving endangered languages, stories, and songs. From mobile apps to oral history repositories, our voices are being stored, protected, and passed on (LaDuke, 1999).

E-Commerce allows Native-made goods to reach global markets. Artists and crafters now use online platforms to sell items that were once only available at powwows.

Telehealth and Education bring essential services to remote areas, supporting both physical well-being and educational access without leaving tribal lands or traditions behind.

Augmented Reality (AR) is being used to teach tribal history by layering historical stories and imagery onto landscapes once thought lost to memory.

Balancing Tradition and Progress

Community Involvement and Leadership

- The most effective models of cultural preservation and modernization are community-led. Cultural direction cannot be dictated by outside consultants or governments—it must be led by elders, youth, and grassroots voices.
- Inclusive Governance ensures decisions about economic growth reflect the tribe's values. Regular community forums, youth councils, and elder advisories keep leadership grounded in tradition.
- Cultural Leadership should be elevated. Spiritual leaders, cultural educators, and language keepers must hold the same influence as economic or political leaders.
- Intergenerational Collaboration is vital. Elders carry memory. Youth carry momentum. Collaboration ensures both are honored.

- Cultural Education Schools in Indian Country should not be cookie-cutter institutions. They must reflect tribal history, language, and values—because identity is protection.
- Bilingual Education restores language while improving cognitive and academic outcomes.
- Cultural Curriculum must be embedded into daily education—not relegated to one week in November.
- Experiential Learning—harvesting traditional plants, participating in ceremonies, building drums or lodges—grounds students in lived cultural understanding.
- Mentor-ship Programs connecting youth to cultural leaders promote continuity, pride, and responsibility.

Cultural Events and Festivals

Community celebrations serve more than social functions—they are reaffirmations of survival, continuity, and visibility.

- Powwows, Seasonal Ceremonies, and Tribal Fairs reinforce collective memory and invite the broader community to witness and learn.
- Public Engagement builds bridges and corrects stereotypes by showing living culture—not museum exhibits.
- Economic Impact from cultural festivals supports artisans, vendors, musicians, and performers, turning celebration into sustainability.

Sustainable Practices

Modern development must not violate our traditional principle of seventh-generation thinking. Sustainability isn't new—it is traditional.

- Environmental Conservation reflects a worldview in which land is sacred, not transactional. Restoration projects are cultural acts.
- Sustainable Agriculture combines traditional planting techniques with modern tools to restore food sovereignty.
- Renewable Energy respects the land while creating jobs and autonomy.

- Sustainable Tourism ensures that cultural sharing does not become cultural exploitation.

Integration of Traditional Healing Practices

Western medicine alone cannot solve the health crises in Native communities. Cultural healing must be integrated.

- Wellness Centers should blend conventional medicine with traditional healing, offering sweat lodge ceremonies, smudging, plant medicine, and prayer as part of care.
- Cultural Competence Training for non-Native healthcare workers ensures respect, safety, and better outcomes for Native patients (Waldram, 2000).
- Partnerships with Traditional Healers are essential. Recognizing their authority and wisdom honors our history and improves health on our terms (Gone, 2010).

Case Studies of Successful Balance

- Hopi Agriculture: Combines dry farming methods with new irrigation techniques—preserving land and legacy (Weatherford, 1991).
- Alaska Native Language Programs: Use apps and digital tools to teach endangered languages, ensuring intergenerational transfer (Krauss, 1992).
- Blackfeet Nation: Wind and solar initiatives reflect cultural values and economic self-sufficiency (Pevar, 2002).
- Zuni Pueblo: Their schools teach traditional arts, language, and ethics alongside STEM education (Tedlock, 1972).
- Navajo Nation Telehealth: Modern delivery, traditional respect. This program meets patients where they are—literally and spiritually (Wilkins, 2011).
- Haudenosaunee Confederacy: Their Seven Generations principle has shaped policies on environmental preservation and education (Wall, 2001).

Conclusion

True progress does not demand the abandonment of the past. Instead, it challenges us to bring the past with us—to remember, reimagine, and restore. Modernization is not the enemy of tradition. The enemy is forgetting who we are.

Tribes that thrive will be those that refuse to choose between being traditional or modern—but instead insist on being both. The ones who create community gardens next to coding camps. Who record ceremonies in high definition while still dancing barefoot on the earth.

Survival is no longer enough. It is time to flourish—rooted in where we come from, reaching toward where we are going.

"Modernization need not mean the erasure of our heritage. Instead, by embracing the best of both worlds—our ancestral knowledge and contemporary innovations—we build a resilient path forward that honors where we come from while embracing where we are going."

Digital Sovereignty – Protecting Tribal Data

"Digital sovereignty is about more than protecting data—it's about safeguarding our stories, our knowledge, and our power to shape our future without interference. For Native communities, asserting control over our digital landscapes is the next frontier in the fight for true sovereignty."

The First Breach

The fight for sovereignty has always been about more than land. It's about power—over decisions, over resources, over story. In the twenty-first century, that fight has moved to a new battlefield: digital space.

Today, data is currency. It's knowledge. It's leverage. But for Native nations, data is also identity—our health records, our history, our songs, our maps, our languages. If we do not control it, someone else will. Digital sovereignty is not a luxury. It's survival.

Why Digital Sovereignty Matters

Every tribal government today runs on information—land management, emergency response, education, healthcare, enrollment, and internal decision-making. If that information is stored off-reservation, managed by third parties, or subject to non-tribal jurisdiction, it becomes vulnerable. Vulnerable to misuse, subpoena, theft, or misrepresentation.

Digital sovereignty is not just about protecting privacy. It is about protecting self-determination, cultural survival, and political authority. When data leaves our hands, so does our voice. When it stays under tribal jurisdiction, we control the narrative.

Historical Patterns Repeating in Digital Form

Just as settlers once mapped Native land to steal it, today's institutions map tribal data for their own gain. The Havasupai DNA case is a warning. Samples given in trust for diabetes research were later used for unrelated genetic studies—without consent. The result? Exploitation under the guise of science. Colonization now wears a lab coat and uses hard drives instead of cavalry (Garrison, 2013; Mello & Wolf, 2010).

Across Indian Country, data collected through education programs, health services, and grant applications often ends up stored on third-party servers, sometimes even owned by the very governments and corporations that have failed our communities time and again.

Current Barriers to Digital Sovereignty

Inadequate Infrastructure

Many tribes lack the broadband access, secure servers, and IT staffing needed to manage and protect their data. This makes them reliant on outside vendors—vendors who may not understand tribal values or sovereignty (U.S. Commission on Civil Rights, 2018).

Jurisdictional Ambiguity

When tribal data crosses jurisdictional lines, legal protection becomes cloudy. Federal laws such as the CLOUD Act or Patriot Act can compel third-party storage vendors to turn over tribal data without tribal consent (Royster, 2021). Without tribal-specific legal frameworks, sovereignty over digital content remains in question.

Cybersecurity Threats

Tribes are increasingly targeted by cyberattacks. In 2021, the Southern Ute Indian Tribe was hit by ransomware, halting healthcare and administrative services (Tribal Business News, 2021). These attacks highlight the urgent need for cybersecurity capacity rooted in tribal systems and values.

Cultural Exploitation in Digital Archives

Digital archives that document language, art, ceremonies, or burial sites must be governed by tribal law—not museum policies. Cultural misappropriation in digital form is still misappropriation.

Strategic Solutions for Digital Sovereignty

Tribal Data Governance Policies

Adopting tribal data governance protocols—such as the OCAP® principles of Ownership, Control, Access, and Possession—protects data from unauthorized use and ensures its use aligns with tribal interests (FNIGC, 2020).

Investment in Infrastructure

Tribal nations must control their own data centers, cloud environments, and broadband systems. Programs like the Tribal Digital Village Network are proving this is possible (Tribal Digital Village Network, 2020).

Cybersecurity Training and Staffing

Using the NIST Cybersecurity Framework (2018), tribes can build internal cybersecurity systems that reflect tribal control. Training Native professionals through institutions like AIHEC (2021) empowers local IT sovereignty.

Legal Recognition and Advocacy

We need new legislation and federal acknowledgment that tribal data is sovereign data. Until then, tribes must negotiate aggressively for protections in every partnership, contract, or storage agreement.

Ethical Research and Consent Agreements

No data should be collected or shared without informed tribal consent, enforced by tribal law. Whether universities or government agencies, all partners must comply with culturally appropriate data protocols.

Technology for Cultural Preservation

From the Cherokee Nation's language-learning app to digital land maps and VR cultural tours, tribes are turning digital tools into platforms for cultural resilience—not erasure.

Conclusion

Data is the new resource war. It can be mined, stolen, manipulated, or sold. But it can also be reclaimed.

Digital sovereignty means we protect our own stories, define our own records, and determine our own future. Without it, the next century will repeat the thefts of the last. With it, we become authors of our next chapter—not subjects of someone else's research.

"Controlling our digital spaces is not just about technology; it's about protecting our past, empowering our present, and securing our future. The power to govern our own data is the power to write our own story—one that remains authentically ours."

SECTION V: Vision, Language, and the Long Future

"The future of our people rests not only in reclaiming our sovereignty but in the courage to confront our greatest challenges with clarity and determination."

Lifting the Veil

As we enter the final section of this journey into the layered realities of business and politics in Indian Country, we shift our gaze forward—not to escape the past, but to honor it by envisioning what lies ahead. The path forward is not paved in ease or certainty. It is complex, nuanced, and full of tension between who we have been, who we are, and who we must become.

The future of Native American communities hinges on our ability to balance two forces: the preservation of what is sacred and the pursuit of what is necessary. We must learn how to carry our ancestral wisdom while mastering the systems that govern the world today. This is not a matter of choosing between tradition and modernity; it is about forging a future in which both are honored.

Youth: The Foundation of Our Future

The future rests on the shoulders of our youth—but they cannot walk into that future empty-handed. They must be armed with knowledge, sharpened by education, guided by cultural grounding, and emboldened by the truth. Sovereignty is not a mythic destination. It is a responsibility. One that demands legal literacy, economic savvy, and a fierce, unyielding commitment to community.

It is not enough to teach our youth to be proud of who they are—we must teach them how to lead, how to advocate, and how to build. That means ensuring they are fluent in their own history and equally fluent in the systems of law, governance, and economics that shape the world they must navigate. Empowerment without preparation is just rhetoric. Preparation is power (National Indian Education Association, 2023).

Legal Reforms and Policy Advocacy: Tools, Not Afterthoughts

Too often, legal reform is treated as a reactive process—a tool only wielded in moments of threat. But true sovereignty demands proactivity. It means codifying our rights, shaping our policies, and driving legislation that affirms—not just defends—our place in this country. Legal advocacy must move beyond preservation. It must push into innovation. Into nation-building. Into rewriting the rules of engagement with federal and state governments (Cornell & Kalt, 2007).

We must not wait for injustice to act. The future of Indian Country depends on tribal nations defining their terms, writing their laws, and asserting their place with confidence and clarity.

Facing the Hard Truths of Sovereignty

Let us be honest. Sovereignty is not romantic. It is difficult, relentless, and often unpopular. It means saying no to short-term gain for the sake of long-term security. It means choosing accountability over popularity. And it means confronting the painful realities that exist within our own communities—poor governance, nepotism, corruption, apathy. These are not comfortable conversations, but they are necessary if sovereignty is to mean more than ceremonial speeches and tribal seals (Wilkins, 2011).

Real sovereignty demands leadership that is ethical, transparent, and future-focused. We must hold ourselves to higher standards than those who once sought to extinguish us. Our survival is not enough. We must thrive—and thriving requires integrity.

Digital, Economic, and Environmental Frontiers

The next generation of tribal leadership must also be fluent in the new frontiers of power—digital sovereignty, environmental stewardship, and diversified economic development. Our data is valuable. Our lands are valuable. Our knowledge is valuable. But these assets mean little if we do not control them.

We must confront the digital divide with aggressive investment in broadband, cybersecurity, and AI literacy (Tribal Business News, 2021). We must assert ownership of our environmental decisions, our natural resources, and our ecological legacies. And we must move beyond the false comfort of casino revenue into a future built on multiple, sovereign-owned industries—from renewable energy and tech, to healthcare and cultural preservation enterprises (Jorgensen, 2007).

The Weight of Legacy and the Promise of Tomorrow

In every decision we make, we are laying stone for a path others will walk. This is not just about policy or economics—it is about legacy. Will our grandchildren inherit strong tribal institutions? Will they be fluent in their language? Will they know the stories? Will they have choices?

This chapter is a mirror and a blueprint. It asks us to reflect and demands that we build. It does not promise ease—but it promises meaning.

Conclusion: Guardians of Tradition, Pioneers of Progress

The road ahead will demand that we become both guardians and pioneers. We must preserve the sacred, but we must not become frozen in it. We must lead not with nostalgia, but with vision.

Our ancestors survived colonization. We must now survive complacency.

And in doing so, we must remember this truth: sovereignty is not a slogan—it is a structure. One that must be built. One that must be protected. And one that must serve not only us, but those who come after.

Let this section be our charge. To confront what must be changed. To build what must endure. And to ensure that the future of Indian Country is not written by others—but by us, with boldness, truth, and the unwavering resolve of a sovereign people.

"We are the descendants of those who refused to vanish—and the architects of a future that refuses to settle."

Observations:

Youth and the Future of Native Leadership

"True leadership is not taught—it is awakened. When we empower our young people, we are not merely preparing them for the world ahead; we are reconnecting them to the roots of who we are, so that in every step they take forward, they carry their heritage with pride and purpose."

Lighting the Match

Empowering Native American youth is more than a strategy for future success—it's a sacred responsibility. Our ancestors knew that the survival of our people depended on preparing the next generation, not only for the battles they would face but also for the wisdom they would carry forward. Today, those battles are fought in boardrooms and courtrooms, in schools and on social media. Our youth stand at the crossroads of tradition and modernity, tasked with honoring the sacred while leading us into a rapidly changing world. How we prepare them for that journey will define the future of our nations.

The Importance of Education

Access to Quality Education

Ensuring that Native youth have access to education that honors their identity is critical. Academic excellence must go hand-in-hand with culturally relevant curricula, so that our young people know not only how to excel in mainstream society but also how to carry forward the values, language, and history of their people. As Deloria & Wildcat (2001) remind us, true education for Native students must start by affirming who they are at their core.

Culturally Relevant Curriculum

Too often, Native history is written by those who colonized us, not by those who lived it. A culturally relevant curriculum gives our youth the chance to reclaim their stories and shape their identities. Schools that integrate Native traditions, languages, and cultural practices alongside modern subjects allow young people to connect to their heritage while preparing them to be leaders in the wider world (Deloria & Wildcat, 2001).

Higher Education and Vocational Training

Higher education is not a departure from Native traditions but a continuation of them. Whether pursuing academic degrees or vocational training, our youth are building on the strength of their ancestors. They walk in two worlds, excelling in modern disciplines while holding tightly to cultural values. Programs that support educational attainment for Native youth are essential for creating the leaders of tomorrow, be it through scholarships or training tailored to the specific needs of our communities (Deloria & Wildcat, 2001).

Balancing Two Worlds

Native youth carry a unique responsibility—they are heirs to centuries of tradition, yet they must also master the intricacies of a modern, often foreign, economic and political system. Balancing the teachings of their ancestors with the demands of mainstream business and governance is no small feat. Our young leaders must understand that their role is not to assimilate but to incorporate the best of both worlds to build a future that honors our past (Deloria & Wildcat, 2001).

Mentorship and Role Models

Mentorship Programs

We have always known the importance of elders teaching the young. Mentorship is not a modern concept; it is a traditional one. Today, the stakes are higher, but the principle remains the same.

Our future depends on those who guide our youth, showing them how to lead with integrity and wisdom. Formal mentorship programs, where young people are connected to experienced leaders, can be powerful tools for growth. Mentors help youth navigate not only professional challenges but also cultural ones, grounding them in values while encouraging them to dream big (Gipp, 2009).

Role Models

Native communities are filled with role models, both historical and contemporary. These leaders show our youth what is possible, even in the face of adversity. Highlighting the accomplishments of Native leaders across sectors—from business to education to the arts—offers powerful examples of resilience and success. Our youth need to see that they too can rise to lead, just as their ancestors did (Gipp, 2009).

Case Study – ANSEP

One shining example is the Alaska Native Science and Engineering Program (ANSEP). By focusing on mentorship, hands-on learning, and long-term support, ANSEP has engaged Native youth in the fields of science and engineering, showing them that STEM can be a path not just for personal success but also for the betterment of their communities (Gipp, 2009).

Cultural Resilience and Identity

Preserving Cultural Heritage

Without a strong cultural identity, leadership loses its foundation. Cultural resilience is what keeps our communities strong, and it is what will ensure that our youth lead with both wisdom and pride.

Our ceremonies, languages, and histories are gifts handed down through the generations. They are not relics of the past but living legacies. Programs that teach traditional practices and engage youth in cultural preservation are critical. These efforts instill pride and provide a strong sense of identity, ensuring that our youth understand their responsibility to carry forward what was entrusted to them (Jojola, 2013).

Language Revitalization

Language is more than words; it is a worldview. Revitalizing our languages is key to strengthening cultural ties and helping youth feel connected to their communities. Language immersion schools and digital resources are breathing new life into endangered Native languages, ensuring they remain vibrant for future generations (Jojola, 2013).

Cultural Centers and Activities

Establishing cultural centers provides spaces where our youth can gather to learn, practice, and celebrate their culture. These spaces foster intergenerational dialogue and help solidify the bonds between the past, present, and future (Jojola, 2013).

Community Involvement and Leadership Opportunities

Youth Councils and Committees

Leadership cannot be learned in isolation. It requires community involvement and direct experience in governance and service.

Youth councils offer young people the chance to step into leadership roles early, gaining practical experience while contributing to their communities. These councils provide platforms for Native youth to engage in governance, preparing them for future responsibilities (Cornell & Kalt, 2000).

Leadership Training Programs

Specialized programs that teach leadership skills—public speaking, negotiation, project management—are essential. These training programs help youth develop the confidence and competence they need to lead effectively within their communities (Cornell & Kalt, 2000).

Service Learning and Community Projects

Engaging youth in community service teaches them the importance of giving back. Service-learning projects provide hands-on experience in addressing community needs, deepening their sense of responsibility and leadership (Cornell & Kalt, 2000).

Case Study – White Earth Tribal and Community College

In Minnesota, the White Earth Tribal and Community College combines academic learning with community service. This approach allows students to develop leadership skills while addressing local issues, fostering a strong sense of community and responsibility (Johnson, 2019).

Health and Well-being

Addressing Health Disparities

The future of Native leadership also depends on health and well-being. Without strong bodies and minds, our youth cannot fully step into their roles as leaders.

Our youth face significant health challenges, from diabetes to substance abuse to mental health struggles. Holistic health programs that combine modern healthcare with traditional healing practices are critical for supporting their overall well-being (Gone & Trimble, 2012).

Mental Health Support

Native youth carry the weight of historical trauma along with the pressures of modern life. Access to mental health services that are culturally appropriate is essential. These services, when combined with traditional healing practices, can provide the resilience needed to overcome personal and community challenges (Gone & Trimble, 2012).

Physical Activity and Nutrition

Promoting physical activity and healthy eating habits within our youth fosters a sense of discipline and strength. Programs that encourage traditional diets and outdoor activities connect youth to their cultural roots while promoting overall health (Gone & Trimble, 2012).

Conclusion

Empowering Native youth is not just an investment in the future—it is an investment in the preservation of our culture, our sovereignty, and our resilience. By focusing on education, mentorship, cultural preservation, and health, we ensure that the next generation is ready to lead. It is through our youth that we will continue to thrive, honoring the wisdom of our ancestors while embracing the possibilities of tomorrow.

"Our youth are the living threads that weave together the past and the future. Their strength lies not just in the knowledge they gain from books, but in the wisdom passed down through stories, songs, and the land itself. It is our sacred duty to guide them, so they may lead with both the spirit of their ancestors and the vision of a new tomorrow."

Observations

The Real Cost of Sovereignty and Self-Determination

"True self-determination is not without its trials, but it is in these trials that we find the resilience of our people, the fire that sustains our cultures, and the path to a future where our voices are heard, respected, and empowered."

Prelude to Truth

Sovereignty and self-determination stand as cornerstones of Native American tribal identity. They signify not only the right to self-govern but the freedom to manage resources, safeguard traditions, and preserve cultural integrity free from external interference.

However, the journey toward achieving and maintaining sovereignty comes with substantial costs—financial, social, and political. This chapter explores these challenges and opportunities, analyzing the profound costs involved in achieving genuine self-governance for Native American communities.

Historical Context

For centuries, Native American tribes have endured persistent attacks on their sovereignty. From forced relocations to destructive assimilation policies such as the Dawes Act, the U.S. government systematically undermined tribal governance and dissolved communal landholdings (Prucha, 1984).

The Indian Reorganization Act of 1934 aimed to reverse some of these destructive policies, encouraging tribes to restore self-governance and regain control over their lands. Yet, despite these efforts, the path to true sovereignty remains fraught with legal, financial, and political obstacles.

Financial Costs

Infrastructure and Services

Achieving self-determination requires tribes to finance and maintain essential services like healthcare, education, and law enforcement. Unlike state and local governments, tribes often lack a broad tax base and must rely heavily on federal grants, which can be inconsistent. The Navajo Nation, for instance, which spans three states, struggles to maintain roads, provide clean water, and ensure access to adequate healthcare. The cost of developing and maintaining this infrastructure, particularly in remote and environmentally harsh areas, can be staggering.

Economic Development

Developing sustainable businesses on reservations presents unique challenges, including limited access to capital and navigating complex regulatory systems. Many tribes find themselves balancing economic growth with the need to preserve cultural values. The Choctaw Nation of Oklahoma, for instance, has diversified its economy through gaming, manufacturing, and retail, but doing so required substantial investments in infrastructure and strategic foresight.

Legal and Administrative Expenses

Defending tribal sovereignty often involves expensive legal battles. These can include disputes over land, water, or hunting rights, all of which require significant legal expertise and resources. In McGirt v. Oklahoma (2020), the Muscogee (Creek) Nation fought a protracted legal battle to affirm their historical territory's sovereignty—though they won, the financial cost was immense.

Revenue Generation and Dependency

Many tribes have come to rely on gaming as their primary revenue stream, but this source of income can be volatile and dependent on external market forces. The economic downturns of the past decade have hit tribal gaming operations hard, underscoring the need for diversified revenue streams. The reliance on federal grants further perpetuates economic dependency, limiting tribes' ability to achieve full financial sovereignty (Cornell & Kalt, 1992).

Social Costs

Community Divisions

Sovereignty brings with it the potential for internal conflict, particularly in how resources are allocated. This can lead to disputes over leadership, the direction of economic projects, or cultural preservation efforts. For example, debates over resource extraction—such as mining or oil drilling—can create divisions between those focused on economic growth and those advocating for environmental preservation (Smith & Frehner, 2016).

Cultural Preservation

While sovereignty allows tribes to protect their cultural heritage, the pressures of modernization can challenge cultural preservation. The Blackfeet Nation has worked to revitalize its language and traditions while simultaneously developing tourism and agriculture as vital economic sectors (Bastien, 2004).

Health and Well-being

The stress of self-governance, coupled with historical trauma and ongoing discrimination, can exacerbate health disparities in Native communities. The Pine Ridge Reservation, home to the Oglala Lakota, has one of the lowest life expectancies in the Western Hemisphere, a tragic indicator of the health challenges that persist in Indian Country (Warne & Frizzell, 2014).

Political Costs

Intergovernmental Relations

Maintaining sovereignty requires careful management of relationships with federal, state, and local governments. Tribes must continually assert their rights while fostering cooperative partnerships. The Cherokee Nation's negotiation of a healthcare funding agreement with the federal government illustrates the importance of political acumen in sustaining sovereignty (Smithers, 2019).

Self-Governance Challenges

Sustaining self-governance demands capable leadership and effective administrative structures. Turnover in tribal leadership can disrupt continuity, as evidenced during the Dakota Access Pipeline protests when the Standing Rock Sioux Tribe faced organizational challenges (Zepeda, 2018).

Legal and Regulatory Compliance

Tribes operate within a complex legal landscape that includes federal, state, and tribal laws. Compliance with these laws requires significant administrative resources. The Indian Child Welfare Act (ICWA), which protects Native children from being separated from their culture, imposes legal responsibilities on tribes, often straining their administrative capacities (Fletcher, 2009).

Case Studies

The Navajo Nation

As one of the largest tribes, the Navajo Nation has made strides in self-governance but faces significant challenges in managing natural resources and funding essential services. The tribe's ongoing water rights disputes highlight the financial burden of maintaining sovereignty.

The Ho-Chunk Nation

In Wisconsin, the Ho-Chunk Nation has utilized gaming revenues to stabilize its economy and fund community development. However, the tribe recognizes the need for income diversification and is currently exploring renewable energy projects and other ventures (Johnson, 2019).

Potential Solutions and Recommendations

Federal Support

Continued federal support is critical to sustaining tribal sovereignty. Recent reauthorizations of the Violence Against Women Act (VAWA), which extend tribal jurisdiction over non-Native offenders, exemplify how federal policy can bolster tribal sovereignty (Deer, 2015).

Capacity Building

Investing in education and leadership development within the tribe is crucial for building the administrative capacities necessary for effective self-governance. Programs like the American Indian College Fund offer scholarships to support these goals (Deloria & Wildcat, 2001).

Economic Diversification

Tribes must diversify their economies beyond gaming. Renewable energy projects, technology ventures, and agriculture are promising avenues. For example, the Fort Peck Tribes' wind energy initiative has provided both economic benefits and environmental sustainability (Jojola, 2013).

Proposals for Legislative Reform

Many tribal councils face pressures to hide internal issues, fearing external judgment or loss of control. To address this, legislation could limit council powers, ensuring transparency and accountability. For example, if there is clear evidence warranting termination or prosecution, the council should not have the power to reverse such outcomes, which often perpetuates a lack of accountability.

Conclusion

The path toward sovereignty and self-determination is long and complex. Tribes face considerable financial, social, and political challenges, yet the rewards of true self-governance—cultural preservation, economic stability, and autonomy—are profound. With strategic planning, federal support, and internal capacity building, Native tribes can continue the enduring struggle for sovereignty, a testament to their resilience and strength.

> *"Sovereignty and self-determination are more than lofty ideals; they are hard-won battles demanding sacrifice, resilience, and unwavering commitment. The real cost lies in the constant vigilance required to protect our rights and the enduring effort to build a future on our terms."*

Observations

Legal Reforms and Policy Advocacy

"True justice for Native American tribes is not just about reclaiming land or rights; it's about reclaiming dignity, identity, and the power to shape our own future. Legal reforms must be more than policy—they must be the foundation for healing and renewal."

The Law Was never Ours

The long path toward justice for Native American tribes has always been fraught with legal battles and policy struggles that seek to redress centuries of marginalization. Legal reforms and policy advocacy remain critical to addressing the challenges that affect tribal communities—from land rights and sovereignty issues to the disparities in social justice and economic development.

This chapter delves into the complex legal landscape, highlighting the need for comprehensive legal frameworks that uphold tribal autonomy and sovereignty while providing a roadmap for future generations to carry the mantle of advocacy forward. These reforms are not only about righting historical wrongs but about creating a sustainable, dignified future for tribal nations.

Historical Context of Legal Challenges

The legacy of colonialism and post-colonialism introduced policies aimed at eroding Native American sovereignty and undermining the social fabric of tribal nations. The Doctrine of Discovery, deeply rooted in European colonial thought, laid the foundation for the systematic dispossession of Native lands and the marginalization of tribal governance.

Landmark legal decisions and policies such as the Indian Removal Act of 1830 and the Dawes Act of 1887 only deepened this divide by forcibly relocating tribes and breaking communal landholdings, paving the way for federal control over tribal affairs (Deloria & Lytle, 1983).

The mid-20th century brought the Termination Era, a dark period marked by efforts to assimilate Native peoples and dissolve tribal sovereignty. Policies such as the Termination Act aimed to dismantle tribal legal recognition, resulting in severe losses of land, resources, and political identity for tribes. However, the Indian Reorganization Act of 1934 and the shift toward self-determination in the following decades offered some respite, allowing tribes to regain a semblance of control over their governance (Deloria & Lytle, 1983).

Land Rights and Sovereignty

Restoring Land Ownership

The fight for land rights continues to stand at the forefront of Native American legal reforms. Generations of tribal land dispossession have left many communities with fragmented territories. Efforts toward legal reform must prioritize the restoration and protection of these lands, taking into account the cultural, spiritual, and ecological importance of the land to Native communities.

A prime example of this ongoing struggle is the Black Hills land dispute involving the Sioux Nation. Although the 1980 U.S. Supreme Court ruling awarded financial compensation for the illegal seizure of the Black Hills, the Sioux continue to seek the return of the land itself, emphasizing its sacred significance over monetary redress (Pevar, 2012).

Enhancing Sovereignty

At the heart of Native American self-determination is tribal sovereignty. True sovereignty extends beyond symbolic recognition—it requires real, functional autonomy that enables tribes to manage their lands, resources, and governance structures. Strengthening sovereignty through legal reforms can empower tribes to fully govern their lands and people without federal or state encroachment.

Self-governance compacts, which enable tribes to assume control over federal services, have emerged as a powerful tool. These agreements allow tribes to tailor programs to fit their unique needs and values, thereby reinforcing tribal sovereignty (Cornell & Kalt, 2000).

Social Justice and Civil Rights

Addressing Historical Injustices

The legacy of forced relocations, cultural erasure, and systemic discrimination continues to resonate across Native American communities. Legal reforms aimed at achieving reparative justice, such as the return of lands and financial compensation for historical injustices, remain vital to the restoration of tribal dignity and autonomy. However, true justice must also include formal apologies and the institutional recognition of these past wrongs.

Criminal Justice Reform

Native Americans face stark disparities within the criminal justice system, ranging from higher incarceration rates to inadequate legal representation and protection against violence. The passage of the Violence Against Women Reauthorization Act (VAWA) of 2013, which restored tribal jurisdiction over non-Native perpetrators of domestic violence on tribal lands, marked a pivotal step in correcting systemic injustices (Deer, 2015). However, more is needed to ensure that Native peoples receive fair treatment and protection under the law.

Voting Rights and Political Representation

Native Americans have historically faced significant barriers to voting, from stringent voter ID laws to the lack of accessible polling stations on reservations. Legal reforms must focus on eliminating these obstacles and ensuring greater representation of Native Americans in local, state, and federal politics.

Economic Development and Resource Management

Promoting Economic Sovereignty

Economic sovereignty is an essential pillar of tribal self-determination. Legal frameworks that enable tribes to manage their natural resources and enter into economic partnerships and business ventures play a critical role in fostering economic growth and independence. The Navajo Nation's development of coal, oil, and renewable energy resources demonstrates how legal reforms can help tribes harness their economic potential while balancing environmental and cultural stewardship (Royster & Blumm, 2008).

Regulatory Challenges

Tribal enterprises often face multiple regulatory hurdles, including federal and state oversight that limits economic development. Legal reforms should streamline these processes, offering financial incentives, infrastructure development, and increased access to capital.

Health and Education Reforms

Healthcare Access and Equity

Native American communities face some of the most significant health disparities in the country. Reforms that improve access to healthcare through expanded funding for the Indian Health Service (IHS) and culturally tailored healthcare practices are urgently needed. The Affordable Care Act's permanent reauthorization of the Indian Health Care Improvement Act (IHCIA) provided a framework for improving healthcare services, but much remains to be done to achieve health equity (Warne & Frizzell, 2014).

Education and Cultural Preservation

Preserving Native languages, traditions, and history is central to the long-term vitality of tribal communities. Legal reforms should aim to enhance access to culturally relevant education, increase funding for tribal colleges, and support language revitalization programs. Laws such as the Native American Graves Protection and Repatriation Act (NAGPRA) have made significant strides in safeguarding cultural heritage, but continued advocacy and legal protections are essential for ensuring these gains are sustained (Echo-Hawk, 2010).

Environmental Protection and Sustainability

Protecting Sacred Sites

Tribal lands are not just economic resources—they are sacred landscapes imbued with cultural and spiritual meaning. Legal reforms that recognize and enforce the protection of these sacred sites are necessary to prevent further desecration and exploitation.

Climate Change Adaptation

Native American tribes are among the communities most vulnerable to the effects of climate change. Rising sea levels, changing ecosystems, and extreme weather events threaten the very survival of many tribal nations. Legal reforms must prioritize climate resilience through infrastructure development, disaster preparedness, and sustainable resource management (Whyte, 2017).

Advocacy Strategies and Collaborative Efforts

Building Coalitions and Mobilization

True change requires collective action. Advocacy must extend beyond tribal communities to include alliances with environmental, civil rights, and social justice organizations. Grassroots movements such as the Standing Rock Sioux's fight against the Dakota Access Pipeline (DAPL) showcase the power of unified voices in defending tribal sovereignty and environmental rights (Estes, 2019).

Legal Advocacy and Litigation

The legal system remains a critical battleground for Native American rights. Tribes must continue to use litigation as a tool to challenge unjust laws and defend their sovereignty. Whether through legal challenges to state overreach or advocating for progressive policies in Washington, legal advocacy is essential for protecting the gains achieved and securing new victories for tribal communities.

Conclusion

The future of Native American sovereignty and self-determination hinges on the strength of legal reforms and policy advocacy. By addressing land rights, sovereignty, social justice, health, education, and environmental stewardship, we can lay the foundation for a more just and sustainable future. The work ahead is immense, but with strategic advocacy, coalition-building, and a steadfast commitment to justice, tribal nations can forge a path toward true autonomy and lasting prosperity.

"Legal reform is not just about the laws we change, but about the futures we protect."

Observations

Hard Answers – Ensuring Tribal Success and Thriving

"The truth is, the road to tribal success isn't easy or without sacrifice. It requires hard decisions and even harder truths. But through those truths, we forge a path to sovereignty, dignity, and prosperity for generations to come."

Introduction

Achieving success and ensuring the long-term prosperity of Native American tribes demands more than good intentions—it requires a willingness to confront uncomfortable realities and take bold, strategic actions. This chapter explores the "hard answers" necessary for tribes to navigate both internal and external challenges. From qualified leadership and governance reforms to economic strategies and cultural resilience, these elements form the foundation for sustainable growth and self-sufficiency. Tribes must address these issues head-on to secure a future where success is not just achieved, but where communities thrive.

The Necessity of Qualified Leadership

Challenges of Unqualified Leadership

Many tribes have historically adhered to a practice of appointing tribal members to key leadership positions, often placing kinship and internal connections above merit. While this practice is rooted in the desire to preserve cultural integrity and ensure tribal members benefit from leadership roles, it can create inefficiencies and mismanagement. Leadership positions that require expertise in modern governance, finance, and business operations are too often filled by individuals without the necessary qualifications. When leaders lack these skills, the overall effectiveness of tribal government and enterprises is compromised, setting back progress and development (Cornell & Kalt, 2000).

Incompetence and Nepotism

Nepotism, which often favors family relationships over merit, can further exacerbate this problem. It undermines the principles of governance and accountability by promoting individuals based on connections rather than ability. This weakens the tribal government's overall functionality and hinders the progress of community projects. Worse yet, it creates an environment where accountability is scarce, decisions are unchecked, and performance is not rigorously evaluated. The consequences include poor decision-making, resource mismanagement, and the deterioration of public trust in leadership (Cornell & Kalt, 2000).

Impact on Business Ventures

Poor leadership in tribal enterprises can result in the failure of vital economic ventures. Business success in today's complex economy requires strategic vision and skilled management. When leadership lacks these elements, tribal businesses are unable to grow, compete, or sustain themselves. Failed projects, financial losses, and missed opportunities for diversification are the inevitable outcomes of unqualified leadership

Case Study

In one unfortunate instance, a tribal casino's mismanagement by an unqualified executive led to financial failure. Due to a lack of financial oversight and strategic planning, the casino—a primary source of revenue for the tribe—suffered severe losses, putting the entire community's economy at risk. This stark example underscores the importance of skilled leadership to ensure the success and sustainability of tribal enterprises (Smith, 2018).

Implementing Minimum Qualifications

To prevent such failures, tribes must establish and enforce minimum qualifications for leadership roles. This entails setting clear criteria for education, experience, and relevant skills that candidates must meet before assuming leadership positions. Implementing standards for professional qualifications ensures that those entrusted with governing or leading tribal enterprises are equipped to make informed decisions (Cornell & Kalt, 2000).

Governance Reforms and Accountability

Establishing Governance Standards

Successful governance requires a clear framework that prioritizes accountability, transparency, and ethical leadership. Tribes must establish governance structures that prevent corruption, mismanagement, and inefficiencies. Such frameworks should include codified policies, procedures, and ethical guidelines that all officials are required to follow. Ensuring these standards are in place is essential for preventing the destructive effects of nepotism and incompetence (Cornell & Kalt, 2000).

Code of Ethics and Accountability

A formal code of ethics sets the tone for responsible governance. This code should emphasize transparency, ethical decision-making, and the avoidance of conflicts of interest. When all tribal officials and employees are held to these standards, the government operates more efficiently and with greater trust from the community.

Case Study

A tribe in the Pacific Northwest implemented governance reforms, which included a robust code of ethics and regular audits. These reforms helped the tribe avoid the mismanagement that had plagued previous administrations. With clearer governance standards, the tribe experienced increased economic growth and stronger partnerships with external entities (Johnson, 2019).

Leveraging Federal Programs and Support

Utilizing Federal Programs

Federal programs, such as the SBA 8(a) Business Development Program, offer invaluable support to tribal businesses. These programs provide access to government contracts, business training, and financial assistance—resources that significantly enhance the capabilities of tribal enterprises. Taking full advantage of federal support can be a game changer for tribes seeking to diversify their revenue streams (Cornell & Kalt, 2000).

Case Study

An Alaskan tribe successfully leveraged the SBA 8(a) program to secure a multi-million-dollar contract for building military infrastructure. This contract not only provided immediate financial benefits but also established the tribe's reputation as a reliable government contractor. The tribe's success highlights the importance of strategic use of federal programs to bolster economic growth (Smith, 2018).

Promoting Accountability and Transparency

Internal Audits and Public Reporting

Accountability must be embedded in the governance framework through mechanisms such as regular internal audits and public reporting. Independent audit committees play a crucial role in ensuring financial transparency, while regular public reports provide tribal members with access to key governance decisions and financial data.

Case Study

A tribe in the Midwest implemented a transparency initiative that required all leadership actions and financial operations to be publicly reported. This transparency increased trust within the community and prevented the kind of financial mismanagement that had previously destabilized tribal governance (Johnson, 2019).

Building External Partnerships

Collaborating for Growth

Strong external partnerships are vital for tribal success, offering access to resources, expertise, and markets. Tribes should actively seek strategic alliances with private businesses, non-profits, and governmental agencies. Such partnerships can drive economic development, provide technical support, and open new avenues for growth and diversification (Cornell & Kalt, 2000).

Embracing Innovation and Sustainability

Innovative Economic Development

Innovation is key to ensuring long-term success. Tribes must explore new technologies, business models, and sustainable practices to remain competitive in today's economy. Embracing sustainable development, renewable energy projects, and technology integration will not only ensure economic resilience but also align with the traditional values of environmental stewardship.

Case Study

A Pacific Northwest tribe embraced sustainable practices by developing renewable energy projects and promoting eco-tourism. These initiatives, rooted in respect for the environment, generated significant revenue while preserving cultural values. This model of innovation and sustainability offers a roadmap for other tribes seeking to balance economic growth with environmental responsibility (Johnson, 2019).

Conclusion

Ensuring tribal success and long-term thriving requires addressing tough realities and making bold decisions. Qualified leadership, governance reforms, federal support, accountability, and sustainability are the pillars upon which successful tribal futures are built. By confronting these hard truths and embracing innovative strategies, Native American tribes can secure a prosperous and self-sufficient future—one rooted in resilience, strength, and cultural integrity.

> *"True success for our tribes demands that we confront hard truths and make difficult decisions with courage and clarity. Thriving means not only preserving our heritage but also forging new paths with integrity and resilience, always guided by our collective wisdom."*

Observations

Decay of Tribal Languages: From Thousands to a Few

"To reclaim our languages is not merely to preserve words; it is to breathe life back into our culture, our history, and our future. In every syllable, we find the strength of our ancestors and the hope for generations yet to come."

When Silence Took the Place of Song

Language is the soul of a culture, carrying within it the stories, values, and identity of a people. For Native American tribes, language has always been a fundamental part of their identity, connecting generations through oral traditions, songs, ceremonies, and daily communication. Yet, despite its central importance, the survival of these languages has been under relentless threat for centuries. Today, what remains is a fraction of the linguistic diversity that once flourished across Native lands.

The Decline of Tribal Languages: From the 1700s to Present

In the early 1700s, over 300 distinct Native American languages were spoken across what is now the United States (National Geographic Society, 2018). These languages reflected the rich diversity of tribes, each capturing the essence of their geography, history, and worldview. Today, however, the number of languages still spoken or remembered has shrunk dramatically.

According to the National Congress of American Indians (NCAI), 2019, approximately 175 Native languages are still spoken to some degree, with many teetering on the brink of extinction. Shockingly, only about 20 of these languages are being learned by children, signaling an alarming trend toward language death. Without intentional and comprehensive efforts, many Native languages will be lost forever, severing the lifeline to a cultural heritage.

Reasons for the Decay of Tribal Languages

Assimilation Policies and Boarding Schools

In the 19th and 20th centuries, the U.S. government pursued assimilation policies aimed at erasing Native identity. Boarding schools were established to "civilize" Native children, forcibly removing them from their families and forbidding them to speak their languages. Generations of children were punished for speaking in their mother tongues, resulting in a profound loss of linguistic continuity (Smithsonian Institution, 2020). The legacy of these policies lingers today, manifesting in the broken chain of language transmission across Native families.

Missionary Influence

Missionaries contributed to the suppression of Native languages, often perceiving them as impediments to religious conversion. By introducing the Bible and religious instruction in English or European languages, missionaries further eroded the use of tribal languages in both daily life and sacred practices. This spiritual colonization displaced Native tongues from their cultural contexts, leading to further marginalization.

Cultural Influence and Changing Values

Over time, as American values and media infiltrated Native societies, a shift occurred. The appeal of fitting into mainstream society often pushed Native individuals to prioritize English over their ancestral languages. Practical considerations such as employment, education, and social mobility made English seem like a necessity, but the cost of this pragmatism was the gradual erosion of cultural identity.

Shifting Identity and the Desire to Be "American"

For many young Native Americans today, there is an ongoing internal conflict between maintaining cultural roots and navigating modern American society. The pressure to assimilate, to be seen as "American," can overshadow the desire to preserve traditional languages and values. This identity struggle reflects a broader issue of marginalization, where Indigenous identities are often overlooked or misunderstood by the dominant culture.

"Language is our soul, our memory, and our future. To lose it is to lose ourselves."

A Personal Reflection: The Loss of Fluency

The decay of tribal languages is not just an abstract or academic problem—it is deeply personal and impacts the very core of Native families and communities. I will never forget a particular moment with my grandmother, a powerful symbol of this loss. She lived to be 104, a woman fluent in three Native languages, effortlessly switching between dialects that she knew instinctively. During a large powwow, she greeted two elders in their respective native languages, replying fluently and with grace. After they walked away, she chuckled to herself.

I asked, *"Why do you laugh, Grandma?"*

"They are so old," she replied softly, *"yet they are speaking in baby talk."*

Her words struck me deeply. These elders were once surrounded by fluent speakers, yet as time passed, their command of the language had withered. What remained was a fragmented echo, a vestige of a once-thriving culture. My grandmother had witnessed the gradual decay, and her response was not mere amusement but a recognition of the painful truth that we, as a people, are slowly losing our most valuable inheritance.

The Path Forward: Preservation and Revitalization

Despite the tragic loss of many Native languages, there is hope. Across tribal communities, language revitalization efforts are growing, rooted in the recognition that these languages are essential to cultural survival. Language immersion schools, digital archives, and community programs offer pathways for young generations to reconnect with their linguistic heritage. Tribes have made language preservation a cornerstone of their cultural revival efforts, understanding that language is the key to sovereignty, identity, and continuity.

Technology has also become a powerful ally in these efforts. AI-driven language platforms, digital dictionaries, and online classes allow for unprecedented access to Native languages, particularly for those living far from their tribal lands. The Cherokee Nation's development of language apps and virtual classrooms illustrates how technology can play a transformative role in this battle for survival.

As I reflect on my grandmother's words, I realize that language is far more than a tool for communication—it is the essence of who we are as Native peoples. Every word carries the weight of our ancestors, every phrase echoes the wisdom of generations past. Revitalizing our languages means reclaiming our past and ensuring that our stories, songs, and traditions live on.

"Our identity as Native peoples is woven into the words of our languages. When we lose that connection, we are not just losing a language—we are losing the heartbeat of who we are."

The Future of Native America – 100 Years Ahead

"The future is not a place we arrive at—it is a legacy we shape with every decision we make today. If we fail to act with courage and clarity now, the silence that follows will not be because we disappeared, but because we surrendered our voice."

Introduction: The Spirit Beyond the Horizon

To gaze 100 years into the future of Native America is to peer through the mist of time and memory, where the echoes of our ancestors mingle with the challenges of today. The truth, often difficult to confront, lies in the confluence of historical wounds and ongoing struggles, both within and outside our communities. Our survival, our identity, and the sacred bond between the land and our people stand at a crossroads. What will we choose? To walk the path of resilience and renewal, or to allow the forces of erasure and assimilation to silence the very heartbeat of our nations?

The past haunts us, but it also teaches us. And as we face the uncertain horizon, we must have the courage to acknowledge that our future will be shaped not only by external pressures but also by the decisions we make from within. The spirit of our people, though tested, has not been extinguished. But to survive the next century, we must ask ourselves: What are we willing to do to ensure the survival of our cultures, our sovereignty, and our very existence?

Economic Disparities and Dependency: The Chains We Forge

"What good is sovereignty if our hands remain bound by the chains of dependency?"

The story of economic dependency is an old one in Indian Country, woven into the very fabric of our existence since the first treaties were broken and our lands were taken. Federal funds, casino revenues, and grant cycles have become lifelines for many Native communities. But a lifeline is not the same as freedom. Economic sovereignty is not a handout—it is a condition earned through vision, risk, and rebuilding.

The concept of the "Hang Around the Fort Indians," born from forced dependency, still echoes in our communities today. If we do not confront this mindset head-on, we risk waking up a century from now and realizing we mistook survival for strength. Economic dignity will not be secured through federal budgets or the volatile tides of gaming. It will come from bold decisions—to innovate, to diversify, to lead.

Tribes that fail to invest in sustainable industries, technologies, agriculture, and energy independence will find themselves shackled to systems they cannot control. Those that break free—that elect leaders of integrity, reject nepotism, and cultivate partnerships rooted in sovereignty—will stand as models of Native self-determination (Kalt & Singer, 2004).

Cultural Preservation vs. Assimilation: The Battle for Our Souls

"If we lose our language, our stories, and our ceremonies, what is left of us? We may live, but will we still be Native?"

Cultural preservation is not a side project. It is our frontline. Language, ceremony, and ancestral knowledge are not simply artifacts—they are living threads in the spiritual fabric of our nations. And they are unraveling.

The loss of Native languages is not just a linguistic crisis—it is an identity crisis. Each elder who passes without passing down the songs, the stories, the words, takes with them a piece of our collective soul. If we fail to invest now in language immersion programs, cultural mentorship, and the sacred duties of oral tradition, we will lose more than memory—we will lose ourselves (Smithsonian Institution, 2023; National Indian Education Association [NIEA], 2024).

In the century to come, our children must not inherit only photographs and regalia. They must inherit living knowledge. Let our classrooms echo with Native tongues. Let our youth learn the ways of ceremony, not from documentaries, but from their grandmothers and uncles. The world will not mourn the cultures we neglect. It is on us to carry them forward (NIEA, 2024).

Digital Sovereignty: Algorithms, AI, and the Blended Society

"Platforms are not neutral. If we do not shape the code that shapes our people, someone else will."

The next hundred years will not be defined only by land, water, and courts—but by attention, data, and code. Our children are growing up in a blended world where ceremony meets scrolling, where a meme travels faster than an elder's story, and where a rumor can topple a leader before truth has time to stand. The question is not whether social media will shape Native nations—it already does. The question is whether we will govern it, or be governed by it.

Algorithmic assimilation is real. Platforms reward what is loud, short, angry, and easy to sell, while our teachings are slow and relational. Unchecked, the feed can shape identity and mental health in ways that undermine language and lifeways (Office of the Surgeon General, 2023). At the same time, deepfakes, AI voice models, and bot swarms can impersonate leaders, amplify division, and distort elections—pressures that demand new capacities in cyber and crisis communications (Cybersecurity and Infrastructure Security Agency [CISA], 2024; National Institute of Standards and Technology [NIST], 2024).

This is also about data sovereignty—who owns the faces of our children, the recordings of our songs, the locations of our medicines. Indigenous data governance frameworks like CARE (Collective Benefit, Authority to Control, Responsibility, Ethics) and OCAP® (Ownership, Control, Access, Possession) insist that community data be managed on our terms (Global Indigenous Data Alliance [GIDA], 2020; First Nations Information Governance Centre [FNIGC], n.d.).

Mental and spiritual health cannot be ignored. The attention economy is designed to keep us restless and reactive; balance requires new disciplines for a digital age (Office of the Surgeon General, 2023). Governance—not retreat—is the path forward: constitutions that speak to pixels as well as parcels; authenticity standards so citizens can trust official messages; media-literacy curricula beside language programs; and community rules that keep our conversations aligned with our values (CISA, 2024; NIST, 2024; GIDA, 2020; FNIGC, n.d.).

What choosing sovereignty looks like (starting now):

- Establish Digital Sovereignty policies: consent, ownership, and respectful use of cultural content online.

- Create a Tribal Communications & Crisis Playbook: verified channels, authenticity seals, and rapid myth-busting protocols.

- Fund language and culture creators: pay youth and elders to produce lessons, songs, and stories for our platforms.

- Launch media-literacy and mental-health curricula grounded in culture.

- Build data governance that treats community data as a sacred resource.

- Train cybersecurity and AI monitors to detect deepfakes, bots, and coordinated harassment targeting leaders and elections.

If we steward the digital as we steward the sacred, our nations will not just survive the blended century—they will lead it.

Political Sovereignty: A Right, Not a Symbol

"Sovereignty is not a gift to be granted by others. It is a right that we must defend every day, in every decision, with every breath."

We speak often of sovereignty. We celebrate it. We invoke it. But if we do not practice it with discipline, it becomes nothing more than a symbol. The erosion of tribal sovereignty will not come solely from federal pressure—it will come from within, from apathy, disunity, and failed leadership.

Leadership turnover, nepotism, and cronyism have crippled many tribal governments, as detailed in The Politics of Leadership Change: Disrupting Potential. Without stable, principled governance, visionary strategies collapse under the weight of short-term thinking. True sovereignty requires leaders who do more than occupy positions—it requires those willing to sacrifice, to listen, to serve with accountability. Institutions rooted in cultural values and constitutional clarity endure; those built on personalities do not (Kalt & Singer, 2004).

Health and Wellness: Healing the Body, Spirit, and Future

"What does it mean to live as Native if our bodies and spirits are broken?"

The health crisis in Indian Country is not just a matter of medicine—it is a spiritual emergency. Generations of systemic neglect, compounded by poverty, trauma, and inadequate care, have left deep wounds. Disparities in diabetes, heart disease, mental health, and suicide persist at unacceptable levels (Centers for Disease Control and Prevention [CDC], 2024; U.S. Department of Health and Human Services, Office of Minority Health [HHS OMH], 2024). The Indian Health Service is chronically underfunded; culturally grounded care remains more aspiration than norm.

We must change this. We must fund our own clinics, train our own healers, and embrace both traditional and modern medicine without shame or hesitation. A century from now, let them say we were the generation that made wellness sacred—that we understood sovereignty to include the right to live fully and well (Warne & Frizzell, 2014).

Land and the Environment: The Sacred Trust

"The land is not just where we live. It is who we are."

Climate change, pollution, and resource exploitation threaten not just the environment, but the Indigenous worldview itself. Our relationship with the land is not transactional. It is sacred. And it is under siege.

In the next hundred years, Native communities will face unprecedented environmental challenges. Water will be fought over. Sacred sites will be targeted. Lands will be poisoned for profit. The question is not if these pressures will come—but whether we will be ready to defend what is sacred (Indian Law Resource Center, n.d.). We must train environmental lawyers and water protectors, and we must write and enforce laws that reflect our values, not just the colonial frameworks forced upon us.

"The land cannot protect itself. That duty is ours."

Conclusion: The Warrior's Path Forward

The future of Native America will not be handed to us. It must be fought for. It must be chosen. The next century holds peril and promise in equal measure. Our traditions, our sovereignty, our very identity hang in the balance.

But we are not without tools. We have our ancestors. We have our teachings. We have each other.

Now is the time to walk the warrior's path—with clarity, with unity, and with an unshakable commitment to the generations yet to come.

"The truth is, we are still here. And as long as we are here, we have the power to shape our future. But we must choose to rise, to fight, and to reclaim what is ours."

Native Service in the U.S. Military – Pride and Betrayal

"Despite centuries of betrayal, we have stood on the front lines, fighting for a nation that has often turned its back on us. Our service is not about duty to Washington—it is about who we are. We serve because it is in our blood."

Warriors Still, Under a Different Flag

I am a Native, and I am a U.S. Army veteran. When I speak of Native military service, I am not reciting statistics—I am speaking about my brothers, my sisters, my people. We have carried rifles under the American flag for generations, even while that same government tried to erase us.

We didn't start this tradition in the World Wars. It goes back further—to the 1800s, when Crow and Pawnee scouts fought alongside U.S. soldiers, tracking and battling other tribes. They were promised respect, but when the wars ended, the Army disarmed them and sent them back to reservations like broken tools (Smithsonian NMAI, 2023). Their service was disposable. That betrayal didn't end in the 19th century. It continues today. We are used in war, then forgotten in peace.

A Legacy We Chose—From World War I to Today

In World War I, before America even recognized us as citizens, more than 12,000 Native men and women volunteered (Smithsonian NMAI, 2023). We stepped forward not because the United States deserved us, but because we are warriors.

In World War II, 44,000 of us put on the uniform—over 10% of our entire population at the time (U.S. Department of Defense, 2022). The Navajo Code Talkers turned the very language boarding schools tried to beat out of us into an unbreakable code that helped win the Pacific (Smithsonian NMAI, 2023). That is our way: turning survival into strength.

From Korea and Vietnam to Desert Storm, Iraq, and Afghanistan, we kept enlisting. In Vietnam alone, more than 42,000 Natives fought (National Congress of American Indians, 2021). Some came home draped in medals. Some came home in coffins. Some never came home at all.

The Cost We Carry

For every 100 Native men, nearly 20 have served (U.S. Census Bureau, 2021). That is higher than any other group in America. We have shed blood in every major conflict this country has fought. We have carried the cost of loyalty.

But the burden goes beyond the battlefield:

Sidebar: The Numbers Don't Lie

When I say we serve at higher rates than anyone else, here's what that really looks like:

- **Enlistment** – For every 100 Native men, nearly 20 of us have worn the uniform (U.S. Census Bureau, 2021). Service isn't the exception in our communities—it's the expectation.
- **Combat Deaths** – In Vietnam alone, more than 200 of our warriors didn't come home (National Museum of the American Indian, 2023). In every war since World War I, Native names have filled casualty lists far out of proportion to our numbers.
- **PTSD** – Roughly 1 in 5 of us wrestle with severe PTSD (Veterans Health Administration, 2022). But many never get treatment because VA care is hours away, or because the system doesn't understand our culture and our healing ways.
- **Suicide** – We lose Native veterans to suicide at nearly twice the rate of white veterans (American Psychological Association, 2022). These aren't statistics to me. They are brothers-in-arms. Friends. Family.
- **Homelessness** – Too many of us come back to no jobs, no homes, and no support. Native veterans are overrepresented in homeless counts across the country (HUD, 2022). That is the price of a grateful nation that forgets its promises.

These numbers are not just data points on a government chart. They are proof of what we already know: we give this country more than it gives back.

The Betrayal After Service

Here is the part America doesn't want to hear: once we take off the uniform, the country that welcomed us in war abandons us in peace.

I have seen it. Native veterans driving hours for a VA appointment that never comes (U.S. Department of Veterans Affairs, 2020). IHS clinics with no staff trained to treat combat trauma. Bureaucracies blind to our languages, our ceremonies, our healing traditions.

We bury too many of our own because they cannot carry the weight of untreated wounds. Suicide. Addiction. Homelessness. These are not failures of the warrior—they are failures of the nation that sent us to fight and then turned away.

And it's the same old story. In the 1800s, Native scouts were disarmed and discarded when no longer needed (Smithsonian NMAI, 2023). Today, we are thanked with parades and forgotten when the news cycle ends. The uniform changes, but the betrayal does not.

Why We Still Serve

So why do we keep enlisting? Why do we still fight for a country that breaks its promises?

Because service is not about loyalty to Washington. It is about loyalty to who we are. We are warriors. It is in our blood, our history, our tradition. When we fight, we protect our families, our homelands, and the generations to come.

I served because that warrior spirit still lives in me. My brothers and sisters served for the same reason. We did not do it because America earned it. We did it because we carry a legacy older than America itself.

The Demand for Justice

But let me be clear: honoring Native veterans cannot stop at parades and plaques. If America values our service, then it must value our lives when we return. Healthcare that heals. Housing that shelters. Jobs that lift us up instead of casting us aside.

Until that happens, our story will always be told in two parts: pride in our service, and betrayal after our service.

Conclusion

We have always served. We will always serve. But we will not stay silent about the price.

From the scouts of the 1800s to the soldiers of today, the pattern is the same: welcomed in war, discarded in peace. That is the truth.

And yet we endure. We stand. We serve—not because of what this country has done for us, but because of who we are.

We are Native. We are veterans. And we will not be forgotten.

Native American Military Service and Casualties by Conflict

Conflict	Estimated Native Service Members	Estimated Deaths
World War I	~12,000	~600
World War II	~44,000	~1,250
Korean War	~10,000	~194
Vietnam War	~42,000	226–248
Desert Storm (1991)	Not specified	At least 1
Afghanistan (OEF)	Not specified	30
Iraq (OIF)	Not specified	43

Eugene D Samuels

Born April 1, 1913
Died June 9, 1945 in Okinawa, Japan
Enlisted: April 23, 1942

Bronze Star *Nez Perce Tribe*
Army Infantry

One of many KIA during WW2. Over 44,000 Native Americans Served.

Acknowledging Our Greatest Challenge

"True empowerment lies not in the absence of external barriers but in the strength to overcome our internal struggles. Only by acknowledging the challenges within can we rise above them and shape a future where our people thrive, resilient in culture and unity."

The Hardest Truth to Face

The journey of Native American tribes toward self-sufficiency, prosperity, and cultural revitalization is marked by numerous obstacles. Throughout this book, we have explored the myriad internal and external forces that have hindered progress—from systemic injustices to historical traumas inflicted by external oppressors.

Yet, while it is essential to recognize the harm caused by these external forces, it is equally crucial to confront the internal struggles that we, as Native peoples, must address. Acknowledging and understanding our greatest challenge—ourselves—is the first step toward meaningful change and lasting empowerment.

Self-Inflicted Wounds: The Barriers We Must Face to Heal

Understanding Internal Barriers

The notion that "we are our own worst enemy" is difficult to accept but necessary to examine. This concept suggests that, alongside the external forces of oppression and marginalization, there are internal dynamics within Native American communities that may obstruct progress.

These internal barriers include leadership conflicts, economic dependency, cultural erosion, and divisions within communities. Addressing these issues requires deep introspection, courage, and a readiness to implement necessary changes (Smith, 2019).

Leadership and Governance

Leadership is the cornerstone of any thriving community, yet many Native American tribes face significant challenges in this area. Conflicts in leadership, nepotism, and a lack of qualified leaders have created barriers to progress. In some cases, frequent leadership changes disrupt continuity, stalling critical initiatives. Nepotism, which places unqualified individuals in key positions, undermines governance and divides communities (Jones, 2018).

To overcome these challenges, tribes must implement governance reforms that emphasize merit over kinship. Clear criteria for leadership roles, professional development, and a culture of accountability are essential. Leadership committed to long-term well-being, rather than short-term gain, can become the engine of sustainable development (Wilson, 2020).

Economic Dependency

Federal assistance remains vital for many tribes, but long-term dependency creates cycles that discourage initiative and stifle innovation. True economic sovereignty will require tribal nations to build economic ecosystems that do not rely solely on outside aid (Taylor, 2021).

This shift involves investments in infrastructure, workforce development, and industries such as renewable energy, agriculture, and digital technologies. With strategic planning and community-led innovation, Native economies can evolve into self-sustaining systems (Garcia, 2020).

Cultural Erosion

Forced assimilation policies have led to the loss of language, traditions, and spiritual practices—fraying the cultural fabric of many communities. The damage inflicted by boarding schools and colonial education has left generations disconnected from their roots (Smith & Brown, 2022).

Cultural revitalization efforts—language immersion programs, traditional arts, and community storytelling—are central to restoring that identity. When culture is restored, unity and pride naturally follow (Wilson, 2018).

Community Divisions

Political rivalries, generational divides, and differing visions often pit community members against one another. These internal fractures paralyze collective action and make even well-meaning initiatives unsustainable (Jones, 2019).

Open forums, inclusive leadership models, and values-based vision statements can help restore cohesion. Healing internal divides must be a strategic, intentional effort rooted in transparency and respect.

Embracing Change and Empowerment

Promoting Education

Education is the cornerstone of modern empowerment. A dual-track approach—one that merges traditional knowledge with modern skills—is vital for preparing Native youth to lead (Miller, 2021).

By building partnerships with universities and technical institutes, tribes can increase access to higher education while grounding it in cultural values. Culturally infused education creates a foundation for sovereignty, innovation, and economic resilience (Jones, 2020).

Fostering Economic Resilience

Economic diversity is no longer optional. Tribal nations must develop industries aligned with cultural values and ecological sustainability. Renewable energy, ecotourism, sustainable agriculture, and AI-driven entrepreneurship represent real paths forward (Taylor, 2020).

Access to startup capital, tribal business incubators, and mentorship programs will nurture entrepreneurship at all levels—from youth to elders (Smith & Brown, 2022).

Strengthening Governance and Accountability

Accountable governance is not a luxury—it is a survival tool. Strong governance structures, clear leadership criteria, annual audits, and performance benchmarks are essential for restoring trust and producing results (Wilson, 2019).

Leadership rooted in service, guided by ethics, and protected by law can safeguard sovereignty in ways that no federal policy ever will (Garcia, 2020).

Revitalizing Culture and Community

Cultural revitalization is an act of resistance and survival. From language camps to ceremonial renewals, tribes must make culture a daily part of life. Programs that connect youth with elders are particularly vital (Smith, 2018).

Culture is not just a legacy—it is a leadership tool. It teaches values, builds cohesion, and prepares people to lead with honor (Jones, 2019).

Addressing Health Disparities

Native communities continue to face unacceptable health outcomes. Solutions must be holistic—combining physical care, nutrition, mental health, and traditional healing (Taylor, 2021).

Tribes must invest in local clinics, telehealth, mental wellness programs, and addiction recovery—grounded in cultural frameworks.

Embracing the Mystical: The Role of Spirituality

Spiritual Leadership

Spiritual leaders—elders, medicine people, ceremonial guides—must be supported and respected. Their teachings offer not only cultural continuity but emotional grounding and spiritual clarity (Harper, 2017).

Ceremonies and Rituals

Ceremonial life is essential to community health. Rituals anchor identity, remind us of our obligations, and foster deep intergenerational bonds (Jones, 2018).

Connection to the Land

Land is sacred. Traditional practices in land stewardship, seasonal ceremonies, and ecological respect must inform tribal policy. Culture and climate resilience go hand in hand (Smith & Brown, 2022).

Vision Quests and Meditation

Traditional practices like vision quests offer individual clarity and community guidance. In times of chaos, these rituals reconnect us with the land, the spirit, and ourselves (Garcia, 2020).

Conclusion: Acknowledging Our Greatest Challenge

To acknowledge our greatest challenge—ourselves—is not defeat. It is the moment we begin to rise. From governance to education, economy to spirit, the transformation of Indian Country will begin the moment we face our reflection with honesty and resolve.

With discipline, vision, and cultural commitment, Native nations can reclaim their future. This path demands courage—but it offers something even greater in return: dignity, prosperity, and the restoration of generational strength.

"Our greatest challenge is not the forces that work against us but the doubt that lives within us. When we confront the shadows of our past with honesty and courage, we illuminate the path to a future where sovereignty, identity, and self-determination flourish together."

Summary and Path Forward

"Our path forward requires not just the will to survive, but the courage to transform. By embracing change, honoring our heritage, and committing to unity, we ensure that the future for Native America is not just one of survival, but of thriving prosperity."

The journey toward economic self-sufficiency and political stability for Native American tribes is fraught with historical and contemporary challenges. However, as this book has illustrated through chapters and case studies, many tribes have navigated these obstacles successfully, forging a path toward prosperity.

This chapter synthesizes the key insights, strategies, and best practices discussed and outlines a comprehensive path forward for tribes aiming to achieve sustainable development and thriving communities.

Historical Context and Current Challenges

Native American tribes have faced centuries of systemic discrimination, displacement, and marginalization. Historical policies such as the Indian Removal Act and the Dawes Act were designed to dispossess tribes of their lands and cultural heritage, resulting in lasting socioeconomic challenges, including poverty, unemployment, and limited access to education and healthcare (Deloria & Lytle, 1983).

Many tribes remain economically dependent on federal assistance, which has hindered long-term self-sufficiency and economic resilience (Cornell & Kalt, 2000). Additionally, health disparities continue to affect Native American populations, with elevated rates of chronic illnesses such as obesity, diabetes, and heart disease, exacerbated by limited access to healthcare (Warne & Frizzell, 2014).

Strategies for Success

Economic Diversification

One of the critical solutions for sustainable development is diversification beyond traditional revenue sources such as casinos. Tribes can explore industries like renewable energy, sustainable agriculture, and technology to build a robust economic base.

Renewable Energy Projects: Leveraging tribal land to develop solar, wind, and other renewable energy projects provides tribes with sustainable income and reduces reliance on external energy resources (Royster & Blumm, 2008).

Sustainable Agriculture and Aquaculture: Investments in organic farming, permaculture, and aquaponics can improve food security and create new economic opportunities for tribes.

Technology and Innovation: Tribes must embrace technology and invest in industries such as IT services, software development, and tech innovation. This will provide high-paying jobs and reduce reliance on federal aid.

Qualified Leadership

Competent and experienced leadership is critical for effective governance and economic development. Tribes must implement governance reforms that establish and enforce minimum qualifications for elected officials, ensuring leaders have the necessary education and experience to make informed decisions.

Educational Requirements: Tribal leaders should possess relevant degrees in business administration, law, public policy, or similar fields that equip them to manage complex operations effectively.

Professional Development: Ongoing training and professional development in governance, financial management, and strategic planning should be mandatory to ensure leaders stay current with best practices.

Governance Reforms and Accountability: High standards of governance, transparency, and accountability are critical for preventing corruption and ensuring efficient management of tribal resources.

Code of Ethics: Adopting a comprehensive code of ethics ensures tribal officials adhere to the highest standards of conduct, including addressing conflicts of interest and promoting financial transparency.

Audit Committees: Establishing independent audit committees will ensure regular financial audits, which help tribes address potential issues early and maintain transparency.

Health and Wellness: Addressing the health disparities within Native American communities is critical for improving economic productivity and quality of life.

Health-care Services: Tribes can invest in healthcare infrastructure that serves both the tribal and broader communities. Partnerships with providers and insurers can create sustainable healthcare systems.

Access to Healthy Foods: Tribes can enhance access to healthy foods through community-supported agriculture programs, farmers' markets, and partnerships with local food producers.

Education and Workforce Development: Educational investments are vital for building a skilled and adaptable workforce. Vocational training programs in fields such as healthcare, technology, and construction can prepare tribal members for diverse career paths.

Higher Education Partnerships: Partnering with colleges and universities for scholarships, internships, and joint research initiatives will support educational and leadership opportunities for tribal members.

Building External Partnerships: Strong relationships with external businesses, organizations, and government agencies are essential for tribal success. Collaborating with external partners provides tribes access to resources, expertise, and growth opportunities.

Leverage the SBA 8(a) Business Development Program: The Small Business Administration's 8(a) program offers tribes significant advantages, such as larger sole-source contracts and expedited procurement processes. This provides tribes with reliable revenue streams and strengthens economic stability (Cornell & Kalt, 2000).

Conclusion

This book has illustrated through case studies, including the Choctaw Nation, Mohegan Tribe, Oneida Nation, and others, that success is possible through diversified economic strategies. By embracing qualified leadership, implementing governance reforms, addressing health disparities, and building strong external partnerships, Native American tribes can overcome historical challenges.

The path forward involves a commitment to strategic planning, cultural revitalization, and economic diversification. Tribes must balance tradition with modern realities to build a prosperous future for generations to come. With determination and a commitment to excellence, Native communities can rise above the challenges that have historically constrained them and achieve lasting self-sufficiency, political stability, and economic resilience.

"Charting our path forward requires a blend of wisdom from our ancestors, innovative thinking for the present, and a steadfast commitment to the future. It's through this harmonious balance that we will truly thrive."

Reparations? We've Got the Receipts

"They didn't just take our land. They took our names, our wombs, our languages, and then had the audacity to ask what we wanted in return. We don't want handouts. We want history acknowledged—and debts paid."

Let's begin with a statement that shouldn't be controversial, but somehow still is: if the United States ever gets serious about reparations, Native Americans shouldn't be in line—we should already be at the register.

We're not talking about vague historical guilt. We're not asking anyone to feel bad about things their ancestors did. We're talking about ongoing harm—federal policies, enforced by law, funded by tax dollars, that were intentionally designed to erase us. And not 400 years ago. Try 50. Try last week.

We have receipts.

Let's tally a few.

Exhibit A: The Land Theft Ledger

Over 1.5 billion acres taken. Not just seized—signed away through treaties the U.S. government never intended to honor. Over 370 treaties, and nearly all of them broken (Prucha 1997). We made deals. They made promises. We kept ours. They brought bayonets.

When the Dawes Act of 1887 rolled through Indian Country, the government said it was promoting self-reliance. What it actually did was strip tribal lands into individual plots, assign them to Native families, then sell the "surplus" to white settlers. It was theft with a paper trail (Wilkinson 2005).

Exhibit B: Genocide in a White Coat

Between the 1960s and 1970s, thousands of Native women were sterilized—without consent, without knowledge, often while under anesthesia for unrelated procedures. The Indian Health Service and contracted hospitals executed this quietly, like bureaucratic warfare. A report in 1976 estimated that 25% to 42% of all Native women of childbearing age had been sterilized (Lawrence 2000). Let that sink in.

This isn't ancient history. It's within the lifetime of the women still carrying that wound—sometimes literally.

Exhibit C: Boarding Schools and Cultural Erasure

Imagine someone taking your child at five years old, cutting their hair, beating them for speaking their language, and telling them their God was a lie. That was the policy. Not the exception—the policy. Carlisle. Haskell. Chilocco. These weren't schools. They were re-education camps (Fixico 1986).

They didn't just try to kill the Indian and save the man. They tried to make sure the Indian never came back.

Exhibit D: Termination and Relocation

In the 1950s, entire tribes were legally "terminated"—stripped of their federal status and rights. Urban relocation programs promised opportunity and delivered poverty. They took us from the rez, dropped us into cities, and left us to rot in the corners of forgotten neighborhoods (Fixico 1986).

No land. No services. No tribe. Just paperwork that said we didn't exist anymore.

Exhibit E: The Casino Mirage

Whenever reparations are mentioned, some wise soul points to Indian casinos and says, "You guys already hit the jackpot."

Here's the truth: only a small percentage of tribes operate profitable casinos. Many don't have the population base, the infrastructure, or the political leverage to even get one off the ground. And those that do? Their profits go toward filling the holes that federal neglect blasted wide open—healthcare, housing, education.

Casinos didn't fix the damage. They've just helped some of us survive it.

So Let's Talk Numbers

The U.S. government still holds billions in tribal trust funds—often mismanaged, misplaced, or outright lost. The Cobell settlement in 2009 finally awarded $3.4 billion to resolve decades of gross mishandling of Indian trust assets (U.S. Department of the Interior).

That was a payout—not a payoff. It didn't come close to balancing the ledger.

If Anyone Deserves Reparations, It's Us

We're not asking for guilt money. We're asking for what was promised. What was signed. What was stolen. And what was silenced.

We don't need a commission. We don't need a task force. We need the United States to do what it said it would do, going back over two centuries. Honor the treaties. Restore the land where possible. Compensate where it's not.

We don't want to be paid for being Native. We want to be paid back for what was taken from us because we're Native.

If this country is serious about justice, start where the blood is still fresh.

"If reparations are about justice, then let's start with the first lie, the first treaty, the first grave. Ours is not a forgotten claim—it's an open wound stitched with silence."

Observations

Unfinished Conversations: Tough Topics Beyond This Book

"The truths most worth confronting often exceed the pages we can give them—but acknowledging their importance ensures they're never truly silenced."

This volume moved fast on purpose. But a handful of fault lines demand more pages, more receipts, and more hard math than a single spine can hold. Consider the following a map of the next battles—not an apology for brevity, but a promise to finish this work in daylight.

Core Fault Lines We Will Not Leave Behind

1) Indian Gaming Regulatory Act (IGRA, 1988) — Wealth, Wedges, and the Discipline of Governance

Casinos rebuilt payrolls and clinics, but they also taught us what happens when cash outruns controls. The real question isn't "gaming good or bad?" It's whether governance can out-govern envy: transparent distributions, clean compacts, audits on time, and reinvestment that survives downturns. Strong policy beats strong personalities—every time. [IGRA 1988; NIGC Overview]

2) Indian Child Welfare Act (ICWA) — Protecting Children and Nations

ICWA is not nostalgia; it's survival. The fight is won or lost in practice: early notice to tribes, qualified expert witnesses, kinship placement capacity, and state-court compliance that happens in weeks, not months. Measure sovereignty here by two outcomes: do our children come home, and do they stay? [ICWA 1978; Haaland v. Brackeen 2023; NICWA Guidance]

3) Cobell v. Salazar — Ending Old Theft Without Inventing New Confusion

A settlement check is not a system. We still need trust accounting people can actually read, probate paths that don't turn families into land fragments, and fractionation fixes that build wealth instead of

443

paperwork. Justice is more than a payout; it's a ledger you can explain to your aunt. [Cobell 2010]

4) Standing Rock / DAPL — Treaties, Permits, and "Never Again"
Treaty rights met global cameras. "Never again" isn't a slogan; it's pre-planned NEPA strategy, cultural resource work done early, injunction readiness, and intertribal coordination that moves faster than a pipeline crew. Solidarity matters. So do survey maps, affidavits, and timing. [Estes 2019; NEPA]

5) McGirt v. Oklahoma — Law on Paper, Safety on the Ground
A jurisdictional earthquake followed by aftershocks. Translation work remains: cross-deputization, prosecutor capacity, detention logistics, and funding formulas that match the law with delivery. Safety is a chain; fix the weakest link first and stop pretending the others are unbreakable. [McGirt 2020]

6) Cannabis, Hemp & Regulated Markets — Sovereignty Without Illusions
Headlines are easy; compliance is not. Banking, taxation, diversion risk, age control, testing, and public health will make or break any market. If you can't fund enforcement, don't fund the sign. The win is a narrow lane where sovereignty and safety both stand. [NCAI 2019; Tribal Cannabis Policy Notes]

7) Tribal Taxation Authority — Compacts, Codes, and Courtroom-Ready Data
Fuel, tobacco, lodging, and e-commerce revenues face constant state encroachment. Airtight tax codes, smart compacts, joint audits, and clean datasets resolve more conflict than speeches ever will. If you can't prove it, you can't keep it. [Taylor 2019; CICD Papers]

8) Labor Sovereignty & Unionization — Protecting Workers and Nations
Worker dignity and national sovereignty are not enemies. The path forward is designed: clear HR policy, real grievance processes, and bargaining frameworks that respect jurisdiction without importing someone else's politics wholesale. Safe jobs, fair pay, sovereign law—that's the point. [Fletcher 2018]

9) The Digital Divide — Fiber, Spectrum, and the Last Mile of Sovereignty

Broadband isn't a luxury; it's payroll, school, telehealth, and public safety. Realities: middle-mile partnerships, EBS/2.5 GHz Tribal spectrum, take-rates, maintenance budgets, and field crews with spare parts. Connectivity is not a ribbon cutting; it's a utility. [FCC 2021; GAO Broadband 2022]

10) COVID-19 & Relief Funding — From Emergency to Endurance

The pandemic exposed our cracks and our courage. Build permanent capacity: public-health staffing, supply chains, emergency finance, and data systems that report in days, not months. Clean audits aren't vanity; they're the price of faster help next time. [CRS 2021; Treasury 2020]

Additional Fronts for the Extended Edition

11) The Marshall Trilogy — The Crooked Foundation and How We Stand Anyway

Johnson, Cherokee Nation, Worcester: the floor we didn't choose but must understand. Learn it in plain language—then fight smart: where to litigate, where to compact, and when to win in spreadsheets instead of courtrooms. [Johnson 1823; Cherokee Nation 1831; Worcester 1832]

12) Jurisdiction That Holds — *Oliphant, Castro-Huerta*, VAWA 2013/2022

If your police can't arrest and your courts can't sentence, criminals read the same headlines you do. This is paperwork and practice: special jurisdiction requirements, evidence handling, defense counsel access, and victim services that actually work. [Oliphant 1978; Castro-Huerta 2022; VAWA 2013/2022]

13) Capital Stacks That Close — CDFI, SSBCI, NMTC and Friends

Projects die where financing is fuzzy. Blend federal, philanthropic, and private dollars within the lines. Collateral realities on trust land, debt-service coverage, governance that comforts lenders without selling the store—money follows clarity. [Treasury SSBCI 2022; CDFI/NMTC Overview]

14) Federal Contracting Masterclass — 8(a), HUBZone, Buy Indian, IIP
Opportunity is not entitlement. Do the self-performance math, avoid bona fide-office traps, structure JVs that help instead of harm, and document for audits before the award. Past performance isn't a trophy; it's a staircase. Climb it. [SBA 8(a) Regs; HUBZone; Buy Indian Final Rule; IIP/FAR]

15) Urban Indian Undercounts — When Seventy Percent Goes Missing
Most of our people live off-reservation; many budgets pretend otherwise. Fix undercounts with urban–tribal partnerships, data-sharing agreements, and reporting that turns "invisible" families into funded services. Identity isn't a ZIP code; allocations keep acting like it is. [IHS Urban Indian Fact Sheets; NCUIH/UIHI Reports]

16) Model Policy Deep Dives (Narrative Only) — Ethics, Procurement, Whistleblower, Language at Work
We won't print templates here. We will tell the truth about features that work: disclosure that actually discloses, recusal with teeth, bid thresholds that stop theater, protected channels that save careers, and language policies that make culture daily, not decorative. [Governance Best-Practice Syntheses]

17) Digital Sovereignty 2.0 — AI, Datasets, and Cultural IP
Our languages and stories shouldn't be scraped into someone else's profit. Guard data, license what you choose to share, and prevent cultural motifs from turning into clip art. The future is already training on our past; decide whether it learns with permission or without it. [Data Sovereignty Discussions]

18) Workforce Sovereignty — Apprenticeships to Executive Pipelines (CCC-ID Lessons, Modernized)
The CCC-ID proved an old truth: work plus dignity builds nations. Update the formula—apprenticeships tied to real projects, credentials that travel, retention pay bands, and leadership paths that don't require leaving home forever. Jobs aren't numbers; they're futures with last names. [CCC-ID Histories]

Throughlines That Bind Them

- **Jurisdiction → Safety → Economy.** If people aren't safe, investment is pretend.

- **Data is the new treaty.** What you can prove, you can fund; what you can't, you'll lose.

- **Ethics beats charisma.** Codes and procurement guardrails outperform strong personalities, every time.

- **Language is policy.** If it isn't spoken at work, it's being curated for tourists.

- **Sovereignty isn't a speech.** It's contracts honored, audits clean, and a payroll that clears on Friday.

Author's Note — About the Extended Edition

This book was built to move, not meander. If it earns its keep—if councils use it, if readers push for more—we will publish **Book Two: *Business & Politics in Indian Country — The Extended Edition***. No "toolkits," no fluff—just deeper chapters where the fights are real. Its release is **contingent on the success of this first volume** and a clear need to take the next hill. Until then, use what's here. Build what's next. Our grandchildren deserve the proof.

Some topics in these pages are the opening move, not the endgame. They're named, framed, and pushed forward—but the **Extended Edition** will take them the rest of the way: deeper, harder, and more technical. Expect the operational mechanics—jurisdiction that holds, capital stacks that close, contracting and compliance that survive audit, broadband that actually turns on, and language policies that live at work, not on posters. This volume lights the fire; the next one brings the fuel and the match.

Epilogue

To the world. To my people. To those still brave enough to face the truth.

We've reached the line where excuses end and choices begin. Our greatest obstacle is no longer history's injustice or outside oppression—it is ourselves.

Our story has been one of survival. But too often, that survival fractures under the weight of mistrust, division, and our refusal to confront hard truths. We have learned to fight external enemies. Now, we must face the one within.

For generations, we've been conditioned to look outward for the source of our pain. Colonization, erasure, displacement—they are real, and they cut deep. But if we stop there, we give away the very power we need to heal. I am asking you now: look inward. It is not enough to reclaim land or declare sovereignty. We must reclaim our unity, our will, and our direction.

In this book, *Business and Politics in Indian Country: You Can't Handle the Truth*, I have tried to lay bare the systems that hold us back—from broken governance to economic dependency, from cultural erosion to compromised leadership. But none of that will change unless we change.

The essence of true sovereignty lies not just in self-governance—but in self-reliance. Economic. Cultural. Spiritual. We cannot continue waiting for permission to heal. We cannot allow comfort or complacency to dictate our destiny. We must challenge traditions that breed complacency and leadership that fears change.

Our youth deserve more than a legacy of survival. They deserve a future built on thriving. They must inherit more than government programs—they must inherit real, usable power rooted in identity and strategy. The sacred knowledge of our ancestors—our languages, ceremonies, stories—these aren't relics. They are living instructions, and they will guide us forward if we choose to carry them.

We need leadership that is qualified, courageous, and unafraid of accountability. We must replace political games with vision, division with unity, and dependency with strength. That is how we reclaim our future—not from Washington, but from within.

This final word is not an ending. It's a beginning—a declaration for those willing to lead. Our legacy will not be defined by what was taken, but by what we chose to build. It is time to rise—not just in protest, but in purpose.

Let them say we were the generation that stopped surviving—and started building.

In unity and strength,

—D.G. Comer

Acknowledgments

This book was never written in isolation. It was carried—at times fiercely, at times quietly—on the shoulders of those who poured into me when I had nothing left to give. It is the product of long nights, unflinching truths, and the steady presence of people who stood beside me, even when they could not fully see the weight I bore.

To our eldest sister: your calm has been my compass. Your strength—often silent, always unwavering—has steadied me through storms I could not name.

To my grandparents, Ann and Titus Samuels: your wisdom shaped the very bones of this work. The powwows, the road trips, the stories shared in darkness and daylight alike—they echo on every page. You have walked on, but you still walk with me.

To the Native leaders, elders, and everyday warriors—some I met, most I did not—your endurance is the backbone of this book. Your courage to speak when it cost you something, and your wisdom to remain silent when words would have been wasted, taught me what real leadership looks like. I have only tried to honor what you already lived.

To my brothers and sisters in the United States Army: the fire we endured together left its mark. The discipline, the tension, the clarity that distance and danger alone can bring—it is here, stitched between the lines. For those of us—Native or not—who wore that uniform, service never truly ends. We carry it forward, each in our own way.

To the parts of me that broke during this journey—thank you for breaking. And to the parts that refused to stay broken—thank you for rising again.

To Denise—my wife, my constant, my fiercest ally since 1977. No words can equal the depth of what you have carried with me. You held steady when I staggered. You gave silence when I needed space, and strength when I had none. This book exists because you refused to let it remain unwritten.

And finally, to you—the reader. Whether you arrived here by accident or intention, I ask only this: read with an open mind, sit with what unsettles you, and allow the hard truths to do their work. May these words not merely inform, but ignite. We cannot afford silence any longer.

With deepest respect and gratitude,
—D.G. Comer

What Was Left Unsaid: A Letter to the Reader

Final Chapter: Carry the Flame

I didn't write everything that could be written. That would take volumes.

There are truths—hard, urgent, and unresolved—that live beyond the borders of this book. Forces that continue to shape Indian Country, both from within and without. Some are wounds we inflict on ourselves. Others are the quiet manipulations and loud injustices imposed by outside systems.

What I've shared here are the fires I could tend—the battles most urgent, most dangerous, most overdue. But let's be clear: this is not the full story. It cannot be.

No single book can carry the entire weight of Native struggle, sovereignty, betrayal, and resilience. What you've read are just chapters in a much larger saga—one still being written in tribal courts, along dirt roads, around kitchen tables, and in the lives of generations yet to come.

There is more to learn. More to face. More we must be willing to speak aloud.

Let this book be a beginning—not a boundary.

To the Reader

You made it to the end.

That sounds simple. It isn't. Not with a book like this—not with truths this sharp. You didn't just turn pages—you walked through fire. I see that, and I honor it.

This was never written to comfort or coddle. It was built to confront—and, if I did my job, to change something in you.

You've seen cracks in our foundations; stories that don't make headlines; patterns we've trained ourselves to ignore. You've seen how cycles of dysfunction feed on silence, and how sacred promises bend under politics, pride, and fear.

But this isn't the end. It's the start.

The pages behind you are a mirror. They reflect the parts of Indian Country we don't put on brochures—the things we only whisper about. A mirror alone does nothing. What you do after you look into it—that's what matters.

So what now?

Maybe you're a Native reader who saw your own story in these chapters.
Maybe you're a non-Native ally, trying to understand sovereignty, identity, and struggle.
Maybe you're a tribal leader who feels called out—or called forward.

Whatever your role, know this: you are now a keeper of these truths. Carry them. You don't need a title or a platform to lead—only the courage to speak what others avoid, to question what others accept, and to build what others only dream about.

Let these truths be fuel. Let them start hard conversations—around dinner tables, in council chambers, and in classrooms. Let them push you to demand better—from your leaders, your community, and yourself.

We cannot heal what we refuse to face. We will never rise while protecting the systems that keep us low.

I wrote this book because I've seen what becomes possible when we stop pretending. If we can face the truth together, we can reclaim the future together.

You've walked through the fire.
Now—carry the flame.

Lim lemt·sh,
—D.G. Comer

Access the Complete Works Cited

The full, hyperlinked Master Works Cited is available as a free and anonymous download—no signup, no email, no tracking.

Visit: **www.heckfuzzy.com**

Every source used in this book—including government documents, academic works, news articles, and oral histories—is available for review, citation, or further exploration. This book was built on truth. You deserve full access to the trail that led here.

Note: Extreme diligence was applied to ensure the accuracy and completeness of all citations and quotes. Given the scope—over 60 pages of referenced works—some minor errors may remain. Every effort was made to honor the sources and voices represented.

"This book was built on truth—not just the kind you find in archives or court rulings, but the kind you carry in your bones. If it unsettles you, good. That means the truth is still alive—and still capable of demanding something from us."

Who Is D.G. Comer?

D.G. Comer is a U.S. Army veteran, tribal executive, business strategist, and unapologetic truth-teller with more than four decades of experience at the intersection of Native governance, federal policy, and economic development. Raised with a deep respect for cultural sovereignty—and with firsthand knowledge of the systems working against it—Comer brings both insider clarity and outsider honesty to *Business & Politics in Indian Country – You Can't Handle the Truth*.

An enrolled member of the Coeur d'Alene Tribe and a shareholder of the Northwest Arctic Native Association (NANA), Comer's roots and responsibilities run deep. He knows that real representation isn't inherited—it's earned, one truth and one hard decision at a time.

As CEO of Red Lake Construction, a tribally owned SBA 8(a) enterprise, Comer has led federal projects across the country, built multi-million-dollar joint ventures (five currently), and fought to ensure that tribal ownership means more than a legal formality. He is also spearheading the development of a nationwide Native American Governance Accord—a voluntary framework designed to raise ethical standards, enforce financial transparency, and restore trust in tribal leadership throughout Indian Country.

Comer holds a Bachelor's degree in Business Administration and a Master's in Business Administration, but his true education came from a lifetime of challenges—some in uniform during the Cold War, others in tribal boardrooms, statehouses, and job sites.

He has previously published a short story, but this is his first full-length book—and it will not be his last.

He and his wife, Denise Ann—his partner since 1977 and his lifelong pillar—have five children and live between Northern Idaho and Northern Minnesota, where they remain deeply involved in tribal affairs, creative projects, and community building. Comer restores his rural Minnesota property, and when in Idaho, he works on their 1967 GTO and continues raising the questions others would prefer to leave unasked.

D.G. Comer & Tony

BUSINESS AND POLITICS IN INDIAN COUNTRY
You Can't Handle the Truth.

To: Educators and Leaders:

This book wasn't written as a lesson—it was written as a challenge. How you teach it is part of how you answer it. What you choose to ignore will be the next generation's burden to carry."

---

www.heckfuzzy.com

www.ingramcontent.com/pod-product-compliance
Lightning Source LLC
Chambersburg PA
CBHW052126030426
42337CB00028B/5047